Canadian Living
Cooks Step by Step

**150 recipes with at-a-glance cooking lessons and tips
from The Canadian Living Test Kitchen**

Daphna Rabinovitch
and The Canadian Living Test Kitchen

Transcontinental
PUBLISHING

Random House Canada

A Canadian Living® Book

Random House of Canada Limited	Canadian Living
One Toronto Street	Transcontinental Publications Inc.
Suite 300	25 Sheppard Avenue West
Toronto, Ont.	Suite 100
Canada	North York, Ont.
M5C 2V6	Canada
	M2N 6S7

Canadian Cataloguing in Publication Data

Rabinovitch, Daphna
Canadian living cooks step by step : 150 recipes with at-a-glance cooking
lessons and tips from The Canadian Living Test Kitchen

"A Canadian living book".
Includes index.

ISBN 0-679-30924-1 (bound)   ISBN 0-679-31122-X (pbk.)

1. Cookery. 2. Cuisine. I. Title.

TX715.6.R27 1999   641.5
C99-931442-4

Canadian Living® is a trademark owned by Transcontinental Publications Inc.
and licensed by Random House of Canada Limited. All trademark rights,
registered or unregistered, are reserved worldwide.

A Denise Schon/Kirsten Hanson Book
Produced by Denise Schon Books Inc.

Editorial Assistance: Beverley Renahan, Julia Armstrong
Index: Barbara Schon
Book Design: Counterpunch/Linda Gustafson
Colour Separation: Quadratone Graphics
Front cover photograph: Roasted Herb Chicken with
Lemon Wine Sauce, page 98, Robert Wigington

Printed and bound in South Korea
9 8 7 6 5 4 3 2

Contents

Introduction

When I was training as a chef in California, I rushed home after class each day to try out recipes and techniques on my roommate. It was so exciting: learning how to debone a chicken, exactly how long to simmer fish stock, how to whisk egg whites to glossy, thick peaks – by hand! Mastery of one dish spurred interest in another and curiosity about yet another. That same sense of exhilaration still characterizes my cooking endeavours, whether at home or in the *Canadian Living* Test Kitchen. And it's that sense of excitement, possibility and accomplishment that I hope to convey to you with *Canadian Living Cooks Step by Step*.

Learning to cook is full of rewards, tangible and intangible. The tangible benefits are, of course, mouth-watering or, at the very least, edible. The intangible returns, however, are equally important: self-esteem and confidence are as much the fundamental building blocks in the kitchen as are knowing how to fold, season and stew. The cooking lessons in this book were chosen to strengthen those building blocks. Individually, they clarify various techniques; together they offer a spectrum of skills that, once mastered, will inspire you to create new recipes or experiment with old favourites. For the novice cook, there are lessons on how to make the perfect omelette, your first stew and a topnotch meat sauce. If you're a more experienced cook, coordinating a summertime lobster feast may be just the challenge you're looking for.

Canadian Living Cooks Step by Step is organized to facilitate your learning process. The cooking lessons, more than 75 in total, showcase the relevant technique in six detailed photos. Each was selected because the technique involved is pivotal to success in the kitchen and because the recipe is a classic or based on one. The collections of must-do recipes that immediately follow the cooking lessons build on the specified techniques. For example, once you've learned how to make and assemble a basic lasagna, try the Many-Mushroom Manicotti and the Sky-High Roasted Red Pepper Lasagna, which, although they employ slightly differing methods, reinforce the principal technique and are just as electric in taste.

Before You Begin

Successfully completing a recipe is just one step in becoming master of your culinary destiny. Knowing how to work efficiently helps. Learning how to wield a knife is primary (the introductory cooking lesson on page 6 shows you how). Understanding the assumptions and tacit rules that so many recipe resources blithely make is also useful. Some of these are deciphered in the boxes and tips scattered throughout the book. I'd like to share a few more with you here.

- Read recipes (ingredients and method) thoroughly before you even don an apron. This arms you with all the foreknowledge you'll need, from what technique is used, to which steps you can do while some other components are cooking, to whether or not you have all the requisite ingredients and equipment. Believe me, there is nothing more frustrating than finding yourself halfway through a recipe only to discover you're out of baking powder!

- Have as many ingredients as possible ready and chopped or premeasured before you even preheat the skillet or oven. This means the cooking process will move along seamlessly. It's especially important in baking, when you cannot stop mid-recipe to search for the brown sugar.

- Some assumptions that are particularly handy for you to know are that in almost every case, when the size of an ingredient such as a potato or an onion is not specified, the recipe assumes you will use the medium size. One salient exception is eggs: all *Canadian Living* recipes are tested using large-size eggs. Another assumption our recipes make is that you will use salted butter unless unsalted is called for. And finally, unless otherwise noted, all vegetables should be peeled.

In the *Canadian Living* Test Kitchen, we know that every stove and oven is different and so we try to offer two tests for doneness, one based on time and one based on a visual cue. For example, our recipes usually read "cook for about 5 minutes or until onions are softened and golden." Those same onions may take 3 minutes on your neighbour's stove and 7 on yours, but at least you'll both be looking for them to turn that identifiably golden colour. Get to know the unique behaviour of your oven and stove top.

One Final Word

Last, I want to encourage you to taste as you go along. It can make the difference between a dish that just barely makes the grade and one that sings with perfect balance and depth. But mostly, have fun. Make mistakes. Make some more. Eat them all. Taste, and learn.

A Note on the Nutrient Analysis

To meet nutrient needs each day, moderately active women aged 25 to 49 need about 1,900 calories, 51 g protein, 261 g carbohydrate, 25 to 35 g fibre and not more than 63 g total fat (21 g saturated fat). Men and teenagers usually need more. Percentage of recommended daily intake (% RDI) is based on the highest recommended intakes (excluding those for pregnant and lactating women) for calcium, iron, and vitamins A, C and folate.

Figures have been rounded off. They are based on the first ingredient listed when there is a choice and do not include optional ingredients. Variations have not been analysed. ABBREVIATIONS: cal = calories; pro = protein; carb = carbohydrate; sat. fat = saturated fat; chol. = cholesterol.

Knife Skills

One of the essential skills that will take you the furthest in the kitchen is knowing how to wield a knife. This lesson comes first because it's simply that important. With practice, chopping, mincing and dicing will become second nature. Clockwise from top left: shred A; chop; cube; dice; julienne; shred B; slice; mince.

1 **Chop:** Peel onion or other round vegetable. On cutting board, cut onion in half lengthwise; place cut side down. With knife held horizontally, cut to (but not through) root end into thick or thin slices depending on use.

2 With knife held vertically, cut onion lengthwise almost to (not through) root end into same-size thickness of slices.

3 Keeping fingernails parallel to blade, hold onion securely with fingertips. Keeping tip of knife on cutting board, slice across onion with rocking motion, moving fingers away from blade while chopping onion into pieces.

Mince: Follow steps 1, 2 and 3, cutting into pieces no more than about ⅛ inch (3 mm) for most vegetables, smaller for garlic, gingerroot and shallots.

Slice: Peel vegetable if necessary. On cutting board, cut crosswise into thick or thin slices as desired. For diagonal slices, cut at 45-degree angle.

Julienne: Peel carrot or other dense vegetable if necessary. Cut crosswise into 2-inch (5 cm) lengths. Slice thin strip off 1 side; lay flat side down. Cut lengthwise into thin slices. Stack slices; cut lengthwise into thin matchstick-size strips.

Dice or Cube:
Dice: Gather julienned strips together in bundle; cut crosswise into tiny cubes.
Cube: Cut slices and strips thicker; cut crosswise into similar-size cubes.

Shred A (spinach, lettuce, herbs or other pliable leaves): Stack leaves on top of one another. Starting at long edge, tightly roll up into cylinder; cut crosswise into desired width of strips.

Shred B (cabbage and iceberg lettuce): Cut head in half, then into quarters lengthwise; cut out core. Place wedge cut side down; thinly slice crosswise.

Appetizers, Soups, Salads

Entertaining has been popular ever since our distant ancestors "broke bread" together. While the venue may have changed and the available ingredients expanded, our basic desire to share nourishment and culinary pleasure has remained constant. Of course, the ways in which we entertain have changed dramatically. Long gone are the spreads of days of old, with their attendant lavish expenditures of time and money. For a small dinner party or cocktail party, the new rules dictate fresh, seasonal and, above all, delicious but doable dishes.

Our recipes for starter courses and hors d'oeuvres reflect the new entertaining reality. They equip you with all the necessary tips and make-aheads to keep you happy and creative and your guests nibbling away. Phyllo need never again give you cause for worry after you've tried our provocatively flavoured Mushroom Red Pepper Pleated Puffs. The Chinese Pot Stickers, Sushi and Crispy Spring Rolls lessons will demystify the methods and ingredients so common to Asian cooking. Our soup lessons run the gamut from the essential chicken stock to thick, vegetable-based meals-in-a-bowl that will surely inspire many other combinations. So tuck into these irresistible dishes that whet and completely satisfy not only your appetite but also your culinary endeavours.

Mushroom Red Pepper Pleated Puffs

There's no question that phyllo has earned a bad rap. Most people think (incorrectly) that it's difficult to work with and that it is full of fat. This wonderful recipe dispels both rumours. It shows you just how easy working with phyllo can be – even when the package is full of pleats. Using a mustard-water combination with a minimum of butter proves that phyllo doesn't have to be dependent on layer after layer of fat.

Ingredients

1 lb	small mushrooms	500 g
2 tbsp	red wine vinegar	25 mL
¼ tsp	each salt and pepper	1 mL
1	jar (340 mL) roasted sweet red peppers	1
1 cup	fresh bread crumbs	250 mL
1 tbsp	liquid honey	15 mL
½ tsp	crushed dried mint	2 mL
10 oz	Oka or Port du Salut cheese	300 g
3 tbsp	sweet mustard	50 mL
12	sheets phyllo pastry	12
2 tbsp	butter, melted	25 mL
1	egg white, beaten	1

Makes 8 servings

Per serving: about 233 cal, 11 g pro, 14 g total fat (7 g sat. fat), 18 g carb, 2 g fibre, 46 mg chol. % RDI: 21% calcium, 12% iron, 15% vit A, 37% vit C, 11% folate.

Variation

Mushroom Prosciutto: Omit red pepper, honey and mint. Increase mushrooms to 2 lb (1 kg). Increase red wine vinegar to ¼ cup (50 mL). Cook mushrooms for 40 to 45 minutes. Add 4 oz (125 g) chopped prosciutto or thinly sliced ham to filling. Omit bread crumbs in filling; sprinkle about ½ cup (125 mL) bread crumbs among phyllo circles. Top each with 1 cup (250 mL) filling.

Tips

A 1-lb (454 g) package of frozen phyllo pastry usually contains 20 sheets. To thaw, place package in refrigerator for about 24 hours. It's best to refreeze any remaining phyllo only once.

If phyllo tears while working with it, simply mend it by patching torn sections together with melted butter.

Unbaked puffs can be refrigerated for up to 12 hours or wrapped individually and frozen for up to 2 weeks; increase baking time by 5 minutes.

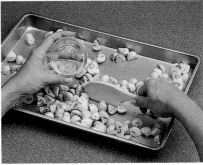

1 Trim and quarter mushrooms; place on 17- x 11-inch (45 x 29 cm) rimmed baking sheet. Sprinkle with vinegar and half each of the salt and pepper; toss to coat mushrooms evenly. Bake in 400°F (200°C) oven, stirring occasionally, for 35 to 40 minutes or until tender and liquid is evaporated. Let cool slightly.

2 Drain red peppers; pat dry with paper towels. Chop and place in large bowl. Add half of the bread crumbs, the honey, mint and remaining salt and pepper; toss to combine. Cut rind from cheese; shred and add to bowl along with mushrooms. Toss again and set aside. *(Filling can be covered and refrigerated for up to 1 day.)*

3 Blend mustard with 1 tbsp (15 mL) water; set aside. Layer 3 sheets of phyllo on work surface. Cover remaining phyllo with waxed paper or plastic wrap then damp towel to prevent drying out. Using sharp knife and 8-inch (20 cm) round cake pan or cardboard template as guide, cut out 2 circles from each sheet, discarding trimmings.

4 Place 2 circles side by side on work surface. Brush each lightly with mustard mixture. Top each with second circle; brush lightly with butter. Top each with remaining circles; brush again with mustard. Sprinkle 1 tbsp (15 mL) of the remaining bread crumbs in centre of each. Top crumbs with heaping ½ cup (125 mL) of the filling.

5 Fold 1 edge of phyllo to centre. Grasp point at edge where first fold begins; fold point over filling, forming pleat. Continue overlapping pleats but leaving ½-inch (1 cm) steam vent in centre; press to seal.

6 Place on parchment paper–lined or greased baking sheet. Brush all over with egg white. Repeat to make 8 puffs. Bake in 400°F (200°C) oven for 20 minutes or until golden brown and crisp.

drying out. Using ruler and sharp knife, cut sheet lengthwise into 5 strips, each about 2½ inches (6 cm) wide.

3 Using pastry brush, lightly brush each strip with butter. Spoon heaping teaspoonful (5 mL) of the filling about ½ inch (1 cm) from end of each strip.

4 Fold 1 corner of phyllo over filling so bottom edge of phyllo meets side edge to form triangle.

5 Fold up triangle. Continue folding triangle sideways and upward until end of phyllo strip is reached. Fold end flap over to adhere. Working quickly, form triangles with remaining strips. Repeat with remaining phyllo sheets and filling.

6 On baking sheets, brush phyllo triangles lightly with butter. *(Triangles can be prepared to this point and frozen on baking sheets. Store in airtight containers for up to 2 months. Do not thaw before baking.)* Bake in 375°F (190°C) oven for 15 to 18 minutes or until golden. Serve hot.

Makes 50 hors d'oeuvres
Per piece: about 46 cal, 1 g pro, 3 g total fat (2 g sat. fat), 3 g carb, 0 g fibre, 8 mg chol. % RDI: 2% calcium, 2% iron, 5% vit A, 2% folate.

Phyllo Triangles

Inspired by the Greek pie called spanakopita, these scrumptious bundles utilize the classic method of folding one sheet of phyllo into triangles, creating the illusion of a many-layered delicacy. Don't limit yourself to savoury ingredients; once you've mastered this technique, be sure to try a sweet rendition, such as blueberry or cherry turnovers.

10	sheets phyllo pastry	10
½ cup	butter, melted	125 mL

Spinach Cheese Filling:
1 tbsp	olive oil	15 mL
2 tbsp	minced onion	25 mL
2	cloves garlic, minced	2
1 cup	ricotta cheese	250 mL
¾ cup	chopped drained cooked spinach (10 oz/284 g pkg fresh)	175 mL
⅓ cup	freshly grated Parmesan cheese	75 mL
½ tsp	grated lemon rind	2 mL
Pinch	each salt, pepper and nutmeg	Pinch

1 **Spinach Cheese Filling:** In skillet, heat oil over medium-high heat; cook onion and garlic, stirring often, for 2 minutes or until softened. In bowl, stir together onion mixture, ricotta, spinach, Parmesan cheese, lemon rind, salt, pepper and nutmeg; set aside.

2 Place 1 sheet of phyllo on work surface. Cover remaining phyllo with waxed paper or plastic wrap then damp towel to prevent

Variation

Mushroom Sausage Cheese Filling: Increase olive oil to 2 tbsp (25 mL). Add 2½ cups (625 mL) chopped mushrooms and ¼ tsp (1 mL) hot pepper flakes to onion mixture; cook, stirring, for 3 to 5 minutes or until mushrooms are tender. Transfer to bowl. To skillet, add 8 oz (250 g) crumbled hot Italian sausage; cook, stirring, for 3 to 5 minutes or until golden. Add to bowl along with remaining ingredients, but omit spinach and nutmeg. Use 1½ tsp (7 mL) filling per triangle.

Fast Phyllo Cups

These easy, perfectly sized cups are the answer to a hostess's prayers. Ideal for the two following fillings, they can also simply be filled with a dollop of cream cheese and a dot of jalapeño jelly, or your favourite chutney and a sliver of roasted chicken or turkey.

6	sheets phyllo pastry	6
¼ cup	butter, melted	50 mL

1 Place 1 sheet of phyllo on work surface. Cover remaining phyllo with waxed paper or plastic wrap then damp towel to prevent drying out. Brush sheet lightly with butter. Top with second sheet; brush with butter. Top with third sheet; brush with butter. Cut lengthwise into 4 strips and crosswise into 6 strips to make 24 squares.

2 Press each square into 24 greased mini muffin or tart tins. Bake in 400°F (200°C) oven for about 5 minutes or until golden. Let cool in pan on rack. Repeat with remaining phyllo. *(Cups can be frozen in single layer in airtight container for up to 1 month; recrisp in 350°F/180°C oven for 3 minutes.)*

Makes 48 cups
Per cup: about 18 cal, trace pro, 1 g total fat (1 g sat. fat), 2 g carb, 0 g fibre, 3 mg chol. % RDI: 1% iron, 1% vit A.

Quick Fillers for Phyllo Cups

- Beat herb-flavoured cream cheese to soften and spoon or pipe into phyllo cups; top with toasted pecans or walnuts.
- Mix together light mayonnaise, Dijon mustard, hot pepper sauce and flaked crabmeat; spoon into phyllo cups.
- Mix together thin slivers of fresh peeled mango, light mayonnaise, Dijon mustard, curry powder and golden raisins; spoon into phyllo cups.
- Mix together small cubes of cooked lamb or chicken breast, store-bought baba ghanoush and slivered peeled cucumber; spoon into phyllo cups.

Warm Thai Shrimp

Fill your phyllo cups with these spicy shrimp at the last minute to prevent the pastry from becoming soggy.

2 tsp	vegetable oil	10 mL
1	small onion, chopped	1
½ tsp	red curry paste	2 mL
½ cup	coconut milk	125 mL
2 tsp	fish sauce	10 mL
1 lb	large raw shrimp, peeled and deveined	500 g
1½ tsp	lime juice	7 mL
2 tbsp	chopped fresh coriander	25 mL

1 In skillet, heat oil over medium heat; cook onion and curry paste, stirring, for about 5 minutes or until onion is softened.

2 Stir in coconut milk and fish sauce; bring to boil. Reduce heat and simmer for 2 minutes or until reduced by half.

3 Add shrimp to skillet; cook, stirring, for about 4 minutes or until opaque. Stir in lime juice. (*Shrimp can be covered and refrigerated for up to 1 day; reheat over low heat.*) Sprinkle with coriander.

Makes 8 servings
Per serving: about 87 cal, 9 g pro, 5 g total fat (3 g sat. fat), 2 g carb, trace fibre, 65 mg chol. % RDI: 1% calcium, 9% iron, 2% vit A, 2% vit C, 3% folate.

Thai Crab Salad Phyllo Cups

Here crabmeat takes centre stage amid a wonderful supporting cast of refreshing lime juice, fish sauce, chopped cucumber and sweet pepper. Opt for a light- rather than dark-colour fish sauce, which means it won't have a heavy, bitter tang. Store in the refrigerator. Colour is also a predictor of whether an open bottle has been in the refrigerator too long since the sauce darkens with age.

48	Fast Phyllo Cups (see page 12)	48
Filling:		
3 tbsp	vegetable oil	50 mL
3 tbsp	lime or lemon juice	50 mL
2 tbsp	granulated sugar	25 mL
4 tsp	fish or soy sauce	20 mL
1½ tsp	peanut butter	7 mL
1	clove garlic, minced	1
Dash	hot pepper sauce	Dash
8 oz	crabmeat (fresh or thawed) or salad shrimp	250 g
⅔ cup	each finely chopped English cucumber and sweet red pepper	150 mL
3 tbsp	each finely chopped green onion and fresh basil or mint	50 mL
2 tbsp	finely chopped peanuts	25 mL

1 **Filling:** In large bowl, whisk together oil, lime juice, sugar, fish sauce, peanut butter, garlic and hot pepper sauce until sugar is dissolved.

2 Gently squeeze any excess liquid from crabmeat. Add crabmeat to bowl along with cucumber, red pepper, onion and basil; toss to combine.

3 Spoon into phyllo cups. Sprinkle with chopped peanuts.

Makes 48 pieces
Per piece: about 38 cal, 2 g pro, 2 g total fat (1 g sat. fat), 3 g carb, trace fibre, 6 mg chol. % RDI: 1% iron, 2% vit A, 5% vit C, 2% folate.

Planning for Party Success

- Create a festive and celebratory mood by varying the appetizers in terms of colour, shape, texture and taste. Make sure your platters, napkins and glasses are beautiful and clean, too. Interesting platters in a variety of shapes always add flair.
- Calculate 10 to 12 small hors d'oeuvres per person if no meal is planned. If a meal is to follow, reduce that number to five or six.
- Be a part of the party, too! Make as many of the appetizers ahead of time as possible and factor this into your selection of appetizers. If appropriate, choose appetizers with components that can be made ahead then assembled at the last minute.
- Limit the number of hot appetizers because they usually need last-minute ministration.
- Always serve some items that need no tending, such as bowls of olives or plates of cubed cheese.
- Cold appetizers should actually be served at room temperature to allow the flavours to reach their potential.
- Bite-size appetizers are easy on your guests and you, eliminating the need for small plates.
- Remember that people eat with their eyes as well as their mouths, so stock up on edible flowers and fresh herbs to use as garnishes.
- An assortment of baskets holding a large variety of flatbreads and crackers is always attractive and useful.
- Have backup platters ready for when the plates being passed around start to look sparse.

Crudité Platter with Sesame Seed Dip

Whether you've just invited a few people over for dinner or are throwing a break-the-bank cocktail party, a platter of veggies and dip is always welcome. The array of dips you can concoct and the vegetable combinations and shapes are limited only by your imagination, your timetable and the season.

Ingredients

1 cup	snow peas, trimmed	250 mL
12	Chinese long beans	12
12	garlic chives or green onion strips	12
1	sweet red pepper, cored and seeded	1
Half	English cucumber	Half
2	carrots, peeled	2

Sesame Seed Dip:

½ cup	sesame seeds	125 mL
1	pkg (250 g) light cream cheese, softened	1
½ cup	light sour cream	125 mL
2 tbsp	soy sauce	25 mL
1 tbsp	minced green onion	15 mL
1 tsp	minced gingerroot	5 mL
1 tsp	rice vinegar	5 mL

Garnish:

4	hot red chili peppers	4

Makes 12 servings

Per 1 tbsp (15 mL) dip (without vegetables): about 50 cal, 2 g pro, 4 g total fat (2 g sat. fat), 2 g carb, trace fibre, 10 mg chol. % RDI: 2% calcium, 2% iron, 1% vit A, 2% folate.

1 **Sesame Seed Dip:** In small dry skillet, toast sesame seeds over medium-high heat, stirring constantly, for 5 minutes or until golden. Let cool. Transfer to food processor. Add cheese, sour cream, soy sauce, onion, ginger and vinegar; purée until smooth. (Dip can be refrigerated for up to 1 day.)

3 In saucepan of boiling water, immerse snow peas to blanch for 30 seconds or until colour brightens. With slotted spoon, transfer to bowl of ice water to stop cooking process. Repeat with beans, blanching for 2 minutes and using tongs. Repeat with chives, blanching for 30 seconds.

5 Cut red pepper, cucumber and carrots into 3-inch (8 cm) long sticks about ¼ inch (5 mm) thick. Using each chive as string and wrapping once or twice, tie vegetables into bundles of about 3 sticks each. Arrange on platter. Garnish with chili pepper flowers. Scrape dip into bowl.

2 **Garnish:** Wearing rubber gloves to prevent irritation of hands, trim tip from hot peppers. Starting about 1 inch (2.5 cm) from stem end, cut lengthwise into 6 strips; scrape out seeds. Soak in ice water in refrigerator for about 2 hours or until strips curl to resemble petals.

4 Place bowl for dip on serving platter. Cut out V shape from 1 end of each snow pea; arrange around bowl. Holding each long bean at ends, tie overhand knot in centre, leaving space in knot. Turn upside down so knot is at bottom; tie second knot at top. Arrange on platter.

6 **Variations:** Instead of bundles, cut red pepper into triangles. With channel knife, peel off strips from cucumber; cut into slices. With crinkle cutter, slice carrots diagonally. Other vegetables to try are cherry tomatoes, Belgian endive leaves, blanched asparagus spears and broccoli florets.

Greek Classics

The following three dips pay homage to the wonderful and vibrant flavours of Greece, with a salute to the trinity of lemon juice, olive oil and garlic that supports that wonderful cuisine.

Hummus

1	can (19 oz/540 mL) chick-peas, drained and rinsed	1
⅓ cup	tahini	75 mL
3 tbsp	each lemon juice and water	50 mL
1 tbsp	olive oil	15 mL
¾ tsp	ground cumin	4 mL
¼ tsp	salt	1 mL
2	cloves garlic, minced	2

1 In food processor, purée together chick-peas, tahini, lemon juice, water, oil, cumin and salt until smooth; transfer to bowl.

2 Stir in garlic. *(Hummus can be covered and refrigerated for up to 3 days.)*

Makes 2 cups (500 mL)
Per 1 tbsp (15 mL): about 34 cal, 1 g pro, 2 g total fat (trace sat. fat), 3 g carb, 1 g fibre, 1 mg chol. % RDI: 1% calcium, 2% iron, 2% vit C, 4% folate.

Variations

Herbed Hummus: Omit tahini and cumin. Stir in ¼ cup (50 mL) chopped fresh parsley, 2 green onions, chopped, and 1 tsp (5 mL) dried oregano.

Creamy Hummus: Omit tahini and cumin. Stir in ¼ cup (50 mL) herbed cream cheese, softened.

Black Olive Hummus: Stir in ¼ cup (50 mL) chopped oil-cured black olives.

Sun-Dried Tomato Hummus: Omit tahini, cumin and salt. Substitute sun-dried tomato oil for olive oil and stir in ¼ cup (50 mL) chopped drained oil-packed sun-dried tomatoes.

Roasted Red Pepper Hummus: Omit tahini and cumin. Blend in ¼ cup (50 mL) chopped roasted red peppers.

Minted Tzatziki

2 cups	plain yogurt	500 mL
Half	English cucumber	Half
½ tsp	salt	2 mL
2 tbsp	chopped fresh mint	25 mL
1 tbsp	each olive oil and lemon juice	15 mL
3	cloves garlic, minced	3
¼ tsp	pepper	1 mL

1 Line sieve with double thickness of cheesecloth; spoon in yogurt. Cover and let drain in refrigerator for at least 3 hours or for up to 24 hours to make about 1 cup (250 mL).

2 Peel and grate cucumber into sieve; sprinkle with half of the salt. Let drain for 1 hour.

3 In bowl, stir together drained yogurt and cucumber, remaining salt, mint, oil, lemon juice, garlic and pepper.

Makes 1½ cups (375 mL)
Per 1 tbsp (15 mL): about 18 cal, 1 g pro, 1 g total fat (0 g sat. fat), 1 g carb, 0 g fibre, 2 mg chol. % RDI: 3% calcium, 1% iron, 1% vit A, 2% vit C, 1% folate.

> **Tip**
>
> **Draining yogurt, as in the Minted Tzatziki, results in a divine-tasting product called yogurt cheese – a great replacement for whipping cream, a pleasing spread for sandwiches or a wonderful dip in its own right.**

Grilled Eggplant Dip

2	eggplants (about 2 lb/1 kg total)	2
2	cloves garlic, minced	2
1	green onion, minced	1
2 tbsp	chopped fresh parsley	25 mL
2 tbsp	extra-virgin olive oil	25 mL
1 tbsp	chopped fresh basil	15 mL
1 tbsp	lemon juice	15 mL
1 tsp	Dijon mustard	5 mL
	Salt and pepper	

1 With fork, prick eggplants all over. Grill over medium-high heat, turning occasionally, for 45 to 50 minutes or until tender and charred all over. Let stand on plate until cool enough to handle, reserving juices.

2 Cut eggplants in half lengthwise. With spoon, scoop out flesh to food processor or bowl, reserving any juices on plate; purée or mash with fork. Transfer to bowl.

3 Stir in garlic, onion, parsley, oil, basil, lemon juice, mustard and any juices on plate. Season with salt and pepper to taste.

Makes 2 cups (500 mL)

Per 1 tbsp (15 mL): about 14 cal, 0 g pro, 1 g total fat (0 g sat. fat), 2 g carb, 1 g fibre, 0 mg chol. % RDI: 1% iron, 2% vit C, 2% folate.

Grilled Antipasto Platter

Summer means easy entertaining. What better time for this make-ahead sensation? Choose your favourite vegetables and vary the meats as your tastes dictate, even substituting grilled shrimp, scallops and squid for the cold cuts. In a pinch, jarred marinated artichoke hearts and deli-purchased olives can round out the assortment nicely.

2	eggplants	2
2 tsp	salt	10 mL
1	each sweet red and yellow pepper	1
2	zucchini	2
1	large red onion	1
12	mushrooms	12
⅓ cup	extra-virgin olive oil	75 mL
6 oz	thinly sliced mozzarella or provolone cheese	175 g
6 oz	thinly sliced assorted Italian cold cuts (salami, mortadella, prosciutto, cooked ham)	175 g
1	tomato, cut in wedges	1
½ cup	black olives	125 mL

Dressing:

½ cup	extra-virgin olive oil	125 mL
⅓ cup	chopped fresh basil (or 1½ tsp/7 mL dried)	75 mL
1 tbsp	balsamic vinegar (or 2 tbsp/25 mL red wine vinegar)	15 mL
1 tbsp	Dijon mustard	15 mL
3	cloves garlic, minced	3
½ tsp	each salt and pepper	2 mL

1 Cut eggplants into ½-inch (1 cm) thick slices. In colander, sprinkle eggplant with salt; toss to coat and let drain for 30 minutes.

2 Meanwhile, place red and yellow peppers on greased grill over medium-high heat; cook, turning often, for 15 to 20 minutes or until charred. Let cool slightly. Peel, seed and cut peppers into 1-inch (2.5 cm) wide strips. Set aside.

3 Diagonally cut zucchini into ½-inch (1 cm) thick slices. Cut onion into ½-inch (1 cm) thick slices. Trim stems from mushroom caps. Rinse eggplant under cold running water; pat dry.

4 Lightly brush vegetables with oil. Place on grill and cook, turning occasionally, mushrooms and onions for 8 to 10 minutes, then eggplant and zucchini for 10 to 15 minutes, or until vegetables are tender but not charred. Set aside separately.

5 **Dressing:** In bowl, whisk together oil, basil, vinegar, mustard, garlic, salt and pepper. Add mushrooms and turn to coat; transfer mushrooms to large shallow baking dish. Repeat with onion, then zucchini, peppers and eggplant, arranging vegetables separately in dish. Refrigerate and marinate for at least 8 hours or for up to 24 hours; bring to room temperature before serving.

6 To serve, attractively arrange vegetables and cheese on large platter. If using salami, fold into cornets by overlapping 2 or 3 slices, then folding in half lengthwise before forming into cone shape. Nestle among vegetables along with other cold cuts. Garnish with tomato and olives.

Makes 6 to 8 servings

Per each of 8 servings: about 397 cal, 11 g pro, 32 g total fat (8 g sat. fat), 19 g carb, 5 g fibre, 32 mg chol. % RDI: 15% calcium, 14% iron, 17% vit A, 93% vit C, 19% folate.

Grilled Satays

Once you've tasted these satays with their accompanying peanut dipping sauce, you'll find all sorts of excuses to make this versatile sauce again: to dress a noodle salad accompanied by snow peas, miniature cobs of corn and sweet red pepper; to drizzle onto a pita sandwich filled with sliced grilled chicken and sprouts; or to brush on a pork tenderloin while it's being grilled. Satays are wonderful made with pork, beef or chicken.

Ingredients

1 lb	boneless pork loin	500 g
1	slice gingerroot, ½ inch (1 cm) thick	1
4	cloves garlic, minced	4
¼ cup	teriyaki sauce	50 mL
3 tbsp	vegetable oil	50 mL
2 tbsp	chopped fresh coriander	25 mL
2 tbsp	rice vinegar	25 mL
2 tsp	grated lemon rind	10 mL
1 tsp	lemon juice	5 mL
¼ tsp	hot pepper sauce	1 mL
1 tbsp	hoisin sauce	15 mL
1 tbsp	sherry	15 mL
⅓ cup	smooth peanut butter	75 mL
¼ cup	finely chopped green onions	50 mL

Makes 4 servings

Per serving: about 415 cal, 32 g pro, 27 g total fat (5 g sat. fat), 11 g carb, 2 g fibre, 70 mg chol. % RDI: 4% calcium, 13% iron, 1% vit A, 8% vit C, 13% folate.

Variation

Chicken or Beef Satays: Substitute ¾-inch (2 cm) thick boneless skinless chicken breasts or sirloin tip marinating steak for the pork; cut across the grain into ¼-inch (5 mm) thick strips. Cook chicken for about 4 minutes or until no longer pink inside. Cook beef for 4 to 6 minutes or until browned yet still pink inside.

1 With sharp chef's knife, trim any fat from pork. Cut into 1-inch (2.5 cm) thick slices. Cut across the grain into ¼-inch (5 mm) thick strips. Place in glass baking dish.

2 With sharp paring knife, peel ginger; finely chop with chef's knife. In bowl, whisk together ginger, garlic, teriyaki sauce, oil, coriander, vinegar, lemon rind and juice and hot pepper sauce.

3 Transfer ⅓ cup (75 mL) of the marinade to measuring cup; whisk in hoisin sauce and sherry. Pour over pork, stirring to coat. Cover and refrigerate, stirring occasionally, for at least 2 hours or for up to 4 hours.

4 Meanwhile, whisk peanut butter, onions and 3 tbsp (50 mL) warm water into remaining marinade. *(Peanut sauce can be covered and set aside for up to 4 hours.)*

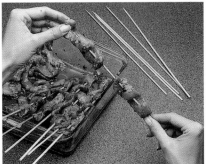

5 In shallow dish, soak 12-inch (30 cm) wooden skewers in water for at least 30 minutes. Reserving marinade, thread 2 or 3 pieces of pork onto each skewer, leaving 1 inch (2.5 cm) between pieces.

6 Place on greased grill over medium-high heat or under broiler; cook, brushing with marinade and turning once, for 3 to 4 minutes or until browned and just a hint of pink remains inside. Serve with peanut sauce.

Chinese Pot Stickers

**Pot stickers, Northern China's celebrated dumplings, have been the sweethearts of dim sum trays for a long time.
With our easy-to-follow steps, you'll soon find yourself making these tempting morsels
not only for your own version of dim sum but for cocktail parties as well.**

Ingredients

2 cups	finely chopped napa or green cabbage	500 mL
1 tsp	salt	5 mL
8 oz	shrimp, peeled, deveined and finely chopped	250 g
1 lb	lean ground pork	500 g
2 tbsp	light-colour soy sauce	25 mL
2 tbsp	rice wine (mirin), sherry or white wine	25 mL
1 tbsp	chopped green onion	15 mL
1 tbsp	sesame oil	15 mL
2 tsp	minced gingerroot	10 mL
1	clove garlic, minced	1
64	wonton wrappers (2 pkg total)	64
¼ cup	vegetable oil	50 mL
1 cup	chicken stock or water	250 mL

Dipping Sauce:

2 tbsp	light-colour soy sauce	25 mL
1 tbsp	rice vinegar	15 mL
1 tsp	minced gingerroot	5 mL

Makes 64 pieces

*Per piece: about 51 cal, 3 g pro, 3 g total fat
(1 g sat. fat), 4 g carb, 0 g fibre, 13 mg chol.
% RDI: 2% iron, 2% vit C, 7% folate.*

Tip

**Uncooked dumplings can be covered
with plastic wrap and refrigerated
for up to 24 hours, or frozen, then
stored in airtight container for up
to 1 week; thaw in refrigerator
before cooking.**

1 In bowl, toss cabbage with salt and let
stand for 5 minutes; squeeze out liquid.
Squeeze any liquid from shrimp. In large
bowl, mix together cabbage, shrimp, pork,
soy sauce, wine, onion, oil, ginger and garlic.
*(Filling can be covered and refrigerated for up
to 6 hours.)*

2 With 3-inch (8 cm) round cutter,
cut wonton wrappers into circles,
keeping covered with damp towel to prevent
drying out. Working with 4 wrappers at a
time, brush edges lightly with water. On
1 half of each round, pinch four ¼-inch
(5 mm) pleats.

3 In rounded hollow of each wrapper,
place 2 tsp (10 mL) filling; fold pleated
side over filling, matching edges and pressing
out all air. Press edges to seal.

4 Arrange, seam side up, on waxed
paper–lined baking sheet, curving into
crescent shape and pressing lightly to flatten
bottom. Cover with damp towel.

5 In 2 large skillets, heat 1 tbsp (15 mL)
oil per pan over medium-high heat;
fry 16 dumplings in each, flat side down,
for 1 minute or until golden on bottom.
Pour ¼ cup (50 mL) stock into each pan;
reduce heat to low. Cover and cook, without
turning, for 7 minutes or until dumplings
are translucent and most of the liquid
is evaporated.

6 Uncover and increase heat to medium;
cook for 5 to 7 minutes or until liquid
evaporates and bottoms are dark brown.
Drain on paper towels. Transfer to dish;
keep warm. Wipe pans; repeat with
remaining dumplings.

Dipping Sauce: Stir together soy
sauce, vinegar and ginger; serve with hot
or warm dumplings.

Sushi

Sushi is one of the most wonderful appetizers because you can get your guests involved in assembling and rolling it, something I've never known anyone to refuse (any guest worth his or her salt, I mean!). This type of sushi is called *futomaki*, or thick sushi roll. Equip yourself with a few rolling mats (available at Japanese specialty stores) or use a folded tea towel as a substitute. For utmost authenticity, use seasoned rice vinegar (it is sweeter and more traditional) and serve with small mounds of pickled ginger and wasabi (Japanese horseradish) and a little bowl of soy sauce for dipping.

Ingredients

2¼ cups	water	550 mL
2 cups	Japanese rice, rinsed and drained	500 mL
⅓ cup	rice vinegar	75 mL
¼ cup	granulated sugar	50 mL
2 tbsp	rice wine (mirin)	25 mL
2 tsp	salt	10 mL
4	sheets nori (pressed seaweed)	4

Filling:

10	dried shiitake mushrooms	10
1 tbsp	soy sauce	15 mL
1 tsp	granulated sugar	5 mL
1 tsp	wasabi powder	5 mL
1	pkg (7 oz/200 g) frozen flaked crabmeat, thawed (or 2 oz/60 g smoked salmon, cut in strips)	1
Quarter	English cucumber, cut in long ½-inch (1 cm) thick sticks	Quarter
Half	bunch watercress	Half
2 tsp	sesame seeds, toasted	10 mL

Makes 32 pieces

Per piece: about 65 cal, 3 g pro, 0 g total fat (0 g sat. fat), 13 g carb, 0 g fibre, 4 mg chol. % RDI: 1% calcium, 2% iron, 2% vit A, 3% vit C, 4% folate.

1 In 8-cup (2 L) saucepan, cover and bring water and rice to boil; boil for 2 minutes. Reduce heat to low; cook for 15 minutes. Remove from heat; let stand, covered, for 15 minutes. Meanwhile, in small saucepan, bring vinegar, sugar, mirin and salt to boil, stirring just until sugar dissolves; let cool.

2 Spread rice in large shallow dish. Sprinkle with half of the vinegar mixture; toss with fork. Toss with remaining vinegar mixture. Cover with damp towel; refrigerate for 45 minutes or until at room temperature. Meanwhile, toast nori sheets by quickly brushing 10 times per side over electric element on high heat or gas element on medium heat.

3 **Filling:** Meanwhile, in small saucepan, soak mushrooms in ½ cup (125 mL) warm water for 30 minutes. Add soy sauce and sugar; simmer for 10 minutes or until no liquid remains. Discard stems; slice caps thinly. Combine wasabi with a few drops of water to form paste.

4 Place rolling mat (*maki-su*) on work surface with shortest side closest; place nori sheet, shiny side down, on mat. With wet fingers, press one-quarter of the rice evenly over nori, leaving 1-inch (2.5 cm) border on far side uncovered.

5 Dab thin line of wasabi over rice ½ inch (1 cm) from edge. Top with one-quarter each of the crab, then mushrooms. Arrange one-quarter of the cucumber in row beside mushrooms; top with one-quarter of the watercress. Sprinkle with ½ tsp (2 mL) seeds.

6 Holding filling in place with fingers, tightly roll mat over filling. Using mat as guide, roll up firmly, jelly roll–style, squeezing to compress. With sharp wet knife, trim ends; cut into eight ½-inch (1 cm) thick slices. Repeat with remaining ingredients.

Crispy Spring Rolls

To make these great spring rolls, look for frozen spring roll wrappers called lumpia skins or Shanghai wrappers, sold in Asian stores and some supermarkets. Egg roll wrappers can be used instead but they're thicker, so the spring rolls won't be as crispy.

Ingredients

8	dried Chinese black mushrooms	8
12 oz	boneless pork loin	375 g
12 oz	raw shrimp	375 g
2 tbsp	sesame oil	25 mL
1 tbsp	vegetable oil	15 mL
1	clove garlic, minced	1
1 tsp	minced gingerroot	5 mL
2 cups	shredded napa cabbage	500 mL
1 cup	bean sprouts	250 mL
½ cup	water chestnuts, slivered	125 mL
4	green onions, sliced	4
2 tbsp	oyster sauce	25 mL
1 tbsp	soy sauce	15 mL
½ tsp	salt	2 mL
2 tsp	cornstarch	10 mL
1	pkg 6-inch (15 cm) frozen spring roll wrappers	1
2	egg whites	2
	Vegetable oil for deep-frying	

Dipping Sauce:

⅓ cup	plum sauce	75 mL
1 tbsp	lemon juice	15 mL
½ tsp	Asian chili sauce	2 mL
1	clove garlic, minced	1

Makes 24 pieces

Per piece: about 92 cal, 7 g pro, 3 g total fat (1 g sat. fat), 8 g carb, 1 g fibre, 30 mg chol. % RDI: 1% calcium, 4% iron, 1% vit A, 5% vit C, 11% folate.

Tip

Cooked spring rolls can be cooled, wrapped and frozen for up to 1 month. To serve, bake frozen rolls in 375°F (190°C) oven for 20 minutes or until hot.

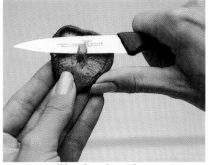

1 In small bowl, soak mushrooms in warm water for 20 minutes; drain. Cut off and discard tough stems; chop caps finely and set aside. Slice pork thinly across the grain; chop finely. Peel and devein shrimp; chop coarsely.

2 In wok or skillet, heat sesame and vegetable oils over high heat; stir-fry pork, shrimp, garlic and ginger for 2 minutes or until pork is no longer pink. Add mushrooms, cabbage, bean sprouts, water chestnuts, onions, oyster sauce, soy sauce and salt; stir-fry for 3 minutes.

3 Push mixture to side of wok. Blend cornstarch with 2 tsp (10 mL) water; pour into liquid in wok and cook, stirring, for 1 minute or until thickened. Stir vegetable mixture back into liquid. Transfer to large bowl; refrigerate for 1 hour or until cooled completely.

4 Working with 1 spring roll wrapper at a time and keeping remaining wrappers covered with moist towel, lay wrapper on work surface with 1 corner toward you. Place 3 tbsp (50 mL) filling about 2 inches (5 cm) from corner.

5 Fold corner over filling. Brush remaining edges with egg whites. Fold in both sides and roll up firmly into cylinder. Set aside in single layer, uncovered. In wok, Dutch oven or deep-fryer, heat oil over high heat until deep-frying thermometer registers 375°F (190°C).

6 Deep-fry rolls, in batches of 4, for 4 to 5 minutes or until golden, turning once. Remove with tongs or slotted spoon; drain well on paper towels.

Dipping Sauce: In small bowl, combine plum sauce, lemon juice, chili sauce and garlic. Serve with spring rolls.

Two-Salmon Pâté

This dynamite appetizer transcends seasons. It's light enough to suit the warm months of spring and summer but elegant enough to adorn any fall or winter entertaining buffet. Serve whole slices for a formal sit-down dinner or merely accompany with toasts and crackers on those occasions when your guests are milling about, drink in hand.

Ingredients

1	pkg (7 g) unflavoured gelatin	1
¼ cup	water	50 mL
1	can (7½ oz/213 g) sockeye salmon	1
1 cup	finely chopped smoked salmon (6 oz/175 g)	250 mL
4 oz	cream cheese	125 g
¼ cup	light mayonnaise	50 mL
2 tbsp	lemon juice	25 mL
¼ tsp	hot pepper sauce	1 mL
2 tbsp	minced green onion	25 mL
2 tbsp	chopped fresh dill	25 mL
¾ cup	whipping cream	175 mL

Garnish:

	Cucumber	
3 oz	thinly sliced smoked salmon	75 g
	Dill sprigs	

Makes 12 to 16 servings

Per each of 12 servings (with garnish): about 150 cal, 8 g pro, 12 g total fat (6 g sat. fat), 1 g carb, 0 g fibre, 42 mg chol. % RDI: 5% calcium, 4% iron, 12% vit A, 2% vit C, 2% folate.

Tips

You can use any decorative mould as long as it has a 4-cup (1 L) capacity. Lining the pan or mould with plastic wrap makes unmoulding easier. Warm a knife under steaming hot water and use it to smooth away any crease lines left by the plastic wrap.

When whipping cream that has to be folded into a batter or mousse, underwhip it slightly so that it still holds peaks but is not yet stiff. The folding process continues to "work" the cream, so if it's stiff to begin with, it will create unpleasant lumps in your mousse or batter.

Pâté can be refrigerated before unmoulding for up to 2 days.

1 In small saucepan, sprinkle gelatin over water; let stand for 1 minute to soften. Warm over low heat, stirring, until dissolved. Remove from heat; set aside.

2 Drain sockeye salmon, discarding juice. In food processor or blender, combine sockeye salmon, half of the smoked salmon, cream cheese, mayonnaise, lemon juice and hot pepper sauce; purée until smooth. Add gelatin mixture; process to blend.

3 Transfer to bowl; stir in remaining smoked salmon, onion and dill. Whip cream; stir about one-quarter into salmon mixture. Fold in remaining cream. Line 8- x 4-inch (1.5 L) loaf pan with plastic wrap; pour in salmon mixture, smoothing top. Cover with plastic wrap and refrigerate for at least 4 hours or until firm.

4 To unmould, unwrap top and invert serving platter over pan. Grasp platter and pan; quickly turn over and lift off pan. Remove plastic wrap.

5 **Garnish:** For cucumber twist, peel cucumber lengthwise at ½-inch (1 cm) intervals; cut 12 to 16 very thin slices. Make cut in each slice from centre to outside edge; twist in opposite directions to form S shape. Arrange around pâté.

6 For each rose, cut salmon into 5- x 1-inch (12 x 2.5 cm) strip. Tightly roll up 1 inch (2.5 cm) to form cone. Pinch cone at base, letting free end dangle. Gather up strip, a little at a time, around cone, bending out upper edges to resemble petals. Garnish pâté with salmon roses and dill sprigs.

Pâté Maison

A welcome addition to any appetizer table, pâté is a great make-ahead since it has to sit for a minimum of
12 hours after it's cooked. Pâté can be coarse or smooth. A pâté maison typically falls into the former
category and uses pieces of ham to make it chunky. Serve with toasted Italian bread slices,
crisped pita triangles, melba toasts or garlic-rubbed slices of French bread.

Ingredients

3 tbsp	butter	50 mL
1	onion, diced	1
4	cloves garlic, minced	4
12 oz	chicken livers, trimmed and halved	375 g
12 oz	each ground pork and ground veal	375 g
4 oz	smoked ham, diced	125 g
¼ cup	dry sherry	50 mL
1	egg, beaten	1
1½ tsp	each salt and pepper (approx)	7 mL
1 tsp	Dijon mustard	5 mL
¾ tsp	dried thyme	4 mL
½ tsp	nutmeg	2 mL
3	bay leaves	3
3 tbsp	cracked peppercorns	50 mL

Makes about 20 servings

Per serving: about 112 cal, 11 g pro, 6 g total fat
(3 g sat. fat), 2 g carb, 0 g fibre, 120 mg chol.
% RDI: 1% calcium, 13% iron, 64% vit A,
5% vit C, 46% folate.

Tips

Sherry can be replaced with chicken stock.

To crack peppercorns, place between sheets of waxed paper on cutting board and smash with rolling pin or bottom of saucepan.

Add pistachio nuts or hazelnuts for even more crunch; avoid softer nuts such as pecans or walnuts.

1 In skillet, melt butter over medium-high heat; cook onion and garlic for 3 minutes or until softened. Add chicken livers; cook, stirring often, for about 5 minutes or until just slightly pink inside. Let cool for 5 minutes.

2 In food processor or blender, purée chicken liver mixture until smooth. Transfer to large bowl. Add pork, veal, ham, sherry, egg, salt, pepper, mustard, thyme and nutmeg; mix well.

3 To test for seasoning, form 1 small patty of meat mixture. Cook in skillet over medium-high heat for about 1 minute per side or until no longer pink inside; let cool. Taste, then adjust seasoning of meat mixture with more salt and pepper if desired.

4 Pack meat mixture into greased 9- x 5-inch (2 L) loaf pan; arrange bay leaves over top. Tap pan on counter to remove air bubbles. Place in larger pan.

5 Pour in enough water to come halfway up sides. Cover pan tightly with foil. Bake in 350°F (180°C) oven for about 2 hours or until meat thermometer registers 160° to 170°F (70° to 75°C).

6 Discard bay leaves; pour off any juices. Let cool, covered, for 30 minutes. Refrigerate for at least 12 hours or for up to 48 hours. To serve, let stand at room temperature for 30 minutes; unmould onto serving platter. Coat top with peppercorns.

Roasted Tomatoes Two Ways

Roasting has become such a popular cooking method that whole cookbooks have been devoted to the subject, and with good reason. Roasting brings out all the depth and sweetness of food, whether it's meat, a pear, an onion or a tomato. Roasted tomatoes have an intensity that fresh tomatoes lack, making them ideal to use for crostini, as the base of a nouvelle pizza or as the foundation of a wickedly pleasing tomato soup.

Ingredients

Roasted Tomatoes

4 lb	ripe plum tomatoes (about 20 whole)	2 kg
4	cloves garlic, minced	4
¼ cup	chopped fresh basil	50 mL
¼ cup	extra-virgin olive oil	50 mL
¼ tsp	each salt and pepper	1 mL

Makes 40 halves

Per half: about 21 cal, 0 g pro, 1 g total fat (0 g sat. fat), 2 g carb, 1 g fibre, 0 mg chol. % RDI: 1% iron, 5% vit A, 12% vit C, 1% folate.

Roasted Tomato Crostini

1	French stick (baguette), 20 inches (50 cm) long	1
4 oz	cream goat cheese (chèvre)	125 g
40	roasted tomato halves	40
20	fresh basil leaves	20

Makes 20 pieces

Per piece: about 104 cal, 3 g pro, 5 g total fat (2 g sat. fat), 12 g carb, 1 g fibre, 5 mg chol. % RDI: 2% calcium, 6% iron, 10% vit A, 22% vit C, 8% folate.

Roasted Tomato Soup

40	roasted tomato halves	40
2 tsp	olive oil	10 mL
1	onion, chopped	1
4 cups	vegetable or chicken stock	1 L
2 tsp	granulated sugar	10 mL
¼ cup	chopped fresh basil	50 mL
½ tsp	pepper	2 mL
¼ tsp	salt	1 mL
2 tbsp	finely shredded Asiago or freshly grated Parmesan cheese (optional)	25 mL

Makes 4 servings

Per serving: about 267 cal, 5 g pro, 18 g total fat (2 g sat. fat), 28 g carb, 6 g fibre, 0 mg chol. % RDI: 5% calcium, 18% iron, 49% vit A, 110% vit C, 17% folate.

1 **Roasted Tomatoes:** Trim stem end of tomatoes; cut in half lengthwise. Arrange, cut side up and without crowding, on large foil-lined rimmed baking sheet.

2 Stir together garlic, basil and oil; brush over tomatoes. Sprinkle with salt and pepper. Bake in 400°F (200°C) oven for 2 hours or until softened, shrivelled and edges begin to darken.

3 **Roasted Tomato Crostini:** Cut bread into 20 slices; broil on baking sheet until toasted. Spread evenly with goat cheese; top each with 2 tomato halves and 1 basil leaf.

1 **Roasted Tomato Soup:** Chop 6 of the tomato halves; set aside. In large saucepan, heat oil over medium heat; cook onion, stirring occasionally, for 5 minutes or until softened. Add remaining tomatoes, stock, 1½ cups (375 mL) water and sugar; bring to boil. Reduce heat and simmer for 15 minutes.

2 Transfer to blender or food processor; purée until smooth. Return to saucepan. Stir in basil, pepper and salt; heat until steaming.

3 Ladle into warmed soup bowls. Sprinkle with cheese (if using). Scatter reserved chopped tomatoes over top.

Chicken Noodle Soup with Homemade Stock

The first time I made chicken stock and soup, I felt a sense of personal victory. That very first pot aligned me with the generations of women in my family who had always produced wondrous chicken soups, as well as with a professional lineage to which I aspired. Truthfully, I still feel that same sense of pride each and every time I make chicken soup.

Ingredients

2 tbsp	butter	25 mL
½ cup	minced onion	125 mL
1½ cups	each sliced carrots and celery	375 mL
1 cup	sliced parsnips	250 mL
1½ cups	egg noodles	375 mL
¼ cup	chopped fresh parsley	50 mL
	Hot pepper sauce	
	Salt and pepper	

Homemade Chicken Stock:

5 lb	stewing hen or roasting chicken	2.2 kg
2	carrots, chopped	2
2	stalks celery, chopped	2
1	onion, chopped	1
1	leek, chopped (optional)	1
3	sprigs fresh parsley	3
1	bay leaf	1
1 tsp	salt	5 mL
½ tsp	dried thyme	2 mL
½ tsp	whole black peppercorns	2 mL

Makes 6 to 8 servings

Per each of 8 servings: about 185 cal, 16 g pro, 7 g total fat (3 g sat. fat), 13 g carb, 2 g fibre, 45 mg chol. % RDI: 4% calcium, 11% iron, 56% vit A, 8% vit C, 11% folate.

Variation

Oriental Chicken Soup: Add 1 tbsp (15 mL) chopped gingerroot to onions while softening. Reduce carrots and celery to 1 cup (250 mL) each, diagonally sliced. Substitute 1 cup (250 mL) diagonally sliced bok choy for the parsnips. Omit noodles. Cook soup for 10 to 15 minutes or until vegetables are softened. Substitute slivered chicken for diced. Add 1 cup (250 mL) snow peas, ¼ cup (50 mL) sherry and 2 tbsp (25 mL) soy sauce along with the chicken. Omit parsley and pepper sauce.

1 **Homemade Chicken Stock:** Place hen or roasting chicken in stockpot or Dutch oven; add 16 cups (4 L) water. Bring to boil; skim off froth. Add carrots, celery, onion, leek (if using), parsley, bay leaf, salt, thyme and peppercorns. Reduce heat and simmer, partially covered, for 2 to 2½ hours for hen, 1 to 1½ hours for chicken, or until juices run clear when thigh is pierced.

3 Remove fat from surface. Set aside 8 cups (2 L). Refrigerate remaining 7 cups (1.75 L) for up to 3 days or freeze for up to 4 months for another use.

5 Add noodles; cook, uncovered, for 8 to 10 minutes or until noodles and vegetables are tender.

2 Remove chicken and refrigerate. Strain liquid through cheesecloth-lined sieve into large shallow bowl, pressing vegetables to extract as much liquid as possible. Let cool, cover and refrigerate for at least 6 hours or for up to 12 hours.

4 **Chicken Noodle Soup:** In large saucepan, melt butter over medium heat; cook onion, stirring occasionally, for 3 minutes or until softened. Add reserved 8 cups (2 L) chicken stock; bring to boil. Add carrots, celery and parsnips; cover and cook over medium-high heat for 5 minutes.

6 Remove skin and bones from chicken. Dice meat and add 2 cups (500 mL) to soup; heat through. Stir in parsley; season with hot pepper sauce, salt and pepper to taste. Refrigerate remaining chicken for another use.

Tips

You can make this soup ahead of time and refrigerate it for up to 5 days. To freeze for up to 1 month, omit potatoes and pasta. Potatoes do not freeze well, because they break down when thawed; pasta continues to absorb liquid, becoming flabby. Add them when reheating by simmering, covered, for 10 to 15 minutes or until potatoes are tender, adding more chicken stock if desired.

Refrigerate the pesto separately for up to 5 days. To freeze it for up to 1 month, omit the Parmesan, then stir it in after thawing.

Grate Parmesan cheese right after buying it and store it in the freezer until needed. But don't throw out the rind. It's great used in soups as a flavouring agent that gets discarded just before serving.

Minestrone with Parsley Pesto

This thick soup warms both the body and the soul. It's chock-full of vegetables, beans and pasta, with a cheesy, gutsy pesto to top it all off. Try to use authentic Parmigiano-Reggiano cheese – identified by the stencilling on the rind – for the best flavour.

1 cup	dried red or white kidney beans	250 mL
4 oz	pancetta or bacon, unsliced	125 g
1 tbsp	olive oil	15 mL
2	onions, chopped	2
2	cloves garlic, minced	2
8 cups	chicken stock	2 L
2	each carrots and celery stalks, diagonally sliced	2
Half	small cabbage, finely shredded	Half
1	can (28 oz/796 mL) tomatoes, mashed	1
1	bay leaf	1
1 tsp	each dried basil and oregano	5 mL
½ tsp	salt	2 mL
¼ tsp	pepper	1 mL
3	potatoes (1 lb/500 g)	3
1 cup	rotini, macaroni or tubetti pasta	250 mL

Parsley Pesto:

1 cup	packed fresh parsley	250 mL
¼ cup	extra-virgin olive oil	50 mL
2 tbsp	pine nuts or walnuts	25 mL
1	clove garlic, minced	1
¼ cup	freshly grated Parmesan cheese	50 mL
	Salt and pepper	

1 In bowl, cover beans with 3 cups (750 mL) water. Cover and soak overnight; drain, discarding water. Cut pancetta into cubes.

2 In Dutch oven, heat oil over medium-high heat; cook pancetta, onions and garlic, stirring occasionally, for 5 minutes or until softened. Add beans and stock; bring to boil, skimming off foam. Reduce heat, cover and simmer over medium-low heat for 1 hour or until beans are tender.

3 Add carrots, celery and cabbage to pot along with tomatoes, bay leaf, basil, oregano, salt and pepper; bring to boil. Reduce heat, cover and simmer for 20 minutes.

4 Meanwhile, peel and cube potatoes; add to pot along with rotini. Simmer, covered, for 10 to 15 minutes or until potatoes are tender. Discard bay leaf.

5 **Parsley Pesto:** In food processor, purée together parsley, oil and pine nuts until smooth; transfer to bowl. Stir in garlic and Parmesan cheese. Season with salt and pepper to taste. Ladle soup into bowls; top each with 1 tbsp (15 mL) pesto.

Makes 8 servings
Per serving: about 419 cal, 17 g pro, 21 g total fat (5 g sat. fat), 42 g carb, 9 g fibre, 12 mg chol. % RDI: 13% calcium, 32% iron, 56% vit A, 60% vit C, 58% folate.

Variations

Garden Minestrone: Use unpeeled new potatoes. Omit cabbage. Add 3 cups (750 mL) cubed zucchini and 1 cup (250 mL) peas along with potatoes.

Basil Pesto: Substitute basil for the parsley; reduce oil to 2 tbsp (25 mL).

Roasted Vegetable Stock

Freeze stock in 1-cup (250 mL) portions for easy use in soups, vegetarian stews or even risotto.

3	carrots	3
3	onions	3
3	stalks celery (with leaves)	3
1 cup	sliced mushroom stems or caps	250 mL
3	cloves garlic	3
2 tsp	vegetable oil	10 mL
10	sprigs fresh parsley	10
1 tsp	crumbled dried mushrooms	5 mL
10	peppercorns, cracked	10
2	bay leaves	2
8 cups	cold water	2 L
½ tsp	salt	2 mL

1 Cut carrots, onions and celery into chunks; place in roasting pan. Add fresh mushrooms, garlic and oil, stirring to coat vegetables. Roast in 450°F (230°C) oven, stirring halfway

through, for 40 minutes or until softened and browned at edges.

2 Transfer to stockpot. Add parsley, dried mushrooms, peppercorns, bay leaves and all but 1 cup (250 mL) of the water.

3 Pour remaining water into roasting pan, stirring with wooden spoon and scraping up any brown bits from bottom of pan. Pour into stockpot; bring to boil. Skim off foam. Reduce heat to medium; simmer for 40 minutes.

4 Strain through fine sieve, gently pressing vegetables to extract liquid. Stir in salt.

Makes about 5 cups (1.25 L)
Per 1 cup (250 mL): about 19 cal, 0 g pro, 2 g total fat (0 g sat. fat), 1 g carb, 0 g fibre, 0 mg chol. % RDI: 1% calcium, 1% iron, 6% vit A.

Basic Vegetable Stock

A flavourful alternative to chicken stock, this versatile stock can accommodate most of the vegetables found in your crisper.

1 tsp	vegetable oil	5 mL
2	carrots	2
2	onions, coarsely chopped	2
1	leek, coarsely chopped	1
1	stalk celery (with leaves), chopped	1
10	sprigs fresh parsley	10
3	sprigs fresh thyme (or ½ tsp/2 mL dried)	3
10	peppercorns, cracked	10
2	bay leaves	2
8 cups	cold water	2 L
½ tsp	salt	2 mL

1 In stockpot, heat oil over medium heat; cook carrots, onions, leek and celery, stirring often, for 10 minutes or until softened but not coloured.

2 Add parsley, thyme, peppercorns, bay leaves and water; bring to boil. Skim off foam. Reduce heat to medium; simmer for 40 minutes.

3 Strain through fine sieve, gently pressing vegetables to extract liquid. Stir in salt.

Makes about 5 cups (1.25 L)
Per 1 cup (250 mL): about 11 cal, 0 g pro, 1 g total fat (0 g sat. fat), 1 g carb, 0 g fibre, 0 mg chol. % RDI: 1% calcium, 1% iron, 4% vit A.

Soup Savvy

- *Bisque:* Usually made with shellfish, this soup is rich and creamy with a velvety smoothness.
- *Broth:* Made by simmering either poultry, meat, fish or vegetables in water to produce a subtly flavoured and lightly coloured soup, broth is either eaten on its own or used as a foundation for other soups.
- *Chowder:* A hearty soup containing chunks of fish, shellfish and/or vegetables that generally also contains milk and potatoes. Most commonly started with a roux (a thickener made of equal parts butter and flour).

- *Consommé:* A clear, richly flavoured soup made by reducing stock, which is then clarified and filtered.
- *Gumbo:* A classic Cajun dish that is a cross between a thick soup and a stew. Flavoured with bay leaves, Worcestershire sauce and cayenne, containing a variety of vegetables, seafood and meat, and usually thickened with okra and served over rice.
- *Stock:* A clear, well-flavoured liquid made by simmering poultry, meat or fish and their bones in water along with root vegetables; used as a base for other soups and cooking of grains and/or vegetables.

Two-Mushroom Barley Soup

In the *Canadian Living* Test Kitchen, I have occasionally been accused of overselling barley, a grain I admittedly love and admire. This hearty soup, with its woodsy mushroom base, is the perfect vehicle for this versatile grain, which lends both creaminess and bulk to a comforting and nourishing meal in a bowl.

Ingredients

1 oz	dried mushrooms (porcini or shiitake)	30 g
4	carrots	4
1 lb	button mushrooms (about 8 cups/2 L)	500 g
2 tbsp	vegetable oil	25 mL
2	onions, finely chopped	2
3	cloves garlic, minced	3
1¼ tsp	dried thyme	6 mL
¾ tsp	crumbled dried sage	4 mL
½ tsp	pepper	2 mL
¼ tsp	salt	1 mL
2 tbsp	tomato paste	25 mL
2 tbsp	soy sauce	25 mL
1 tbsp	balsamic vinegar or red wine vinegar	15 mL
1 cup	pearl or pot barley	250 mL
6 cups	chicken or vegetable stock	1.5 L
3 cups	water	750 mL
4 cups	packed fresh spinach	1 L

Makes 6 servings

Per serving: about 280 cal, 11 g pro, 7 g total fat (1 g sat. fat), 46 g carb, 10 g fibre, 0 mg chol. % RDI: 10% calcium, 36% iron, 152% vit A, 18% vit C, 45% folate.

1 In small bowl, cover dried mushrooms with 1 cup (250 mL) boiling water; let stand for 20 minutes or until softened. Strain through cheesecloth-lined sieve, reserving liquid. If using shiitake, cut off tough stem end. Slice mushrooms into thin strips; set aside.

2 Meanwhile, peel carrots. On cutting board and using sharp chef's knife, slice carrots diagonally; set aside. Using damp cloth or paper towel, wipe button mushroom caps clean. Cut off tough stem ends; slice caps thickly.

3 In large saucepan, heat oil over medium heat; cook onions and garlic, stirring often, for 5 minutes or until softened. Add carrots and dried and button mushrooms; cook, stirring often, for 15 to 20 minutes or until mushrooms are lightly browned and liquid is evaporated.

4 Stir in thyme, sage, pepper and salt. Stir in tomato paste, soy sauce, vinegar and reserved soaking liquid. Add barley; cook, stirring, for 1 to 2 minutes or until well coated and liquid is absorbed.

5 Add stock and water; bring to boil. Reduce heat, cover and simmer, stirring occasionally, for 50 minutes. Uncover and cook for 20 minutes or until slightly thickened. *(Soup can be prepared to this point and refrigerated in airtight container for up to 2 days; reheat gently, adding up to ½ cup/ 125 mL more water to thin if desired.)*

6 Trim spinach; flatten and stack leaves with stems at 1 end. Starting at long side, roll up tightly. Using sharp chef's knife, slice crosswise into ½-inch (1 cm) wide strips; stir into soup. Cover and cook for 3 minutes or until wilted.

Gazpacho

Fiery-looking in a bowl but cool on a spoon, gazpacho is a hot-weather dish that hails from Spain. Half salad, half soup, this refreshing dish is low in fat and eminently adaptable. Try the pepped-up Fire and Ice variation as well as the more mildly spiced classic version.

Ingredients

3	tomatoes, peeled	3
1	each sweet red and green pepper, halved and seeded	1
1	English cucumber, peeled	1
2	cloves garlic, chopped	2
2 tbsp	red wine vinegar	25 mL
1 tbsp	olive oil	15 mL
3½ cups	vegetable cocktail (approx)	875 mL
¼ tsp	hot pepper sauce	1 mL
	Salt and pepper	

Garnish:

1 tbsp	olive oil	15 mL
1	clove garlic, minced	1
2	slices day-old bread, crusts removed	2
2	green onions, sliced	2

Makes 8 servings

Per serving: about 94 cal, 2 g pro, 4 g total fat (1 g sat. fat), 14 g carb, 2 g fibre, 0 mg chol. % RDI: 3% calcium, 9% iron, 29% vit A, 163% vit C, 22% folate.

Variations

Herbed Gazpacho: To serve, stir in ¼ cup (50 mL) chopped fresh basil, coriander or dill.

Fire and Ice Gazpacho: For medium heat, increase hot pepper sauce to ½ tsp (2 mL). For fiery heat, also add 1 tbsp (15 mL) minced hot pepper.

Tip

To peel a large quantity of tomatoes, immerse in pot of boiling water for 30 to 60 seconds or until skins loosen. Or, for just a few tomatoes, place in bowl and pour boiling water over top. Chill in cold water, then drain immediately and peel.

1 Halve tomatoes; scoop out seeds. Grip chef's knife with fingers meeting thumb underneath. With tip of knife held stationary and palm of other hand on top, coarsely chop 2 of the tomatoes, red pepper and half each of the green pepper and cucumber; set remaining vegetables aside.

3 Slice thin strip off side of remaining cucumber to form flat base. With knife tip at end, cut cucumber lengthwise into ¼-inch (5 mm) thick slices.

5 Refrigerate ¼ cup (50 mL) each of the cucumber and green pepper. Add remaining vegetables to soup; refrigerate for at least 2 hours or until chilled or for up to 12 hours. Thin with more vegetable cocktail if desired. Season with salt and pepper to taste.

2 In food processor, or in blender in batches, purée together chopped vegetables, garlic, vinegar and oil until smooth. Transfer to large bowl; stir in vegetable cocktail and hot pepper sauce.

4 Stacking slices, cut into ¼-inch (5 mm) strips; cut crosswise into ¼-inch (5 mm) dice. Flat side down, slice and dice remaining tomato as for cucumber. Dice remaining green pepper.

6 **Garnish:** Combine oil and garlic; brush over bread. Cut into ½-inch (1 cm) cubes; bake on baking sheet in 350°F (180°C) oven, stirring once, for 10 to 15 minutes or until golden. Serve gazpacho in chilled bowls; sprinkle with reserved chopped cucumber and green pepper, croutons and green onions.

Butternut Squash Cream Soup

Restorative and inherently soothing, creamed soups embrace us with their smooth silkiness and straightforward flavour. The taste of this one is especially honest since the creaminess is derived directly from puréeing the vegetables and not by adding any taste-altering whipping cream.

Ingredients

2 tbsp	butter	25 mL
1	large onion, chopped	1
3	cloves garlic, minced	3
2 tsp	minced gingerroot	10 mL
1½ tsp	curry powder	7 mL
½ tsp	each salt and pepper	2 mL
5 cups	cubed peeled butternut squash	1.25 L
1	large potato, peeled and diced	1
4 cups	vegetable or chicken stock	1 L
2 tbsp	lemon juice	25 mL
2 tbsp	tomato paste	25 mL
⅓ cup	milk or 10% cream	75 mL

Red Pepper Paint:

2	sweet red peppers	2

Makes 6 servings

Per serving: about 158 cal, 4 g pro, 5 g total fat (3 g sat. fat), 28 g carb, 4 g fibre, 11 mg chol. % RDI: 8% calcium, 11% iron, 109% vit A, 142% vit C, 17% folate.

Variations

Cauliflower Cream Soup: Substitute chopped cauliflower florets for the squash. Omit lemon juice and tomato paste.

Carrot Cream Soup: Substitute 4 cups (1 L) chopped peeled carrots for the squash. Add ¼ cup (50 mL) orange juice along with stock.

Broccoli Cream Soup: Substitute ½ tsp (2 mL) dried thyme for the curry powder. Omit gingerroot. Substitute chopped broccoli florets and stalks for the squash. Reduce stock to 3½ cups (875 mL). Omit Red Pepper Paint.

1 **Red Pepper Paint:** On baking sheet, broil red peppers, turning twice, for 20 minutes or until charred. Let cool. Peel, remove membranes and seed; purée in blender or food processor until smooth. Strain through fine sieve. *(Paint can be covered and refrigerated for up to 48 hours.)*

2 In large saucepan, melt butter over medium heat; cook onion, garlic, ginger, curry powder, salt and pepper, stirring, for 3 minutes or until softened.

3 Add squash and potato; stir until well coated. Add stock, lemon juice and tomato paste; bring to boil. Reduce heat, cover and simmer for about 20 minutes or until vegetables are very tender.

4 In batches, transfer soup to blender or food processor; purée. Strain through fine sieve into bowl, mashing any lumps through sieve. *(Soup can be prepared to this point, covered and refrigerated for up to 48 hours.)*

5 In clean saucepan, heat puréed mixture with milk over medium heat until heated through but not boiling. Ladle into warmed serving bowls.

6 Using small spoon, dollop Red Pepper Paint randomly in centre of each. Using toothpick or skewer, drag through paint to make decorative swirl.

The Perfect Salad

Say goodbye to the days when salad meant diet fare or wedges of iceberg lettuce. Today's salads are
enthusiastic and innovative creations of bold new flavours, colourful "greens" and varied textures.
Different kinds of lettuces abound, whether from your own backyard or from the local market,
so let colour and season be your muse and our steps be your guide to the perfect salad.
To make your own croutons, see Garnish in Gazpacho (recipe, page 39).

Ingredients

3	heads assorted greens	3
	Shaved Parmesan cheese and croutons (optional)	

Creamy Garlic Dressing:

1	large clove garlic, chopped	1
¼ tsp	salt	1 mL
1 tbsp	mayonnaise	15 mL
1 tbsp	white wine vinegar	15 mL
1½ tsp	Dijon mustard	7 mL
Pinch	pepper	Pinch
⅓ cup	vegetable or extra-virgin olive oil	75 mL

Makes 4 to 6 servings

Per each of 6 servings: about 153 cal, 3 g pro, 14 g total fat (1 g sat. fat), 5 g carb, 2 g fibre, 1 mg chol. % RDI: 5% calcium, 10% iron, 25% vit A, 40% vit C, 78% folate.

Variations

Classic Vinaigrette: Omit garlic and mayonnaise. Increase vinegar (red- or white-wine or cider vinegar) to 2 tbsp (25 mL) and mustard to 2 tsp (10 mL).

Poppy Seed Dressing: Omit garlic. Substitute lemon juice for the vinegar. Add 1 tsp (5 mL) granulated sugar along with salt. Stir in 1 green onion, chopped, and 2 tsp (10 mL) poppy seeds after whisking in oil.

Light Yogurt Dressing: Omit mayonnaise. Reduce oil to 1 tbsp (15 mL). Stir in ½ cup (125 mL) low-fat plain yogurt and 1 tbsp (15 mL) chopped fresh parsley or dill after whisking in oil.

Tip

The best salad vinegars are wine vinegars, but not the harsh wine-flavoured vinegar. Cider vinegar is a reasonable alternative. Avoid distilled white vinegar: it will overpower the salad.

1 Cut out core or stem from lettuce; separate leaves. In cold water, gently swish leaves to clean well. (For tightly furled heads, such as iceberg and Belgian endive, just remove outer leaves and wash head.) Place leaves in colander or towel, shaking off excess water.

2 Discard any wilted leaves; tear off any discoloured parts. Place greens loosely in salad spinner until half full; spin, pouring off water occasionally. Blot leaves gently with towel to remove any remaining moisture. (Alternatively, by hand, pat leaves dry between towels.)

3 Layer greens loosely between dry towels; roll up and place in plastic bag. *(Greens can be prepared to this point and refrigerated for up to 5 days.)*

4 **Creamy Garlic Dressing:** In bowl and using back of spoon, mash garlic with salt to form paste. Whisk in mayonnaise, vinegar, mustard and pepper.

5 Gradually whisk in oil in slow steady stream until blended. *(Dressing can be covered and refrigerated for up to 5 days; whisk to reblend.)*

6 Tear enough greens into bite-size pieces to make 12 cups (3 L) loosely packed. Place in salad bowl. Drizzle with dressing; toss gently just until coated and glistening. Garnish with Parmesan cheese and croutons (if using). Serve immediately.

Warm Steak Salad

A combination of tender greens, such as Boston, leaf, lamb's and oak lettuce, mixed with some bitter greens, such as arugula, endive and radicchio, provides a great base for a warm salad.

2	cloves garlic	2
½ cup	extra-virgin olive oil	125 mL
1 tsp	Dijon mustard	5 mL
6 cups	torn salad greens	1.5 L
12	thin slices French stick (baguette)	12
¼ cup	vegetable oil	50 mL
8 oz	top sirloin grilling steak, thinly sliced	250 g
⅓ cup	red wine vinegar	75 mL
1	sweet red pepper, thinly sliced	1
2 tbsp	chopped shallots	25 mL
1 tsp	dried thyme	5 mL
	Salt and pepper	

1 Mince 1 of the garlic cloves. In salad bowl, whisk together minced garlic, ⅓ cup (75 mL) of the olive oil and mustard; add greens and toss to coat. Set aside.

2 Halve remaining garlic; rub over bread slices. In large skillet, heat vegetable oil over medium heat; cook bread, turning once, for 3 to 5 minutes or until crisp and golden. Drain croûtes on paper towels. Set aside.

3 In same skillet, heat remaining olive oil over medium-high heat; cook steak, stirring, for 2 to 3 minutes or until lightly browned but still pink inside. Using slotted spoon, transfer to salad bowl.

4 To skillet, add vinegar, red pepper, shallots and thyme; cook over medium-high heat, stirring and scraping up brown bits from bottom of skillet, for 2 to 3 minutes or until liquid is reduced by half.

5 Immediately pour hot dressing over salad; toss well. Season with salt and pepper to taste. Arrange croûtes around salad.

Makes 4 servings

Per serving: about 458 cal, 18 g pro, 29 g total fat (4 g sat. fat), 32 g carb, 3 g fibre, 27 mg chol. % RDI: 7% calcium, 28% iron, 28% vit A, 102% vit C, 54% folate.

Variation

Warm Scallop Salad: Substitute scallops for the beef; cook, stirring, for 3 to 4 minutes or just until opaque. Substitute ¼ cup (50 mL) white wine vinegar and 2 tbsp (25 mL) lemon juice for the red wine vinegar. Substitute 1 tbsp (15 mL) chopped fresh dill or 1 tsp (5 mL) dried dillweed for the thyme.

New Waldorf Chicken Salad

Try this lighter, jazzier version of a turn-of-the-century favourite.

5	black peppercorns	5
1	bay leaf	1
1	clove garlic, halved	1
4	chicken breasts	4
2	green onions	2
1	stalk celery	1
2	red apples	2
¼ cup	toasted coarsely chopped pecans	50 mL

Dressing:

½ cup	plain yogurt	125 mL
⅓ cup	light mayonnaise	75 mL
2 tbsp	chopped fresh parsley	25 mL
2 tsp	lemon juice	10 mL
2 tsp	Dijon mustard	10 mL
¼ tsp	pepper	1 mL

1 In large shallow saucepan, pour in water to depth of 2 inches (5 cm); add peppercorns, bay leaf and garlic. Heat over medium heat until simmering (small bubbles form but do not break surface of water).

2 Arrange chicken, bone side up, in single layer in pan; cook for 15 to 20 minutes or until no longer pink inside. Using tongs, transfer chicken to plate; cover loosely with plastic wrap and let cool in refrigerator for about 1 hour or until chilled. *(Chicken can be covered and refrigerated for up to 4 hours.)*

3 Dressing: In small bowl, whisk together yogurt, mayonnaise, parsley, lemon juice, mustard and pepper. *(Dressing can be covered and refrigerated for up to 8 hours.)*

Great Greens

- *Arugula:* A favourite Italian green, this highly perishable lettuce is a member of the mustard family and is characterized by a peppery taste that intensifies as it ages.
- *Belgian endive:* Grown in darkness to preserve its light colour and mild flavour, endive is part of the chicory family. Its leaves are crisp and tender and have a mild, bitter taste.
- *Bibb lettuce:* A small butterhead lettuce, Bibb has a sweet flavour and is identified by its yellow-green colour. Because the leaves are so tender, they demand very gentle handling.
- *Escarole:* This member of the chicory family has broad, slightly curved, pale green leaves, and a milder flavour and chewier texture than its cousin, Belgian endive.

- *Frisée:* The shoots of a chicory root, frisée has tightly packed, delicately slender leaves and a strong, slightly bitter taste.
- *Mâche:* Also referred to as lamb's lettuce, this green is tender and nutty flavoured.
- *Radicchio:* An Italian chicory, radicchio has burgundy-colour leaves with ivory streaks and a slightly bitter taste. It is eaten both raw and cooked.
- *Red oak leaf:* This loose-leaf variety has crisp, rippled leaves with colourful edges.
- *Romaine:* An essential ingredient in Caesar salads, these elongated crispy leaves have a crunchy texture and subtle nutty overtones.
- *Watercress:* A lively, peppery taste characterizes this member of the mustard family.

4 Meanwhile, thinly slice onions and celery. Pull off skin from chicken. Pressing small paring knife against bone, cut off each breast to remove in 1 piece. Cut lengthwise into ½-inch (1 cm) wide strips; cut crosswise into ½-inch (1 cm) cubes.

5 One apple at a time, slice off 1 side close to core; repeat 3 more times. Lay each piece cut side down; cut in half horizontally. Holding layers together, cut into ½-inch (1 cm) wide strips; cut crosswise into ½-inch (1 cm) cubes.

6 In large bowl, combine chicken, onions, celery, apples and pecans. Add dressing and stir gently to coat well.

Makes 4 servings
Per serving: about 321 cal, 29 g pro, 15 g total fat (2 g sat. fat), 17 g carb, 2 g fibre, 76 mg chol. % RDI: 8% calcium, 11% iron, 3% vit A, 15% vit C, 10% folate.

Four Low-Fat Dressings

A salad dressing should have enough of a presence to enhance the greens, not overshadow them. These dressings happily accomplish this delicate balance.

Buttermilk Ranch Dressing

1⅓ cups	buttermilk	325 mL
⅔ cup	light mayonnaise	150 mL
4 tsp	cider vinegar	20 mL
1 tsp	Dijon mustard	5 mL
¾ tsp	dried dillweed	4 mL
½ tsp	dried parsley	2 mL
¼ tsp	each salt, pepper and granulated sugar	1 mL
Pinch	garlic powder	Pinch

1 In small bowl or glass jar, whisk or shake together buttermilk, mayonnaise, vinegar, mustard, dillweed, parsley, salt, pepper, sugar and garlic powder. *(Dressing can be refrigerated in airtight container for up to 1 week.)*

Makes 2 cups (500 mL)
Per 1 tbsp (15 mL): about 20 cal, 0 g pro, 2 g total fat (0 g sat. fat), 1 g carb, 0 g fibre, 0 mg chol. % RDI: 1% calcium.

Honey Dijon Vinaigrette

⅓ cup	each vegetable oil, apple juice and liquid honey	75 mL
¼ cup	Dijon mustard	50 mL
¼ cup	white wine vinegar	50 mL
½ tsp	each salt and pepper	2 mL

1 In small bowl or glass jar, whisk or shake together oil, apple juice, honey, mustard, vinegar, salt and pepper. *(Vinaigrette can be refrigerated in airtight container for up to 1 week.)*

Makes 1½ cups (375 mL)
Per 1 tbsp (15 mL): about 45 cal, 0 g pro, 3 g total fat (0 g sat. fat), 5 g carb, 0 g fibre, 0 mg chol. % RDI: 1% iron, 2% vit C.

Sun-Dried Tomato Dressing

6	dry-packed sun-dried tomato halves	6
2 tbsp	red wine vinegar	25 mL
2 tbsp	extra-virgin olive oil	25 mL
1	clove garlic, minced	1
¼ tsp	dried thyme	1 mL
¼ tsp	granulated sugar	1 mL
Pinch	salt	Pinch

1 Immerse tomatoes in ½ cup (125 mL) boiling water; let stand for 10 minutes or until softened. In blender or mini food processor, purée tomatoes with water. Add vinegar, oil, garlic, thyme, sugar and salt; pulse until blended. *(Dressing can be refrigerated in airtight container for up to 1 day.)*

Makes ⅔ cup (150 mL)
Per 1 tbsp (15 mL): about 27 cal, 0 g pro, 3 g total fat (0 g sat. fat), 1 g carb, 0 g fibre, 0 mg chol. % RDI: 1% iron, 2% vit C.

Creamy Caesar Dressing

¼ cup	light sour cream	50 mL
3 tbsp	water	50 mL
2 tbsp	light mayonnaise	25 mL
2 tsp	lemon juice	10 mL
1	clove garlic, minced	1
1 tsp	Dijon mustard	5 mL
½ tsp	anchovy paste	2 mL
Pinch	each salt, pepper and granulated sugar	Pinch
4 tsp	freshly grated Parmesan cheese	20 mL

1 In small bowl or glass jar, whisk or shake together sour cream, water, mayonnaise, lemon juice, garlic, mustard, anchovy paste, salt, pepper and sugar. Stir in cheese. *(Dressing can be covered and refrigerated for up to 4 hours.)*

Makes ⅔ cup (150 mL)
Per 1 tbsp (15 mL): about 20 cal, 1 g pro, 1 g total fat (0 g sat. fat), 1 g carb, 0 g fibre, 2 mg chol. % RDI: 2% calcium.

Sugar Snap Pea and Pasta Salad

This simple salad is beautiful and scrumptious. For maximum flavour, be sure to toss the pasta with the dressing while the pasta is still warm.

6 cups	farfalle pasta	1.5 L
8 oz	sugar snap peas	250 g
½ tsp	olive oil	2 mL
2	cloves garlic, minced	2
¼ cup	chopped oil-packed sun-dried tomatoes	50 mL
¾ cup	vegetable stock	175 mL
¼ cup	freshly grated Parmesan cheese	50 mL
2 tbsp	each chopped fresh mint and basil	25 mL
¼ cup	pine nuts, toasted	50 mL

1 In saucepan of boiling salted water, cook pasta for 10 minutes. Add peas; cook for 2 to 3 minutes or until pasta is tender but firm. Drain and refresh under cold water; drain well and transfer to serving bowl.

2 In nonstick skillet, heat oil over medium heat; cook garlic and tomatoes for 1 minute. Add stock; simmer for 5 minutes. Toss with pasta along with Parmesan cheese, mint and basil. Garnish with nuts.

Makes 4 servings
Per serving: about 411 cal, 17 g pro, 10 g total fat (2 g sat. fat), 65 g carb, 7 g fibre, 5 mg chol. % RDI: 12% calcium, 23% iron, 4% vit A, 65% vit C, 20% folate.

Beef, Pork, Lamb

Working in the *Canadian Living* Test Kitchen can mean a strange diet at times. Because of publication deadlines, we typically test our Christmas recipes during summer and sometimes can be heard groaning about excessive consumption of stuffed turkey and fruitcake amid predictions of yet another heat wave. Then there are times when we don't test anything except cookies for two weeks – at which point we all go home at the end of the day craving broccoli and other healthy greens! What we rarely balk at, though, are the days, weeks and even months when we can indulge our carnivore tendencies. Even if you choose to eat meat only a few times a month, you know that the deep, satisfying flavour of a well-seasoned, perfectly cooked cut of beef, pork or lamb is irreplaceable. Cooking meat can be tricky these days since the names of different cuts have changed and they are now all leaner. This chapter will help you recognize what you want at the meat counter and show you how to cook it. If pork ribs are on sale, by all means buy them and then choose from among the three tempting sauces in our Smoky Tex-Mex Ribs cooking lesson. Or if your craving runs more to a rack of lamb or roast of beef, you can rest assured that our steps will guarantee a splendid meal.

Pepper Roast Beef

Attuned to the needs of smaller families and lower-fat diets, supermarkets and distributors have begun supplying smaller and leaner roasts. The question is, of course, how do you cook these new, unfamiliar cuts of meat, especially if you grew up on big marbled roasts? Well, not to worry. This cooking lesson takes you through all you'll need to know to deliver a magnificently cooked, mahogany roast to your dinner table.

Ingredients

3 lb	inside round oven roast of beef	1.5 kg
2	cloves garlic, sliced	2
2 tbsp	peppercorns	25 mL
1 tsp	dried oregano	5 mL
1 tbsp	vegetable oil	15 mL

Gravy:		
2 tbsp	butter	25 mL
1	small onion, finely chopped	1
2 tbsp	all-purpose flour	25 mL
1 cup	beef stock	250 mL
1 cup	red wine or beef stock	250 mL
Pinch	salt	Pinch

Makes 8 to 10 servings

Per each of 10 servings: about 317 cal, 28 g pro, 20 g total fat (8 g sat. fat), 3 g carb, 0 g fibre, 77 mg chol. % RDI: 2% calcium, 20% iron, 2% vit A, 6% folate.

Variations

Italian Herbed Roast Beef:
Substitute 1 small onion, finely chopped, 1 tbsp (15 mL) dried thyme and pinch of pepper for the peppercorns. Increase oregano to 1 tbsp (15 mL).

Oriental Roast Beef: Omit peppercorns, oregano and oil. Combine 2 tbsp (25 mL) each hoisin sauce and ketchup, 1 tbsp (15 mL) soy sauce, 1½ tsp (7 mL) Dijon mustard, ¾ tsp (4 mL) ground ginger and pinch of cayenne; brush over roast. Sprinkle with 1 tbsp (15 mL) sesame seeds.

1 Pat roast dry. With sharp paring knife, make small slits in roast; insert garlic slice in each. Set aside.

3 Brush roast with oil; roll in peppercorn mixture to coat all over. Place on greased rack in roasting pan. Pour 1½ cups (375 mL) water into pan.

5 **Gravy:** Meanwhile, drain juices from pan, reserving ⅓ cup (75 mL); set aside. Melt butter in roasting pan over medium heat; cook onion, stirring occasionally, for about 5 minutes or until golden. Stir in flour; cook, stirring, for 1 minute.

2 Place peppercorns between waxed paper; crush coarsely with mallet. Discard top sheet of paper; mix in oregano and spread out evenly.

4 Roast in 500°F (260°C) oven for 30 minutes. Reduce heat to 275°F (140°C); roast for 1 hour or until meat thermometer registers 140°F (60°C) for rare or 150°F (65°C) for medium-rare. Transfer to warmed platter; tent with foil and let stand for 15 minutes for juices to spread evenly throughout meat. Carve thinly.

6 Add beef stock, wine, reserved pan juices and salt; bring to boil, stirring and scraping up brown bits from bottom of pan. Reduce heat and simmer for about 2 minutes or until thickened. Strain and pour into warmed sauceboat; pass with meat.

Perfect Pot Roast

Braising, or pot roasting, is the perfect method for transforming large, tough cuts of meat into tender, mouth-watering dinners. Slowly simmered and richly flavoured, pot roasts have become the ultimate diner or comfort food. Be sure to have lots of mashed potatoes at the ready to soak up the luscious juices.

Ingredients

⅓ cup	all-purpose flour	75 mL
4 lb	cross rib or blade pot roast	2 kg
3 tbsp	vegetable oil	50 mL
1½ cups	chopped onions	375 mL
¾ cup	each chopped carrots and celery	175 mL
1	clove garlic, minced	1
1 cup	chopped drained tomatoes	250 mL
½ tsp	dried thyme	2 mL
1	bay leaf	1
1 cup	beef stock	250 mL
6	small onions	6
6	carrots, halved crosswise	6
6	potatoes, quartered	6

Makes 6 to 8 servings

Per each of 8 servings: about 490 cal, 42 g pro, 18 g total fat (5 g sat. fat), 40 g carb, 5 g fibre, 89 mg chol. % RDI: 7% calcium, 32% iron, 164% vit A, 27% vit C, 23% folate.

Variations

Onion Pot Roast: Substitute 4 cups (1 L) thinly sliced onions for the chopped onions. Omit chopped carrots and celery. Increase garlic to 2 cloves.

Spicy Cajun Pot Roast: Increase garlic to 2 cloves. Omit chopped carrots and celery. Substitute tomato sauce for tomatoes and add ½ cup (125 mL) chili sauce, 2 tbsp (25 mL) Dijon mustard, 1 tbsp (15 mL) vinegar and ¼ tsp (1 mL) hot pepper sauce. Omit thyme and bay leaf.

Tips

Beef has been relabelled according to cooking methods, so look for cuts identified as pot roasts. Since pot roasts are usually the most economical, there's extra incentive to take advantage of this easy-on-the-cook and easy-on-the-budget method.

Never pierce the roast while cooking because it will release the juices that keep it moist. Instead, turn it with wooden spoons.

1 Spread ¼ cup (50 mL) of the flour on plate. Pat roast dry; roll in flour to coat, brushing off any excess. In Dutch oven, heat oil over medium-high heat; brown roast all over, turning with wooden spoons, about 7 minutes. Remove meat and set aside.

2 Add chopped onions, carrots, celery and garlic; cook, stirring often, for 3 to 5 minutes or until softened. Sprinkle with remaining flour; cook, stirring, for 1 minute.

3 Add tomatoes, thyme and bay leaf; pour in stock and bring to simmer. Return meat to pan; cover and cook over low heat or in 325°F (160°C) oven for 1 hour and 45 minutes.

4 Add whole onions, carrots and potatoes; cook, covered, for 45 to 75 minutes or until meat and vegetables are tender, turning roast every 30 minutes. Remove roast, whole onions, carrots and potatoes; cover and keep warm.

5 To make gravy, discard bay leaf from cooking liquid. Tip pan and skim off all fat.

6 Pour cooking liquid into blender or food processor; purée until smooth. Slice roast and arrange on serving platter; surround with vegetables. Pour gravy into sauceboat and pass separately.

Tangy Beef Pot Roast

Stews that have overtones of both sweet and sour are favourites in the Test Kitchen. This pot roast takes its lead from sauerbraten, with its characteristic touches of vinegar, brown sugar and ginger. Bay leaves, despite sometimes hours of cooking, never soften; remember to discard them before serving.

1 tbsp	vegetable oil	15 mL
1	cross rib or blade pot roast, boneless (3 lb/1.5 kg)	1
3 cups	sliced onions	750 mL
1½ cups	beef stock or water	375 mL
¼ cup	packed brown sugar	50 mL
¼ cup	red wine vinegar	50 mL
1½ tsp	ground ginger	7 mL
½ tsp	each salt and pepper	2 mL
¼ tsp	ground cloves	1 mL
1	bay leaf	1
8	potatoes, halved	8

Sauce:

⅓ cup	all-purpose flour	75 mL
1 cup	light sour cream	250 mL
1	sweet green pepper, sliced	1

1 In Dutch oven, heat oil over medium-high heat; brown roast all over, turning with wooden spoons, about 10 minutes. Drain off any fat.

2 Combine onions, beef stock, sugar, vinegar, ginger, salt, pepper, cloves and bay leaf; pour over roast. Cover and cook in 350°F (180°C) oven for 3 hours.

3 Add potatoes; cook, covered, for 20 to 30 minutes or until potatoes and meat are tender.

4 Discard bay leaf. Transfer meat to cutting board. With slotted spoon, transfer onions and potatoes to platter. Cover and keep warm.

5 **Sauce:** In small bowl, whisk flour into sour cream; whisk in ½ cup (125 mL) of the pan juices. Whisk mixture back into pan. Add green pepper. Bring to boil over high heat; cook, stirring, for about 5 minutes or until thickened. Slice beef; add to platter. Serve with sauce.

Makes 6 to 8 servings
Per each of 8 servings: about 467 cal, 36 g pro, 13 g total fat (5 g sat. fat), 51 g carb, 4 g fibre, 74 mg chol. % RDI: 10% calcium, 31% iron, 2% vit A, 53% vit C, 16% folate.

Roasting Chart for Meat and Poultry

Beef
Quick roasting for smaller cuts of rump oven roast, sirloin tip oven roast, inside round oven roast, outside round oven roast and eye of round oven roast:
- Place roast on rack in roasting pan; pour in water to depth of 1 inch (2.5 cm). Roast in 500°F (260°C) oven for 30 minutes. Reduce heat to 275°F (140°C); roast for 25 to 30 minutes per pound (500 g) longer. The internal temperature should be 140°F (60°C) for rare, 150°F (65°C) for medium-rare, 160°F (70°C) for medium or 170°F (75°C) for well done.
- 2½ to 3 lb (1.25 to 1.5 kg): 1¾ hours

Roasting for large cuts such as prime rib premium oven roast, tenderloin premium oven roast, top sirloin premium oven roast and rib eye premium oven roast:
- Place roast fat side up on rack in roasting pan. Roast, uncovered, in 325°F (160°C) oven for 20 minutes per pound (500 g) for rare or until internal temperature is 140°F (60°C); 25 minutes per pound (500 g) for medium or 160°F (70°C); or 30 minutes per pound (500 g) for well done or 170°F (75°C).

Pork
- Roast in 325°F (160°C) oven for 20 to 25 minutes per pound (500 g) for most loin and leg cuts and 25 to 35 minutes per pound (500 g) for shoulder cuts or until juices run clear when meat is pierced. Internal temperature should be 160°F (70°C) for medium with just a hint of pink remaining inside, or 170°F (75°C) for well done.
- Roast pork tenderloin in 375°F (190°C) oven for 25 to 35 minutes per pound (500 g).

- Rack of pork, 3 lb (1.5 kg): 1 hour
- Boneless single loin, 1½ to 2 lb (750 g to 1 kg): 30 minutes

Lamb
- Roast leg and shoulder cuts in 325°F (160°C) oven for 20 to 25 minutes per pound (500 g). Internal temperature should be 140°F (60°C) for rare, or 160°F (70°C) for medium.
- Roast rack of lamb in 400°F (200°C) oven for 10 to 15 minutes per pound (500 g).
- Rack of lamb, 2 lb (1 kg): 35 minutes
- Single boneless loin, 1½ lb (750 g): 30 minutes

Turkey
- Roast in 325°F (160°C) oven for 18 to 22 minutes per pound (500 g) or until internal temperature is 170°F (77°C) for unstuffed turkey, or 180°F (82°C) for stuffed turkey.

Turkey Breast
- Roast in 425°F (220°C) oven for about 20 minutes per pound (500 g) or until juices run clear when turkey is pierced.
- Single bone-in breast, 2 lb (1 kg): 45 minutes
- Single boneless breast, 1½ lb (750 g): 30 minutes

Chicken
- Roast in 325°F (160°C) oven for 20 to 30 minutes per pound (500 g) or until meat thermometer inserted in thigh registers 185°F (85°C).

Braised Beef Strips with Mushrooms

The key to moist, tender meat, when you've started out with a particularly lean and potentially tough cut, is to cook it at a gentle, even-temperature simmer. This recipe accomplishes just that by oven braising in a moderate 300°F (150°C) oven for 2 hours.

1½ lb	outside round marinating steak, about ¾ inch (2 cm) thick	750 g
2 tbsp	all-purpose flour	25 mL
¼ tsp	salt	1 mL
Pinch	pepper	Pinch
Pinch	cayenne (optional)	Pinch
1½ cups	vegetable cocktail	375 mL
2	cloves garlic, minced	2
1	large onion, sliced	1
½ tsp	crumbled dried rosemary or thyme	2 mL
12 oz	small mushrooms (about 2½ cups/625 mL)	375 g

1 Cut beef into 1-inch (2.5 cm) wide strips. In bowl, combine flour, salt, pepper, and cayenne (if using). Add strips to bowl and turn to coat all over. Place on lightly greased baking sheet. Broil for 5 minutes; turn and broil for 5 minutes longer or until browned.

2 In casserole with tight-fitting lid, combine vegetable cocktail, garlic, onion and rosemary. Add beef along with pan juices. Cover and cook in 300°F (150°C) oven for 1 hour.

3 Stir in mushrooms; cook, covered, for 1 hour, adding up to ¼ cup (50 mL) water if sauce appears thick.

Makes 4 to 6 servings

Per each of 6 servings: about 202 cal, 27 g pro, 6 g total fat (2 g sat. fat), 9 g carb, 2 g fibre, 54 mg chol. % RDI: 2% calcium, 23% iron, 7% vit A, 62% vit C, 12% folate.

Tip

This beef dish can be covered and refrigerated for up to 1 day. Reheat in covered saucepan over medium heat for 15 minutes, stirring often.

Sante Fe Pot Roast

This tangy roast packs quite a punch. If you're a graduate student in the school of fiery dishes, feel free to up the ante by adding 2 tbsp (25 mL) more of the canned chilies. If you're merely an undergrad, reduce the amount to a quarter or replace them entirely with half a sweet green pepper, chopped.

⅔ cup	all-purpose flour	150 mL
3 lb	boneless pork shoulder butt	1.5 kg
1 tbsp	vegetable oil	15 mL
1 cup	chicken stock	250 mL
Half	can (4½ oz/127 mL) peeled green chilies, drained, rinsed and chopped	Half
2	cloves garlic, minced	2
1 tsp	each dried oregano, ground cumin and coriander	5 mL
½ tsp	each salt and pepper	2 mL
4 cups	baby or chopped carrots (1¼ lb/625 g)	1 L
6	small onions, halved	6
⅓ cup	cold water	75 mL

1 Spread ⅓ cup (75 mL) of the flour on plate. Pat pork dry; roll in flour to coat, brushing off any excess. In Dutch oven, heat oil over medium-high heat; brown pork all over, turning with wooden spoons, about 10 minutes. Drain off any fat.

2 Combine stock, chilies, garlic, oregano, cumin, coriander, salt and pepper; pour into pan. Cover and cook in 350°F (180°C) oven for 1½ hours. Add carrots and onions; cook for 1½ hours or until meat and vegetables are tender. Transfer meat and vegetables to platter; cover with foil and keep warm.

3 Meanwhile, in small bowl, whisk remaining flour with cold water; whisk in about ½ cup (125 mL) of the hot liquid from pan. Whisk mixture back into pan. Bring to boil over high heat; cook, stirring, for 5 minutes or until thickened. Serve with meat and vegetables.

Makes 6 servings

Per serving: about 427 cal, 41 g pro, 17 g total fat (5 g sat. fat), 26 g carb, 4 g fibre, 89 mg chol. % RDI: 6% calcium, 26% iron, 185% vit A, 20% vit C, 13% folate.

Beef Stew

Beef stews are made with the more flavourful, less tender cuts of meat that are first coated in flour, then browned and seared. To simplify the process, the Test Kitchen eliminated these steps by adding the beef cubes and flour along with the medley of root vegetables.

Ingredients

4	large carrots	4
2	stalks celery	2
Half	small rutabaga	Half
1½ lb	cross rib or blade simmering steak, 1½ inches (4 cm) thick	750 g
1 tbsp	vegetable oil	15 mL
3	onions, quartered	3
2	large cloves garlic, minced	2
½ tsp	each dried thyme and marjoram	2 mL
¼ cup	all-purpose flour	50 mL
1 cup	beef stock	250 mL
1 cup	dry red wine or beef stock	250 mL
1	can (19 oz/540 mL) tomatoes (undrained)	1
3	large potatoes, peeled and cut in chunks	3
1 cup	frozen peas	250 mL
	Salt and pepper	
2 tbsp	chopped fresh parsley	25 mL

Makes 8 servings

Per serving: about 257 cal, 18 g pro, 6 g total fat (2 g sat. fat), 33 g carb, 5 g fibre, 30 mg chol. % RDI: 7% calcium, 21% iron, 119% vit A, 42% vit C, 22% folate.

Variation

Curried Beef Stew: Substitute 1 tbsp (15 mL) finely chopped gingerroot, 4 tsp (20 mL) curry powder and 1 tsp (5 mL) each ground cumin and coriander for the thyme and marjoram. Omit rutabaga. Cut half a cauliflower into florets; add for last 20 minutes of cooking.

Tip

To make stew ahead of time, cook for the first 1 1/2 hours, then cool and freeze for up to 2 weeks. Thaw in refrigerator and proceed with recipe, cooking for about 15 minutes longer.

1 Peel carrots; cut carrots and celery into 2-inch (5 cm) chunks. Place rutabaga flat side down on cutting board; cut away peel with paring knife. Cut into 2-inch (5 cm) chunks.

2 Remove all visible fat from steak. Slice into 1½-inch (4 cm) wide strips; cut crosswise into 1½-inch (4 cm) cubes.

3 In large heavy Dutch oven, heat oil over medium heat; cook onions, stirring occasionally, for about 5 minutes or until lightly coloured. Add garlic, thyme and marjoram; cook, stirring, for 1 minute.

4 Add beef, carrots, rutabaga and celery; sprinkle with flour and cook, stirring, for about 1 minute or until flour is moistened.

5 Stir in stock, wine and tomatoes, breaking up tomatoes with spoon; bring to boil. Cover and cook in 325°F (160°C) oven for 1½ hours.

6 Stir in potatoes; cook, covered, for 60 to 75 minutes or until meat and potatoes are fork-tender, stirring once. Stir in peas; cook for 2 minutes or until heated through. Season with salt and pepper to taste. Serve sprinkled with parsley.

Thai Curry Pork Stew

This blend of flavours is distinctively Thai with its characteristic ingredients of gingerroot, lime juice and fish sauce. Usually there is no adequate substitute for fish sauce (a fermented sauce called *nam pla* in Thailand), which has a unique taste and aroma; however, if the amount called for is 2 tbsp (25 mL) or less, you can usually substitute soy sauce successfully.

1 lb	boneless pork shoulder butt	500 g
1 tbsp	vegetable oil	15 mL
1 tbsp	Thai red curry paste	15 mL
2	onions, cut in wedges	2
2	cloves garlic, minced	2
2 tbsp	chopped gingerroot	25 mL
2 tsp	grated lime rind	10 mL
2 tbsp	lime juice	25 mL
2 tbsp	fish sauce	25 mL
1 tbsp	granulated sugar	15 mL
¼ tsp	salt	1 mL
8 oz	green beans	250 g
1½ cups	cauliflower florets	375 mL
1	sweet red pepper	1
2 tbsp	each chopped fresh mint and coriander	25 mL

1 Trim any fat from pork; cut into 2-inch (5 cm) cubes. In large heavy saucepan, heat 2 tsp (10 mL) of the oil over medium-high heat; brown pork, in batches. Transfer to plate.

2 Add remaining oil to pan. Add curry paste; cook over medium heat for 1 minute, mashing paste into oil. Add onions, garlic and ginger; cook, stirring, for 1 minute. Add lime rind, lime juice, fish sauce, sugar, salt and 1 cup (250 mL) water; bring to boil.

3 Return meat and any accumulated juices to pan. Reduce heat, cover and simmer, stirring occasionally, for about 40 minutes or until meat is very tender.

4 Meanwhile, trim green beans; cut in half crosswise. Add to pan along with cauliflower florets; cook, covered, over medium heat for 10 minutes.

5 Meanwhile, core, seed and cut red pepper in half crosswise; cut lengthwise into strips. Add to pan; cook, uncovered and stirring often, for about 5 minutes or until vegetables are tender. Stir in mint and coriander.

Makes 4 servings
Per serving: about 262 cal, 27 g pro, 9 g total fat (2 g sat. fat), 19 g carb, 4 g fibre, 65 mg chol. % RDI: 7% calcium, 21% iron, 16% vit A, 135% vit C, 26% folate.

Boeuf Carbonnade

This Belgian-inspired stew derives its unique flavour from a base of beer and onions. As the beef simmers to a mouth-watering tenderness, the beer mellows and the onions caramelize to an enchanting sweetness. Serve over buttered egg noodles or roasted garlic mashed potatoes.

2 lb	boneless blade simmering steak, 1 inch (2.5 cm) thick	1 kg
3 tbsp	all-purpose flour	50 mL
½ tsp	salt	2 mL
¼ tsp	pepper	1 mL
2 tbsp	olive oil	25 mL
6	onions, thickly sliced	6
1	clove garlic, minced	1
1	bottle (341 mL) beer	1
1	bay leaf	1
1 tbsp	chopped fresh thyme (or 1 tsp/5 mL dried)	15 mL
1 tbsp	chopped fresh parsley	15 mL

1 Cut beef into 1-inch (2.5 cm) cubes, trimming off fat. In heavy plastic bag, combine flour, salt and pepper. Add beef and shake to coat, reserving any remaining flour. In Dutch oven, heat oil over medium-high heat; brown beef in batches. Transfer to plate. Drain off any fat.

2 Add onions and garlic to pan; cook over medium heat, stirring occasionally, for about 5 minutes or until softened. Stir in any remaining flour mixture. Add beer and bring to boil, stirring and scraping up brown bits from bottom of pan.

3 Return beef and accumulated juices to pan along with bay leaf and thyme. Reduce heat, cover and simmer for about 1½ hours or until tender, uncovering for last 15 minutes if necessary to thicken sauce. Discard bay leaf. Stir in parsley. *(Stew can be covered and refrigerated for up to 1 day.)*

Makes 6 servings

Per serving: about 296 cal, 29 g pro, 13 g total fat (4 g sat. fat), 15 g carb, 2 g fibre, 72 mg chol. % RDI: 4% calcium, 25% iron, 10% vit C, 10% folate.

Tips

If you do not wish to cook with beer, use de-alcoholized beer, or substitute beef stock and decrease salt to 1/4 tsp (1 mL).

To cook the stew in the oven instead of on the stove, cover and cook in 325°F (160°C) oven for about 2 hours.

Miami Glazed Ribs

Be sure to use regular coffee in this inviting recipe that will undoubtedly become a winter staple. Double-strength coffee will become too bitter as the sauce reduces. Also, fancy molasses is preferred over blackstrap molasses because it's much lighter in both flavour and colour.

4 lb	beef simmering short ribs	2 kg
1⅔ cups	coffee	400 mL
1 cup	fancy molasses	250 mL
⅔ cup	cider vinegar	150 mL
½ cup	tomato paste	125 mL
2 tbsp	Worcestershire sauce	25 mL
1 tbsp	ground ginger	15 mL
1 tsp	salt	5 mL
¼ tsp	allspice	1 mL
¼ tsp	hot pepper sauce	1 mL

1 In large pot, cover ribs with cold water; bring to boil. Reduce heat, cover and simmer for 45 minutes or until fork-tender; drain and transfer to 13- x 9-inch (3 L) baking dish.

2 In saucepan, combine coffee, molasses, vinegar, tomato paste, Worcestershire sauce, ginger, salt, allspice and hot pepper sauce; bring to boil. Reduce heat and boil gently for 15 minutes or until reduced to 2⅔ cups (650 mL). Pour over ribs, turning to coat; let cool. Cover and refrigerate for at least 4 hours or for up to 24 hours.

3 Cover dish tightly with foil; cook in 325°F (160°C) oven for 30 minutes. Turn ribs and cook, uncovered and basting occasionally, for 45 minutes or until meat almost falls off bone and sauce is thickened.

Makes 6 servings

Per serving: about 520 cal, 32 g pro, 25 g total fat (11 g sat. fat), 43 g carb, 1 g fibre, 84 mg chol. % RDI: 12% calcium, 44% iron, 5% vit A, 17% vit C, 5% folate.

Tip

Beef simmering short ribs are great in soups as well, provided you simmer them first to remove the fattiness. In summer, grill them after simmering for a terrific outdoor dinner.

Mellow Liver and Onions

Now is the time to cook liver, especially if you have lived your life in horror at the very prospect. Liver perfectly cooked is perfectly delicious. Fried until golden on the outside but still rosy and tender inside, liver is truly luscious and should become a favourite weeknight or special-occasion meat. Liver, like all variety meats, is very perishable; use on the day of purchase or by the next day at the latest.

Ingredients

3 tbsp	vegetable oil	50 mL
6	onions, sliced	6
½ tsp	dried sage	2 mL
¼ tsp	each salt and pepper (approx)	1 mL
1 lb	calves' or beef liver, about ½ inch (1 cm) thick	500 g
¼ cup	all-purpose flour	50 mL
½ cup	beef stock	125 mL
2 tbsp	balsamic or red wine vinegar	25 mL
1½ tsp	granulated sugar	7 mL
	Chopped fresh parsley	

Makes 4 servings

Per serving: about 352 cal, 26 g pro, 15 g total fat (3 g sat. fat), 29 g carb, 3 g fibre, 401 mg chol. % RDI: 4% calcium, 60% iron, 893% vit A, 45% vit C, 38% folate.

Variations

Apple and Mustard Liver:
Substitute 3 sliced unpeeled apples and ¼ cup (50 mL) chopped shallots or onions for the onions and sage; cook over medium heat for 10 to 15 minutes or until tender. Substitute ½ cup (125 mL) apple juice, ¼ cup (50 mL) white wine and 2 tbsp (25 mL) Dijon mustard for the beef stock, vinegar and sugar.

Mushroom and Bacon Liver:
Cook 4 slices bacon until crisp, reserving fat to use instead of oil; crumble bacon for garnish. Substitute 4 cups (1 L) sliced mushrooms for the onions and sage; cook for 5 minutes or until tender, adding juices to stock.

Tips

Even an extra minute of cooking can toughen liver, so be sure not to over-cook it.

For a milder taste if using the more strongly flavoured beef liver, refrigerate it in milk to soak for at least 30 minutes or for up to 8 hours, then drain and pat dry.

1 In large heavy skillet, heat 1 tbsp (15 mL) of the oil over medium heat; cook onions and sage, stirring often, for 8 minutes or until softened. Reduce heat to medium-low; cook, stirring occasionally, for 20 minutes or until deep golden. Season with salt and pepper to taste. Remove and keep warm.

3 Rinse and dry skillet; heat remaining oil over medium-high heat. Dredge liver in flour mixture to coat, shaking off excess; immediately add to skillet.

5 Turn and cook for 1 to 2 minutes longer or until browned, slightly pink inside and springy to the touch. Transfer to warmed serving plates.

2 Meanwhile, peel away any membrane on liver by loosening with sharp knife and gently pulling away from meat. Trim any tough blood vessels. In shallow dish, combine flour and ¼ tsp (1 mL) each salt and pepper; set aside.

4 Cook liver, in batches if necessary, for 1 to 2 minutes or until underside is browned and blood just comes to the surface.

6 Add stock, vinegar and sugar to pan; bring to boil, stirring and scraping up brown bits from bottom of pan. Boil, stirring, for 1 to 2 minutes or until reduced to about ⅓ cup (75 mL). Mound onions over liver; top with sauce. Sprinkle with parsley.

Steaks with Gremolata Mayo

Gremolata is a garnish made with parsley, garlic and lemon rind that is traditionally sprinkled over the Italian dish Osso Buco (see page 64). Here, combined with mayonnaise, it splendidly complements steak. For parsley, substitute fresh basil, coriander or chives if they grow in your garden.

2	rib eye or strip loin grilling steaks, ¾ inch (2 cm) thick (1 lb/500 g total)	2
½ tsp	coarsely ground pepper	2 mL
2 tsp	vegetable oil	10 mL

Gremolata Mayo:

¼ cup	light mayonnaise	50 mL
2 tbsp	finely chopped fresh parsley, basil or coriander	25 mL
½ tsp	grated lemon rind	2 mL
1	clove garlic, minced	1

1 **Gremolata Mayo:** In bowl, stir together mayonnaise, parsley, lemon rind and garlic. *(Mayo can be covered and refrigerated for up to 8 hours.)*

2 Trim fat from steaks; sprinkle with pepper. In nonstick skillet, heat oil over medium-high heat; cook steaks, turning once, for about 6 minutes or until well browned but still rare inside.

3 Transfer to heated platter; tent with foil and let stand for 5 minutes. Cut each in half; serve with dollop of Gremolata Mayo.

Makes 4 servings

Per serving: about 224 cal, 22 g pro, 14 g total fat (3 g sat. fat), 2 g carb, 0 g fibre, 47 mg chol. % RDI: 1% calcium, 14% iron, 1% vit A, 3% vit C, 5% folate.

Variations

Roasted Garlic Mayo: In baking dish, combine 6 large peeled cloves garlic, 1 tsp (5 mL) olive oil and pinch each salt and dried thyme; cover and roast in 325°F (160°C) oven for about 40 minutes or until tender. Let cool; mash with fork and blend in 2 tbsp (25 mL) light mayonnaise. Makes ¼ cup (50 mL).

Roasted Pepper Mayo: Roast half a sweet red pepper (or use 2 tbsp/25 mL chopped jarred roasted red peppers); peel, seed and purée to make 2 tbsp (25 mL). Add 4 tsp (20 mL) light mayonnaise, ½ tsp (2 mL) chopped fresh chives and dash hot pepper sauce. Makes ¼ cup (50 mL).

Steak and Mushrooms for Two

Steak is one of those foods you simply yearn for sometimes and absolutely nothing else will do. This recipe will satisfy that yen and cement your reputation as a cook extraordinaire.

2 tsp	vegetable oil	10 mL
2	onions, sliced	2
1	clove garlic, minced	1
½ tsp	each dried thyme, salt and pepper	2 mL
2 cups	sliced mushrooms (about 6 oz/175 g)	500 mL
8 oz	rib eye or strip loin grilling steak, about ¾ inch (2 cm) thick	250 g
¼ cup	beef stock	50 mL
½ tsp	grated lemon rind	2 mL
1 tsp	lemon juice	5 mL

1 In nonstick skillet, heat half of the oil over medium heat; cook onions, garlic, thyme, salt and pepper, stirring occasionally, for 10 minutes or until golden.

2 Add mushrooms; cook over medium-high heat for about 5 minutes or until browned. Transfer to plate; cover and keep warm.

3 Trim fat from steak. Add remaining oil to pan; cook steak, turning once, for about 6 minutes or until well browned but still rare inside. Add to mushroom mixture.

4 Add beef stock and lemon rind and juice to pan, stirring and scraping up brown bits from bottom of pan; boil for 1 to 2 minutes or until slightly thickened. Return steak and mushroom mixture to pan, stirring to coat. Cut in half to serve.

Makes 2 servings

Per serving: about 326 cal, 26 g pro, 19 g total fat (6 g sat. fat), 13 g carb, 3 g fibre, 57 mg chol. % RDI: 4% calcium, 24% iron, 15% vit C, 14% folate.

Fruited Pork Chops with Squash

Choose an easy-to-peel squash, such as butternut, or one that can be sliced easily, such as acorn.

4	pork loin chops	4
½ tsp	salt	2 mL
¼ tsp	pepper	1 mL
1 tsp	vegetable oil	5 mL
1	onion, diced	1
1½ cups	apple cider or apple juice	375 mL
2½ cups	thinly sliced peeled squash	625 mL
¼ cup	sliced dried apricots	50 mL

1 Trim fat from chops; sprinkle with salt and pepper. Slash edges at 1-inch (2.5 cm) intervals to prevent curling.

2 In large heavy skillet, heat oil over medium-high heat; brown chops on each side, 6 to 8 minutes. Remove and set aside.

3 Add onion to pan; cook over medium heat, stirring occasionally and adding 1 tbsp (15 mL) water if necessary to prevent sticking, for about 5 minutes or until softened.

4 Pour in apple cider, stirring and scraping up brown bits from bottom of pan. Add squash and apricots; cover and simmer for 7 to 8 minutes or until squash is tender.

5 Return chops to pan; cook for 3 to 5 minutes or until juices run clear when pork is pierced and just a hint of pink remains inside.

Makes 4 servings

Per serving: about 286 cal, 27 g pro, 7 g total fat (2 g sat. fat), 29 g carb, 3 g fibre, 71 mg chol. % RDI: 6% calcium, 17% iron, 8% vit A, 17% vit C, 9% folate.

Ginger Orange Pork Chops

Simpler is often better, and this recipe exemplifies that adage, allowing the tang of orange, the spiciness of ginger and the hint of cinnamon to shine through. Since pork is now raised to be much leaner, it's important to cook the chops only for the required amount of time or they will dry out.

4	boneless pork loin chops	4
1 tsp	grated orange rind	5 mL
⅓ cup	orange juice	75 mL
2 tsp	minced gingerroot	10 mL
1	clove garlic, minced	1
1	green onion, finely chopped	1
Pinch	cinnamon	Pinch
	Salt and pepper	

1 Trim any fat from pork; slash edges at 1-inch (2.5 cm) intervals. Arrange in single layer in shallow dish.

2 Combine orange rind and juice, ginger, garlic, onion and cinnamon; pour over chops, turning to coat. Cover and marinate at room temperature for 30 minutes or in refrigerator for up to 24 hours, turning occasionally.

3 Reserving marinade, place chops on greased grill over medium-high heat; cook, turning once and basting halfway through with marinade, for about 10 minutes or until juices run clear when pork is pierced and just a hint of pink remains inside. Season with salt and pepper to taste.

Makes 4 servings

Per serving: about 151 cal, 22 g pro, 5 g total fat (2 g sat. fat), 2 g carb, 0 g fibre, 61 mg chol. % RDI: 2% calcium, 6% iron, 8% vit C, 3% folate.

Grilled Asian Beef Salad

This salad virtually explodes with flavour. The fish and hoisin sauces, the sesame oil and the gingerroot add an exotic touch to the dressing, which is sure to please your family and friends. And yet the salad is simplicity itself, leaving you free to enjoy the evening, the meal and your guests.

Ingredients

12 oz	flank marinating steak	375 g
2 tbsp	each fish sauce, lime juice and hoisin sauce	25 mL
4 tsp	minced gingerroot	20 mL
1 tbsp	sherry	15 mL
1	clove garlic, minced	1
½ tsp	Asian chili paste	2 mL
½ tsp	sesame oil	2 mL
8 cups	torn red-tipped leaf lettuce	2 L
2 cups	snow peas (6 oz/175 g)	500 mL
1	sweet red pepper	1
Half	small English cucumber	Half
1 cup	bean sprouts	250 mL
1 tbsp	balsamic vinegar	15 mL
½ tsp	granulated sugar	2 mL
2 tbsp	olive oil	25 mL

Makes 4 servings

Per serving: about 299 cal, 24 g pro, 15 g total fat (4 g sat. fat), 18 g carb, 4 g fibre, 35 mg chol. % RDI: 11% calcium, 31% iron, 40% vit A, 168% vit C, 48% folate.

Variations

Thai Pork Salad: Substitute pork tenderloin for the flank steak. Grill, turning once, for 20 to 25 minutes or until juices run clear when pork is pierced and just a hint of pink remains inside.

Thai Chicken Salad: Substitute 3 boneless skinless chicken breasts for the flank steak. Grill, turning once, for 8 to 10 minutes or until no longer pink inside.

Tip

Store sesame oil in the refrigerator, not in the pantry or cupboard; at room temperature it can turn rancid quite quickly.

1 Place steak in large shallow dish. Whisk together fish sauce, lime juice, hoisin sauce, ginger, sherry, garlic, chili paste and sesame oil; pour over meat, turning to coat. Cover and refrigerate for at least 8 hours or for up to 24 hours. Let stand at room temperature for 30 minutes.

2 Place lettuce in large salad bowl. In saucepan of boiling water, cook snow peas for 2 minutes or until tender-crisp. Drain and chill under cold running water; drain again and pat dry. Add to salad bowl.

3 On cutting board and using chef's knife, core red pepper and remove membranes and seeds; cut into thin strips and add to bowl. Slice cucumber in half lengthwise; slice thinly crosswise and add to bowl. Add bean sprouts.

4 Reserving marinade, place steak on greased grill over medium-high heat; cook, turning once, for about 10 minutes or until medium-rare. Transfer to cutting board and tent with foil; let stand for 5 minutes.

5 Meanwhile, in small saucepan, bring marinade to boil; boil gently for 5 minutes. Remove from heat. Whisk in vinegar and sugar; gradually whisk in olive oil. Let cool slightly.

6 Slice meat diagonally across the grain into thin slices; add to salad bowl. Pour dressing over top; toss gently to coat lightly.

Osso Buco

This northern Italian dish, which relies on braising to transform the veal shanks into melt-in-your-mouth tenderness, is tremendously soothing. The flavours meld together deliciously, with the sauce just begging to be sopped up with risotto, polenta or mashed potatoes. Italian cooks insist that the veal shanks get coated with flour immediately before browning in oil; otherwise, the flour gets soggy and the shanks never achieve the requisite dark colour.

Ingredients

6	thick (1½-inch/4 cm) pieces veal hind shank (3½ lb/1.75 kg)	6
2 tbsp	all-purpose flour	25 mL
½ tsp	each salt and pepper	2 mL
2 tbsp	olive oil (approx)	25 mL
1 cup	each chopped onion and carrot	250 mL
⅔ cup	chopped celery	150 mL
2	cloves garlic, minced	2
½ tsp	dried thyme	2 mL
¾ tsp	dried sage	4 mL
¼ tsp	dried rosemary	1 mL
¾ cup	dry white wine	175 mL
1½ cups	canned tomatoes, coarsely chopped	375 mL
½ cup	beef stock	125 mL
2	bay leaves	2

Gremolata Topping:

1	lemon	1
1	clove garlic, minced	1
¼ cup	chopped fresh parsley	50 mL

Makes 6 servings

Per serving: about 367 cal, 42 g pro, 16 g total fat (5 g sat. fat), 11 g carb, 2 g fibre, 171 mg chol. % RDI: 8% calcium, 24% iron, 51% vit A, 20% vit C, 20% folate.

Variation

Chicken: Substitute 12 skinned chicken thighs for the veal and chicken stock for the beef stock. Omit rosemary. Cook covered for 1 hour and uncovered for 15 minutes only. Omit boiling sauce for 5 minutes.

1 Cut six 24-inch (60 cm) lengths of kitchen string; wrap each twice around each shank and tie firmly. On plate, combine flour and half each of the salt and pepper; press shanks into mixture to coat both sides well. Reserve any remaining flour mixture.

3 Add onion, carrot, celery, garlic, thyme, sage and rosemary to pan; cook over medium heat, stirring often, for 10 minutes. Sprinkle with any reserved flour mixture; cook, stirring, for 1 minute. Add wine, stirring and scraping up brown bits from bottom of pan. Bring to boil; boil for 2 minutes or until reduced by half.

5 With tongs, transfer shanks to serving platter; cut off string and keep warm. Place pan over medium-high heat; boil gently, stirring, for about 5 minutes or until desired thickness. Discard bay leaves. Pour over shanks.

2 In Dutch oven large enough to hold shanks in single layer, heat oil over medium-high heat. With tongs, add shanks to pan, in batches if necessary; brown on both sides, adding up to 1 tbsp (15 mL) more oil if necessary. Transfer to plate. Drain fat from pan.

4 Stir in tomatoes, stock, bay leaves and remaining salt and pepper. Nestle shanks in mixture; bring to boil. Cover and cook in 350°F (180°C) oven, basting every 30 minutes, for 1½ hours. Turn shanks and cook, uncovered and basting twice, for 30 minutes or until tender and sauce is thickened.

6 **Gremolata Topping:** Meanwhile, using finest side of grater, grate lemon rind. In small bowl, stir together lemon rind, garlic and parsley; sprinkle over shanks.

Smoky Tex-Mex Ribs

It sometimes seems that a prerequisite for working in the Test Kitchen is a love affair with ribs. Even though this recipe worked pretty well the first time, we all insisted it had to be tested again – and we gleefully dug into yet another portion with our fingers. If possible, look for the meatier and less fatty back ribs, which are cut from the loin section. Side ribs have the least amount of meat and can be quite fatty.

Ingredients

3 lb	pork side or back ribs	1.5 kg
Sauce:		
2 tsp	vegetable oil	10 mL
2	cloves garlic, minced	2
⅓ cup	minced onion	75 mL
¾ cup	ketchup	175 mL
⅓ cup	water	75 mL
2 tbsp	cider vinegar	25 mL
4 tsp	packed brown sugar	20 mL
1 tsp	each chili powder and dried oregano	5 mL
1 tsp	Worcestershire sauce	5 mL
½ tsp	each ground cumin and dry mustard	2 mL
¼ tsp	salt	1 mL
¼ tsp	liquid smoke	1 mL

Makes 4 servings

Per serving: about 457 cal, 34 g pro, 28 g total fat (10 g sat. fat), 16 g carb, 1 g fibre, 128 mg chol. % RDI: 7% calcium, 21% iron, 6% vit A, 12% vit C, 5% folate.

Variations

Honey Garlic Ribs: Instead of Sauce, combine ¼ cup (50 mL) each teriyaki sauce and hoisin sauce, 2 tbsp (25 mL) each sherry, plum sauce and liquid honey, 1 tbsp (15 mL) rice vinegar and 2 cloves garlic, minced. Do not cook. Follow Step 5. To serve, brush reserved boiled marinade over ribs instead of serving as dipping sauce.

Thai Ribs: Instead of Sauce, combine ⅓ cup (75 mL) hoisin sauce, ¼ cup (50 mL) each soy sauce and lime juice, 2 tbsp (25 mL) each minced gingerroot, chopped fresh coriander and sherry, 2 cloves garlic, minced, 1 tsp (5 mL) sesame oil and ½ tsp (2 mL) each granulated sugar and Asian chili paste. Do not cook. Follow Step 5. To serve, brush reserved boiled marinade over ribs instead of serving as dipping sauce.

1 Trim fat from ribs; cut into 2- or 3-rib serving-size portions. Place in large pot; cover with cold water. Bring just to boil; skim off froth.

2 Reduce heat, cover and simmer for about 40 minutes or until fork-tender. Drain well; arrange in single layer in large shallow dish. Set aside.

3 **Sauce:** Meanwhile, in saucepan, heat oil over medium heat; cook garlic and onion, stirring occasionally, for 3 minutes or until softened.

4 Add ketchup, water, vinegar, sugar, chili powder, oregano, Worcestershire sauce, cumin, mustard, salt and liquid smoke; bring to boil. Reduce heat and simmer for about 3 minutes or until slightly thickened. Let cool.

5 Pour sauce over ribs, turning to coat well. Cover and marinate in refrigerator, turning occasionally, for at least 4 hours or for up to 24 hours. Transfer ⅓ cup (75 mL) of the sauce to small saucepan; set aside.

6 Place ribs on greased grill over medium-high heat; cook, brushing often with remaining sauce and turning once, for 10 to 15 minutes or until browned. Add 2 tbsp (25 mL) water to reserved sauce and bring to boil; boil for 3 minutes. Serve as dipping sauce.

Oven-Barbecued Chinese Pork

How lucky we are that pork tenderloins are so widely available now. Tenderloins are extremely tender, low in fat and cook quickly in only 25 to 35 minutes – in the oven, on the grill or under the broiler. And remember, although we used to have to cook pork until very well done, it is now much leaner and the dramatically improved production methods allow us to cook it to an internal temperature of 160°F (70°C) or until just a hint of pink remains in the meat.

Ingredients

| 2 | pork tenderloins | 2 |
| | (1½ lb/750 g total) | |

Marinade:

2 tbsp	light soy sauce	25 mL
2 tbsp	hoisin sauce	25 mL
1 tbsp	sherry	15 mL
1 tbsp	black bean sauce	15 mL
1½ tsp	minced gingerroot	7 mL
1½ tsp	packed brown sugar	7 mL
1	clove garlic, minced	1
½ tsp	sesame oil	2 mL
Pinch	five-spice powder	Pinch

Makes 4 to 6 servings

Per each of 6 servings: about 161 cal, 28 g pro,
4 g total fat (1 g sat. fat), 3 g carb, 0 g fibre,
61 mg chol. % RDI: 1% calcium, 10% iron,
3% folate.

Variations

Barbecued Thai Pork: Substitute fish sauce for the soy sauce, and lime juice for the sherry. Increase gingerroot to 1 tbsp (15 mL). Substitute 1 tbsp (15 mL) chopped fresh coriander for the five-spice powder.

Barbecued Szechuan Pork: Substitute 1 tsp (5 mL) Asian chili paste for the five-spice powder. Add 1 green onion, chopped.

1 Trim any fat from tenderloins; tuck ends under to make uniform thickness and tie each with kitchen string. Place in shallow glass dish.

2 Marinade: In bowl, whisk together soy sauce, hoisin sauce, sherry, black bean sauce, ginger, sugar, garlic, sesame oil and five-spice powder.

3 Pour marinade over tenderloins, turning to coat. Cover and refrigerate for at least 2 hours or for up to 24 hours, turning occasionally. Let stand at room temperature for 30 minutes.

4 Reserving marinade, place tenderloins on rack in roasting pan. Pour 1 cup (250 mL) water into pan. Cook in 375°F (190°C) oven, basting generously 4 times with reserved marinade, for 30 to 35 minutes or until meat thermometer inserted at 20-degree angle registers 160°F (70°C) and just a hint of pink remains inside.

5 Transfer to cutting board and tent with foil; let stand for 10 minutes.

6 Remove string. Using sharp knife, slice pork diagonally into thin slices.

Smoked Lemon Sage Pork Loin

Smoking meats is definitely today's de rigueur method of cooking. This technique infuses whatever meat you're using with the flavour of the particular wood chips – hickory or alder, for example – that you've selected. Purchase wood chips where you get grilling supplies. So don your chef's hat, wrap an apron around your waist and prepare to become a pro.

Ingredients

1	boneless pork loin roast	1
	(4 lb/2 kg)	

Lemon Sage Marinade:

2	lemons	2
¼ cup	chopped fresh sage	50 mL
¼ cup	extra-virgin olive oil	50 mL
½ tsp	pepper	2 mL

Makes 12 servings

Per serving: about 240 cal, 28 g pro, 13 g total fat (4 g sat. fat), trace carb, trace fibre, 61 mg chol. % RDI: 2% calcium, 6% iron, 3% vit C.

Variations

Smoked Orange Thyme Pork Loin: Substitute oranges for the lemons. Substitute 2 tbsp (25 mL) chopped fresh thyme for the sage.

Smoked Lemon Sage or Orange Thyme Turkey Breast: Substitute about 2¼ lb (1.125 kg) turkey breast for the pork. Cook, bone side down, for 2½ hours or until juices run clear when turkey is pierced. Makes 4 to 6 servings.

Tips

When barbecuing, add more soaked wood chips when chips no longer smoke.

If you have a special smoke cooker, it will take 6 to 7 hours to cook the pork, 4 to 5 hours to cook the turkey.

Place oven thermometer in barbecue to ensure temperature is maintained.

1 **Lemon Sage Marinade:** Grate enough rind from lemons to make 2 tbsp (25 mL). Using juicer, squeeze out juice to make ⅓ cup (75 mL). In small bowl, stir together lemon rind and juice, sage, oil and pepper.

2 Place pork in shallow glass dish; pour marinade over top, turning to coat evenly. Cover and marinate in refrigerator for at least 4 hours or for up to 24 hours, turning often.

3 Soak 7 cups (1.75 L) wood chips in water for 30 minutes; drain and place 4 cups (1 L) in foil pan. Set remaining chips aside. Remove 1 grill rack; place foil pan on coals. Heat both sides of barbecue at high heat until chips smoke vigorously, about 20 minutes.

4 Turn off burner opposite pan; reduce heat of remaining burner to medium. Reserving marinade, place pork on greased grill over unlit side of barbecue. Close lid and cook for 45 minutes, adjusting heat to make sure temperature remains at about 325°F (160°C) and does not drop below 225°F (110°C).

5 Brush roast with some of the reserved marinade. Cook, brushing and turning every 45 minutes, maintaining barbecue temperature and adding reserved wood chips if necessary, for 2 to 3 hours or until meat thermometer inserted in centre registers 160°F (70°C).

6 Transfer roast to cutting board. Tent with foil and let stand for about 10 minutes before slicing.

Sweet and Spicy Pork Roast

This roast is truly a winner. The onions in the marinade cook down to a tantalizing sweetness, which is highlighted by the addition of honey and contrasted with a little hot pepper sauce. It's an ideal dish for a dinner party or an extra-special night with the family.

2 tsp	olive oil	10 mL
1	small onion, finely chopped	1
2	cloves garlic, minced	2
¼ cup	cider vinegar	50 mL
¼ cup	fancy molasses	50 mL
¼ cup	liquid honey	50 mL
2 tbsp	Dijon mustard	25 mL
2 tsp	soy sauce	10 mL
¼ tsp	hot pepper sauce	1 mL
1½ tsp	cornstarch	7 mL
1	boneless single-loin pork roast (about 3 lb/1.5 kg)	1

1 In small saucepan, heat oil over medium heat; cook onion and garlic for 1 minute. Reduce heat to low; cover and cook, stirring occasionally, for about 8 minutes or until softened.

2 Stir in vinegar, molasses, honey, mustard, soy sauce and hot pepper sauce; bring to boil. Dissolve cornstarch in 1 tbsp (15 mL) water; whisk into saucepan and cook over medium-high heat for 3 minutes or until bubbly and thickened. Let stand for 5 minutes.

3 Meanwhile, trim excess fat from pork. Place on rack in roasting pan; pour in ½ cup (125 mL) water. Brush ¼ cup (50 mL) of the honey mixture all over pork. Roast in 325°F (160°C) oven, basting with 2 tbsp (25 mL) of the honey mixture every 30 minutes and adding up to 1 cup (250 mL) more water to pan if needed to prevent scorching, for about 1 hour and 40 minutes or until meat thermometer registers 160°F (70°C). Transfer to platter and tent with foil; let stand for 10 minutes before slicing thinly.

4 Meanwhile, skim fat from pan juices. Pour remaining honey mixture into pan. On stove top, bring to boil, stirring and scraping up brown bits from bottom of pan. Reduce heat and simmer, stirring, for about 5 minutes or until slightly thickened. Serve with pork.

Makes 8 servings

Per serving: about 307 cal, 34 g pro, 11 g total fat (4 g sat. fat), 18 g carb, 0 g fibre, 93 mg chol. % RDI: 5% calcium, 14% iron, 3% vit C, 3% folate.

Moroccan-Scented Roast of Pork

The tanginess of orange and lemon in the marinade pairs so beautifully with the Moroccan-inspired selection of spices and herbs that it is an all-time favourite.

2	onions, sliced	2
½ cup	orange juice	125 mL
2 tbsp	lemon juice	25 mL
⅓ cup	olive oil	75 mL
2	cloves garlic, minced	2
1 tbsp	minced gingerroot	15 mL
1 tsp	each cinnamon and dried oregano	5 mL
½ tsp	each ground coriander and cardamom	2 mL
¼ tsp	each salt and pepper	1 mL
3 lb	boneless pork shoulder butt, rolled and tied	1.5 kg
1 tbsp	butter	15 mL
1½ cups	chicken stock	375 mL
1 tbsp	all-purpose flour	15 mL
1 tbsp	maple syrup (or 2 tsp/10 mL packed brown sugar)	15 mL

1 In bowl, combine onions, orange and lemon juices, 3 tbsp (50 mL) of the oil, garlic, ginger, cinnamon, oregano, coriander, cardamom, salt and pepper. Pour over pork in roasting pan; cover and refrigerate for 24 hours, turning often.

2 Let pork stand at room temperature for 30 minutes. Remove pork from marinade, reserving marinade in roasting pan. In large heavy skillet, heat remaining oil with butter over medium-high heat; brown pork all over.

3 Return pork to roasting pan. Pour ½ cup (125 mL) of the chicken stock over pork; roast in 325°F (160°C) oven for 1½ to 2 hours or until meat thermometer registers 160°F (70°C). Transfer pork to cutting board; tent with foil and let stand for 15 minutes before slicing thinly.

4 Meanwhile, skim off all but 2 tbsp (25 mL) fat from pan. Set pan over medium heat; sprinkle in flour and cook, whisking, for 1 minute. Pour in remaining stock; bring to boil and cook for about 3 minutes or until thickened. Whisk in maple syrup. Serve with pork.

Makes 8 servings

Per serving: about 298 cal, 29 g pro, 16 g total fat (6 g sat. fat), 8 g carb, 1 g fibre, 75 mg chol. % RDI: 3% calcium, 14% iron, 2% vit A, 12% vit C, 6% folate.

Buying and Storing Dried Herbs

- Buy dried herbs in a store that has good turnover to ensure they are as fresh as possible. Preferably, buy from a reputable bulk store, purchasing just a little bit at a time.
- Dried herbs have a shelf life of six months. They should be stored in a cupboard or drawer away from any heat sources or direct sunlight, which will shorten their shelf life appreciably. Do not store them above your oven.
- Dried herbs can be substituted for fresh herbs using the three to one rule: For every 1 tbsp (15 mL) of fresh herbs called for, use 1 tsp (5 mL) dried.

Barbecue-Roasted Pork Loin

This super-easy recipe takes the shortcut of using a store-bought barbecue sauce that's rounded out by ingredients you're sure to have on hand in your pantry.

1	single-loin pork roast (1½ lb/750 g)	1
¼ cup	prepared barbecue sauce	50 mL
1	clove garlic, minced	1
1 tsp	molasses	5 mL
½ tsp	rice or cider vinegar	2 mL
Dash	hot pepper sauce	Dash
Pinch	each salt and pepper	Pinch

1 Place pork roast, fat side up, on rack in roasting pan; roast in 450°F (230°C) oven for 25 minutes.

2 In small bowl, whisk together barbecue sauce, garlic, molasses, vinegar, hot pepper sauce, salt and pepper; brush some over roast. Roast, brushing occasionally with remaining sauce, for 10 to 15 minutes longer or until meat thermometer registers 160°F (70°C) and just a hint of pink remains inside.

3 Transfer to cutting board and tent with foil; let stand for 10 minutes before slicing thinly.

Makes 6 servings

Per serving: about 172 cal, 23 g pro, 8 g total fat (3 g sat. fat), 1 g carb, trace fibre, 65 mg chol. % RDI: 2% calcium, 6% iron, 1% vit A, 2% vit C, 1% folate.

Crown Roast of Pork

Extravagant yes, but what a sight to behold! There's nothing quite like an impressive crown roast of pork to elicit exclamatory sighs from your guests while simultaneously pampering their appetites. For easy serving, be sure to request from your butcher a roast with 12 ribs (one rib per person).

Ingredients

1	crown roast of pork (about 6½ lb/3 kg)	1
¾ cup	chicken stock	175 mL

Herb Rub:

2 tbsp	dried rosemary	25 mL
2 tbsp	olive oil	25 mL
1 tbsp	dried sage	15 mL
2 tsp	fennel seeds	10 mL
1½ tsp	salt	7 mL
1 tsp	pepper	5 mL
4	cloves garlic	4

Saffron Rice Pilaf:

⅔ cup	pine nuts	150 mL
2 tbsp	butter	25 mL
1	onion, chopped	1
2 cups	chopped fennel or celery	500 mL
1	each sweet red and green pepper, chopped	1
2 cups	long-grain rice	500 mL
1½ tsp	salt	7 mL
¼ tsp	pepper	1 mL
¼ tsp	saffron threads, crumbled	1 mL
3 cups	chicken stock	750 mL
½ cup	golden raisins	125 mL

Sauce:

½ cup	white wine	125 mL
2 tbsp	all-purpose flour	25 mL
½ cup	chicken stock	125 mL

Makes 12 servings

Per serving: about 504 cal, 36 g pro, 24 g total fat (7 g sat. fat), 36 g carb, 3 g fibre, 69 mg chol. % RDI: 9% calcium, 22% iron, 6% vit A, 44% vit C, 10% folate.

1 **Herb Rub:** With mortar and pestle or in mini chopper, grind together rosemary, oil, sage, fennel seeds, salt, pepper and garlic until paste. Rub all over pork, excluding bones. Place, bone ends up, on rack in roasting pan. Wrap bone ends in foil. Pour stock into pan.

2 Roast in 325°F (160°C) oven for 2½ to 3 hours or until meat thermometer registers 160°F (70°C), adding up to ⅓ cup (75 mL) water if necessary to maintain juices in pan. Transfer to serving platter. Remove foil from bones. Tent roast with foil; let stand for 10 minutes.

3 **Saffron Rice Pilaf:** Meanwhile, in large skillet, toast pine nuts over medium heat, shaking pan often, for about 5 minutes or until golden and fragrant. Remove from pan and set aside.

4 Add butter to pan; cook onion, fennel and sweet peppers for 5 minutes. Stir in rice, salt, pepper and saffron. Pour in stock; bring to boil. Add raisins; reduce heat, cover and simmer for 25 minutes or until rice is tender and liquid is absorbed.

5 **Sauce:** Skim fat from juices in roasting pan; place over medium-high heat. Pour in wine, stirring and scraping up any brown bits from bottom of pan. Whisk flour into stock; whisk into pan and cook, whisking, for 2 minutes or until thickened. Strain into sauceboat.

6 Spoon some of the pilaf into centre of roast; transfer remainder to serving bowl. Sprinkle pine nuts over pilaf. To serve, slice between bones; top each serving with 1 tbsp (15 mL) of the sauce. Serve with pilaf.

Tourtière

Christmas in Quebec means families gathering for Réveillon and tourtière, the traditional savoury pie filled with delicately seasoned ground pork. As with so many heirloom recipes, the number and kind of ingredients depend on your source, but the consensus is always the same on its delicious appeal.

Ingredients

1 tbsp	vegetable oil	15 mL
2 lb	ground pork	1 kg
1½ cups	beef stock	375 mL
3	onions, finely chopped	3
3	cloves garlic, minced	3
2 cups	sliced mushrooms	500 mL
1 cup	finely chopped celery	250 mL
¾ tsp	salt	4 mL
½ tsp	each cinnamon, pepper and dried savory	2 mL
¼ tsp	ground cloves	1 mL
1 cup	fresh bread crumbs	250 mL
½ cup	chopped fresh parsley	125 mL
	Pastry for double-crust 9- or 10-inch (23 or 25 cm) pie	
1	egg	1
1 tsp	water	5 mL

Makes 8 to 10 servings

Per each of 8 servings: about 478 cal, 26 g pro, 29 g total fat (9 g sat. fat), 26 g carb, 2 g fibre, 81 mg chol. % RDI: 4% calcium, 19% iron, 4% vit A, 10% vit C, 16% folate.

Variation

Turkey Tourtière: Substitute turkey or chicken for the pork. Substitute chicken stock for beef stock. Omit cinnamon, savory and cloves. Add ½ tsp (2 mL) dried marjoram and ¼ tsp (1 mL) dried thyme.

Tip

To make tourtière ahead of time, omit pastry cutouts. Wrap and freeze unbaked pie for up to 2 months. Partially thaw in refrigerator for 6 hours or until pastry gives slightly when pressed. Cut steam vents and brush with glaze. Bake in 375°F (190°C) oven for 1 1/4 hours or until heated through and pastry is golden, shielding edge with foil if necessary during last 30 minutes.

1 In large skillet, heat oil over medium-high heat; cook pork, breaking up with wooden spoon, for 7 to 10 minutes or until no longer pink. Drain off fat.

2 Stir in stock, onions, garlic, mushrooms, celery, salt, cinnamon, pepper, savory and cloves; bring to boil. Reduce heat to medium-low; simmer, stirring occasionally, for 35 to 45 minutes or until about 2 tbsp (25 mL) liquid remains.

3 Stir in bread crumbs and parsley. Cover and refrigerate until cold or for up to 24 hours. On lightly floured surface, roll out half of the pastry to ⅛-inch (3 mm) thickness; fit into pie plate.

4 Spoon filling into pie shell, smoothing top. Roll out remaining pastry. Moisten rim of pie shell with water. Cover with top pastry, pressing edges together to seal. Trim and flute edge.

5 Beat egg with water; brush some over pastry. Cut decorative shapes from remaining pastry and arrange on top; brush with some of the remaining egg mixture.

6 Cut steam vents in top; bake in 375°F (190°C) oven for 40 to 45 minutes or until golden. Let cool for 10 minutes before cutting.

Spinach-Stuffed Leg of Lamb

Leg of lamb is consistently an elegant dish but it's elevated to an entirely different stratosphere of remarkable when it's stuffed with a garlic-and-oregano-flavoured spinach filling. The rich, nutty flavour of Asiago cheese lends a supporting role, as do the delicately flavoured pine nuts.

Ingredients

1	boneless butterflied leg of lamb (3 lb/1.5 kg)	1
½ tsp	pepper	2 mL
¼ tsp	salt	1 mL
1 tsp	dried oregano	5 mL
3 cups	chicken stock	750 mL
¼ cup	dry white wine	50 mL
1 tbsp	all-purpose flour	15 mL

Spinach Stuffing:

1	pkg (10 oz/284 g) fresh spinach	1
1 tbsp	butter	15 mL
1	onion, finely chopped	1
2	cloves garlic, minced	2
1 tsp	dried oregano	5 mL
½ tsp	pepper	2 mL
¼ tsp	salt	1 mL
½ cup	shredded Asiago or freshly grated Parmesan cheese	125 mL
½ cup	fresh bread crumbs	125 mL
⅓ cup	toasted pine nuts	75 mL
1	egg, beaten	1

Makes 8 servings

Per serving: about 296 cal, 36 g pro, 14 g total fat (6 g sat. fat), 7 g carb, 2 g fibre, 142 mg chol. % RDI: 11% calcium, 34% iron, 30% vit A, 7% vit C, 27% folate.

Variation

Red Pepper Stuffing: Add 1 tsp (5 mL) dried basil along with oregano. Substitute Fontina cheese for the Asiago. Add ½ cup (125 mL) diced sweet red pepper along with onion.

Tip

To replace wine, substitute chicken stock and add 1 tbsp (15 mL) white wine vinegar.

1 **Spinach Stuffing:** Trim and rinse spinach; shake off excess water. In large pot, cover and cook spinach, with just the water clinging to leaves, over medium heat for about 5 minutes or until wilted. Drain and let cool; squeeze out liquid completely. Chop coarsely; place in bowl and set aside.

2 In nonstick skillet, melt butter over medium heat; cook onion, garlic, oregano, pepper and salt, stirring occasionally, for about 5 minutes or until softened. Add to spinach; let cool completely. Stir in cheese, bread crumbs, pine nuts and egg until well combined.

3 Trim excess fat from lamb, leaving thin layer; place, fat side down, on work surface. Sprinkle with half each of the pepper and salt. Spread with spinach mixture, leaving 1-inch (2.5 cm) border uncovered. Starting at narrow end, roll up jelly roll–style.

4 Fasten each end of roll with poultry pins or skewers; tie at 1-inch (2.5 cm) intervals with kitchen string. Rub with oregano and remaining pepper and salt. Place on greased rack in roasting pan; pour in 1 cup (250 mL) of the chicken stock and wine.

5 Roast in 325°F (160°C) oven, basting occasionally and adding more of the stock if necessary to maintain level, for 1½ hours or until meat thermometer registers 140°F (60°C) for rare or 160°F (70°C) for medium. Transfer lamb to platter and tent with foil; let stand for 15 minutes. Remove string and pins; slice ½ inch (1 cm) thick.

6 Meanwhile, stir flour and 2 tbsp (25 mL) of the remaining stock into pan drippings; cook over medium-high heat, stirring, for 1 minute. Add remaining stock; bring to boil. Reduce heat and simmer, whisking, for 5 minutes or until thickened slightly; strain. Serve with lamb.

Racks of Lamb with Lemon and Mint

Some dishes just naturally say home cooking while others more readily conjure up notions of restaurant dining. Rack of lamb tends to snuggle easily into the latter category, because people perceive it as either difficult or expensive. But everybody should try making this festive dish. It's easy, as our photos show, and you'll be so proud that you'll hardly be able to wait to make it again.

Ingredients

| 2 | racks of lamb | 2 |
| | (12 oz/375 g each) | |

Lemon Mint Marinade:

1 tsp	grated lemon rind	5 mL
2 tbsp	lemon juice	25 mL
2 tbsp	chopped fresh mint	25 mL
	(or 1 tsp/5 mL dried)	
1 tbsp	vegetable oil	15 mL
Pinch	pepper	Pinch

Makes 4 servings

*Per serving: about 145 cal, 14 g pro, 9 g total fat
(3 g sat. fat), 1 g carb, 0 g fibre, 54 mg chol. % RDI:
1% calcium, 9% iron, 1% vit A, 7% vit C.*

Variations

Chutney-Glazed Racks: Combine
2 tbsp (25 mL) chutney, ¼ tsp (1 mL)
each cinnamon and ground ginger and
dash of lemon juice; brush over lamb.
Let stand for 30 minutes before roasting.

Dijon Thyme–Glazed Racks:
Combine 2 tbsp (25 mL) Dijon mustard,
1 tbsp (15 mL) each lemon juice and
olive oil, 1 clove garlic, minced, 1 tsp
(5 mL) dried thyme and ¼ tsp (1 mL)
salt; brush over lamb. Let stand for
30 minutes before roasting.

Tip

**Make sure that the backbone
is removed from rack of lamb
(chined) before you begin or it will
be impossible to carve; your butcher
will be happy to do it for you. It's
possible to buy racks of lamb in
which all trimming from ribs
(Frenching) has already been done.**

1 Place each rack, meaty side up, on cutting board. Using sharp paring knife, cut line across rack where meaty portion begins, about 3 inches (8 cm) down from rib ends. Cut off layer of fat between line and rib ends.

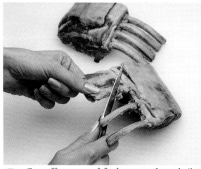

2 Cut off meat and fat between bared ribs to expose bones. Holding each rack firmly and using knife, scrape exposed rib bones clean, removing any remaining meat and fat.

3 Holding knife at 20-degree angle to meat and working with short strokes, trim fat from meaty portion of ribs to ⅛-inch (3 mm) thickness, lifting away fat as you work.

4 With rib ends up, press racks together to interlink bones and form "guard of honour." Separate bases about 1 inch (2.5 cm) to stabilize; place in shallow dish.

Lemon Mint Marinade: Whisk together lemon rind and juice, mint, oil and pepper; brush over lamb. Let stand at room temperature for 30 minutes.

5 Place on greased rack in roasting pan, drizzling with any remaining marinade. Cover exposed ribs with foil to prevent charring. Roast in 450°F (230°C) oven for 10 minutes. Reduce heat to 325°F (160°C); roast for 40 minutes longer or until meat thermometer registers 140°F (60°C) for rare or 150°F (65°C) for medium-rare.

6 Transfer to warmed platter; tent with foil and let stand for 10 minutes. Remove all foil; carve between bones, allowing 3 chops per serving.

Lamb Gyros

Gyros are Greek sandwiches filled with lamb, chopped tomatoes and cucumbers and a tangy tzatziki sauce. Although they're usually made with spit-roasted lamb, our recipe uses a butterflied leg of lamb for its leanness and flavour intensity.

Ingredients

1	butterflied leg of lamb (about 3 lb/1.5 kg)	1
⅔ cup	extra-virgin olive oil	150 mL
1 tsp	grated lemon rind	5 mL
¼ cup	lemon juice	50 mL
3	cloves garlic, minced	3
2 tbsp	chopped fresh oregano	25 mL
1 tbsp	chopped fresh mint	15 mL
	Pepper	
4	zucchini	4
2	small eggplants	2
	Salt	
12	flatbreads (about 8 inches/ 20 cm round) or pita breads	12
2 cups	chopped seeded tomatoes	500 mL

Tzatziki Sauce:

3 cups	plain yogurt	750 mL
1	English cucumber	1
½ tsp	salt	2 mL
2 tbsp	lemon juice	25 mL
1 tbsp	chopped fresh mint	15 mL
2	cloves garlic, minced	2
¼ tsp	pepper	1 mL

Makes 12 sandwiches

Per sandwich: about 466 cal, 30 g pro, 19 g total fat (4 g sat. fat), 45 g carb, 3 g fibre, 74 mg chol. % RDI: 16% calcium, 31% iron, 5% vit A, 25% vit C, 41% folate.

Tip

Lamb can be marinated in the refrigerator for up to 24 hours.

1 Trim fat from lamb; place in glass dish. Combine 3 tbsp (50 mL) of the oil, lemon rind and juice, garlic, oregano, mint and ½ tsp (2 mL) pepper; pour over lamb, turning to coat. Cover and refrigerate for at least 8 hours, turning occasionally. Let stand at room temperature for 30 minutes.

3 Grate cucumber and place in another sieve over bowl; sprinkle with half of the salt. Let drain for 1 hour; press out remaining liquid.

In small bowl, stir together drained yogurt and cucumber, remaining salt, lemon juice, mint, garlic and pepper; set aside in refrigerator.

5 Reserving marinade, add lamb to grill; cook, covered, turning 4 times and basting with marinade once on each side, for 20 to 30 minutes or until meat thermometer registers 140°F (60°C) for rare, or for 35 to 40 minutes for medium-rare (150°F/65°C).

2 **Tzatziki Sauce:** Meanwhile, place yogurt in cheesecloth-lined sieve set over bowl. Cover and refrigerate for at least 6 hours or until reduced to 1½ cups (375 mL), or for up to 24 hours.

4 Slice zucchini and eggplant lengthwise into ¼-inch (5 mm) thick slices. Combine remaining oil and ¼ tsp (1 mL) each salt and pepper; brush over vegetables. Place on greased grill over medium-high heat; close lid and cook zucchini for 10 minutes, eggplant for 15 minutes, turning occasionally, or until tender. Set aside.

6 Transfer lamb to cutting board and tent with foil; let stand for 10 minutes. Sprinkle with ¼ tsp (1 mL) salt. Slice thinly across the grain. Spread sauce over each flatbread; top with lamb, vegetables and tomatoes. Fold flatbread over.

Poultry, Fish, Seafood, Eggs

Poultry is one of those ingredients that cooks love. It's delicious, versatile and relatively inexpensive. Fish and seafood, though more costly, are amazingly adaptable and popular. And with this incredible variety at your disposal, now is a great time to be innovative. Let our steps be your inspiration. Accept that invitation to make Thanksgiving dinner. Our Roast Turkey cooking lesson will take you by the hand and ensure that the bird is the crowning glory – and that you even know how to carve it properly. Experiment! The techniques shown here are as flexible as your imagination. Once you've tenderly tucked some fresh herbs under the skin of a chicken breast, you'll find yourself wanting to apply this treatment to other dishes as well. You'll discover that the sauces you make to accompany smoky grilled turkey breast are just right for grilled tuna. You'll realize that Pad Thai is equally yummy made with chicken instead of pork and scallops instead of shrimp. It is the practicality and applicability of all of these techniques that make cooking so much fun.

Roast Turkey

Roast turkey is one of those glorious dishes that evoke both great
memories (of family gatherings and luscious meals) and great fear (of
overcooking or making lumpy gravy). But actually there's very little
that's more straightforward than roasting a turkey to plump, moist,
golden perfection. In this lesson you'll also learn the best way
to carve that beautiful bird.

Ingredients

15 lb	turkey	6.75 kg
¼ cup	butter, softened	50 mL
½ tsp	each dried sage and thyme	2 mL
	Salt and pepper	

Stuffing:

¾ cup	butter	175 mL
2½ cups	chopped onions	625 mL
1 cup	each chopped celery and fennel (or 2 cups/500 mL celery)	250 mL
4 tsp	dried sage	20 mL
1 tsp	each salt, dried savory, marjoram and pepper	5 mL
½ tsp	dried thyme	2 mL
14 cups	cubed white bread	3.5 L
1 cup	chopped fresh parsley	250 mL

Stock:

4½ cups	chicken stock	1.125 L
1½ cups	dry white wine or water (approx)	375 mL
1	onion, chopped	1
½ cup	each sliced carrots and celery	125 mL

Gravy:

¼ cup	all-purpose flour	50 mL
2 tbsp	butter	25 mL
	Salt and pepper	

Makes 8 to 10 servings

*Per each of 10 servings: about 564 cal, 39 g pro,
32 g total fat (15 g sat. fat), 29 g carb, 2 g fibre,
143 mg chol. % RDI: 10% calcium, 31% iron,
21% vit A, 12% vit C, 27% folate.*

Tips

**Using a trustworthy meat thermo-
meter ensures a bird that's cooked
to the proper temperature. A foil
tent keeps breast meat moist and
basting burnishes the skin to a deep
rich colour. Don't stuff the bird until
just before roasting and always pack
it loosely. If packed too tightly, the
stuffing may not reach the requisite
temperature of 165°F (75°C).**

**Calculate about 1 lb (500 g) per
person to allow for shrinkage and
bones – a little more if you're intent
on leftovers.**

1 **Stuffing:** In skillet, melt butter over medium heat; cook onions, celery, fennel, sage, salt, savory, marjoram, pepper and thyme for 10 to 15 minutes or until tender. Transfer to bowl; toss with bread and parsley. Place turkey giblets and neck in saucepan. Rinse turkey inside and out; pat dry. Stuff neck opening; skewer skin over stuffing to back. Twist wings under back. Stuff body cavity. Tuck legs under band of skin or tie together with kitchen string.

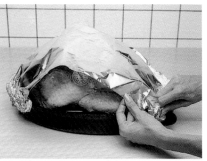

2 Place turkey on rack in roasting pan. Combine butter, sage and thyme; rub over turkey. Sprinkle with salt and pepper. Tent with foil, dull side out, leaving sides open. Roast in 325°F (160°C) oven, basting every 30 minutes, for 4 hours. Remove foil; roast for 1 hour longer or until thermometer inserted in thigh reads 180°F (82°C) and stuffing 165°F (75°C). Transfer to cutting board. Tent with foil; let stand for 30 minutes.

3 **Stock:** Meanwhile, to saucepan with turkey parts, add stock, wine, onion, carrots and celery; bring to boil. Reduce heat to low and skim off fat; simmer for 3 hours. Strain into measuring cup. Add enough more wine to make 3 cups (750 mL). Set aside.

4 **Gravy:** Skim off fat in roasting pan. Stir flour into pan; cook over medium heat, stirring, for 1 minute. Whisk in stock and bring to boil, scraping up brown bits from bottom of pan. Reduce heat and simmer for 5 minutes. Whisk in butter; season with salt and pepper to taste. Strain if desired.

5 Spoon turkey stuffing into bowl; keep stuffing warm.

To carve leg: Steady turkey with back of carving fork. With carving knife and starting at front (neck) end of thigh, cut skin between leg and body up and around to back of thigh.

6 With fork inserted between thigh and body, firmly press thigh outward and down. Probing with tip of knife, locate joint where thigh bone connects to body. Press knife into joint and cut through firmly. Cut through remaining meat to remove whole leg.

7 Cut through joint separating thigh from drumstick. Steady drumstick with fork. Carve thick slice from each side parallel to bone. Turn cut side down; slice remaining meat from sides. Carve meat from thigh parallel to bone.

8 **To carve wing:** With knife at 45-degree angle to cutting board, cut through skin and meat between wing and breast. Press wing down with fork. Using tip of knife (as for leg), locate joint near neck opening; cut wing from body.

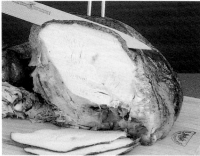

9 **To carve breast:** Pierce turkey with fork at top of breastbone to steady. Starting at breastbone, carve through meat diagonally using long sweeping motion. Lift off each slice. Repeat carving for other side of turkey. Serve with dressing and gravy.

Classic Roast Chicken

What could be more effortless, homey and satisfying than a roast chicken that's golden, aromatic and wonderfully succulent? Knowing just a few tricks of the trade will have you serving one in no time. Most birds are in the mid-size range of 3 1/2 to 5 1/2 lb (1.7 to 2.5 kg), which will serve about four people. Larger chickens are usually ideal candidates for soup (they'll be a little tougher), unless you buy a capon, which weighs 8 to 10 lb (3.5 to 4.5 kg), enough for eight to 10 people.

Ingredients

1	roasting chicken	1
	(about 5 lb/2.2 kg)	
Half	onion	Half
4	cloves garlic	4
Half	lemon	Half
1 tbsp	olive oil or butter	15 mL
¾ tsp	dried thyme	4 mL
¼ tsp	crumbled dried rosemary	1 mL
¼ tsp	each salt and pepper	1 mL
2 tbsp	all-purpose flour	25 mL
¾ cup	chicken stock	175 mL

Makes 6 servings

Per serving: about 379 cal, 38 g pro, 23 g total fat (6 g sat. fat), 3 g carb, trace fibre, 121 mg chol. % RDI: 2% calcium, 14% iron, 6% vit A, 2% vit C, 4% folate.

Variation

Quickie Roast Chicken: Increase oven temperature to 375°F (190°C) and roast for 1¾ to 2 hours in total, basting often after 30 minutes.

Tips

It's always preferable to cook a chicken on a rack in a shallow roasting pan so that the heat can circulate evenly around the bird. Roasting at 325°F (160°C) keeps both white and dark meat moist and tender. The dual tests of juices running clear when the thigh is pierced and an internal temperature of 185°F (85°C) are both necessary to guarantee that the chicken is cooked through.

For a traditional carving method, refer to Roast Turkey cooking lesson (page 86).

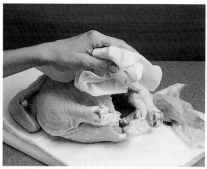

1 Remove giblets and neck, if present, from chicken. Rinse chicken inside and out; pat dry.

2 Place onion and garlic in chicken cavity. Squeeze juice from lemon and set aside; add lemon skin to cavity.

3 Tuck wings under back of chicken; tie legs together with kitchen string. Brush all over with oil; sprinkle with thyme, rosemary, salt and pepper. Place, breast side up, on rack in roasting pan. Roast, uncovered, in 325°F (160°C) oven for 1½ hours.

4 Baste chicken with pan juices. Roast, basting occasionally, for about 1½ hours longer or until juices run clear when thigh is pierced and meat thermometer inserted in thigh registers 185°F (85°C). Transfer chicken to platter and tent with foil; let stand for 10 minutes before carving.

5 Skim fat from juices in pan. Sprinkle flour over juices; cook over medium-high heat, whisking, for 1 minute. Drizzle in chicken stock and 2 tbsp (25 mL) reserved lemon juice; cook, whisking, for about 3 minutes or until thickened. Pour into warmed gravy boat.

6 Cut string holding legs together; discard onion, lemon and garlic. Using poultry or kitchen shears, cut chicken into 2 breast and 2 leg portions. Cut each breast in half diagonally. Cut through each leg at joint to separate into drumstick and thigh. Serve with gravy.

Lemon Rosemary Grilled Chicken

This inexpensive, herby and sweet chicken is sure to be a winner with all-year grillers. Don't be tempted to remove the skin before grilling because it holds in juices while cooking. Feel free to remove it afterward when the meat no longer runs the risk of drying out.

Ingredients

⅓ cup	lemon juice	75 mL
¼ cup	extra-virgin olive oil	50 mL
2 tbsp	chopped fresh rosemary	25 mL
	(or 1 tsp/5 mL dried)	
1	large clove garlic, minced	1
1	chicken (2½ lb/1.25 kg)	1
2 tbsp	liquid honey	25 mL
2 tbsp	Dijon mustard	25 mL
	Salt and pepper	

Makes about 4 servings

Per serving: about 428 cal, 35 g pro, 29 g total fat (6 g sat. fat), 7 g carb, 0 g fibre, 110 mg chol. % RDI: 3% calcium, 13% iron, 6% vit A, 5% vit C, 4% folate.

Variations

Peppery Grilled Chicken: Increase lemon juice to ½ cup (125 mL). Substitute 1 tbsp (15 mL) crushed black peppercorns for rosemary. Increase garlic to 2 large cloves.

Lime Coriander–Grilled Chicken: Substitute lime juice for lemon juice and add 1 tsp (5 mL) grated lime rind. Substitute vegetable oil for olive oil. Substitute 1 tbsp (15 mL) crushed coriander seeds for rosemary.

Tips

To ensure that chicken will be crisp and browned outside and cooked through evenly, grill over medium heat; high heat tends to dry out most meats. Flatten chicken and begin grilling bone side down; the bones diffuse the heat evenly throughout the meat.

To prevent scorching, use sugar-based or tomato sauces only during the last 10 to 15 minutes of cooking.

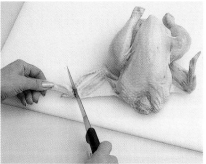

1 Combine lemon juice, oil, rosemary and garlic; pour into shallow glass dish large enough to hold chicken in single layer; set aside. Using sharp knife, remove wing tips from chicken. Place bird, breast side down, on cutting board.

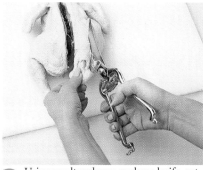

2 Using poultry shears or sharp knife, cut along 1 side of backbone, then along other side; remove and discard backbone.

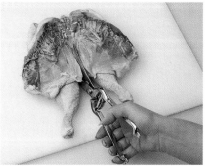

3 Spread chicken apart to lie flat. Using poultry shears or knife, cut along each side of breastbone to separate into halves. Remove and discard breastbone. Trim off all fat and excess skin.

4 Place chicken between 2 sheets of plastic wrap. Using smooth mallet, flatten halves for more even cooking. Place in shallow dish with marinade, turning to coat. Cover and marinate at room temperature for 30 minutes. Or marinate in refrigerator for 2 hours, turning occasionally; let stand at room temperature for 30 minutes.

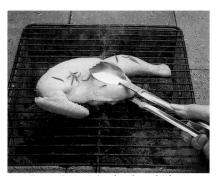

5 Reserving marinade, place chicken, bone side down, on greased grill over medium heat; cook, turning halfway through, for 20 to 30 minutes or until golden brown, watching carefully to avoid flareups. Meanwhile, transfer marinade to small saucepan. Add honey and mustard; bring to boil. Boil for 5 minutes.

6 Brush marinade over both sides of chicken. Cook, turning and brushing with marinade, for 10 to 15 minutes longer or until juices run clear when chicken is pierced. Season with salt and pepper to taste. Cut halves into quarters.

Two Classic Sauces for Grilled Turkey

Inspired by the Italian classic *vitello tonnato*, this update features a boned turkey breast, instead of veal, and two renditions of Italian sauces, both excellent complements to the flavoursome grilled turkey. Great for casual summer entertaining, these sauces are also fabulous with grilled chicken or fish and as part of an antipasto platter replete with sliced cold meats. Pictured, Salsa Verde.

Ingredients

1	boned turkey breast (2 lb/1 kg)	1
2 tsp	olive oil	10 mL
Pinch	each salt and pepper	Pinch

Salsa Verde

1	egg (unshelled)	1
⅓ cup	fresh bread crumbs	75 mL
3 tbsp	red wine vinegar	50 mL
5	anchovies, rinsed	5
1 cup	packed fresh parsley leaves	250 mL
2 tbsp	drained capers	25 mL
1	clove garlic	1
¼ cup	extra-virgin olive oil	50 mL

Basil Tonnato Sauce

1	can (3½ oz/99 g) tuna, drained	1
1 cup	packed fresh basil leaves	250 mL
4	anchovies, rinsed	4
3 tbsp	drained capers	50 mL
2 tbsp	light mayonnaise	25 mL
½ tsp	finely grated lemon rind	2 mL
2 tbsp	lemon juice	25 mL
½ tsp	Dijon mustard	2 mL
¼ cup	extra-virgin olive oil	50 mL

Makes 8 servings

Per serving with Salsa Verde: about 252 cal, 27 g pro, 15 g total fat (3 g sat. fat), 2 g carb, trace fibre, 93 mg chol. % RDI: 4% calcium, 14% iron, 5% vit A, 12% vit C, 10% folate.

Per serving with Basil Tonnato Sauce: about 259 cal, 28 g pro, 15 g total fat (3 g sat. fat), 1 g carb, 0 g fibre, 69 mg chol. % RDI: 3% calcium, 11% iron, 2% vit C, 5% folate.

1 **Salsa Verde:** In small saucepan, cover egg with cold water; bring to boil. Boil for 1 minute. Cover and remove from heat; let stand for 20 minutes. Chill in colander under cold running water. Peel under running water.

2 Meanwhile, in small bowl, soak bread crumbs in vinegar; let stand for 20 minutes. Transfer to food processor. Add egg, anchovies, parsley, capers and garlic; chop finely.

3 With motor running, gradually pour in oil and 3 tbsp (50 mL) water in thin stream. Transfer to serving dish. *(Salsa can be covered and refrigerated for up to 8 hours; stir before serving.)*

4 **Basil Tonnato Sauce:** In food processor, coarsely chop together tuna, basil, anchovies, capers, mayonnaise, lemon rind, lemon juice and mustard. With motor running, gradually pour in oil and 2 tbsp (25 mL) water in thin stream. Transfer to serving dish. *(Sauce can be covered and refrigerated for up to 8 hours; stir before serving.)*

5 Lay turkey on work surface, skin side up. Brush with half of the oil; sprinkle with half each of the salt and pepper. Place turkey, skin side down, on greased grill over medium heat; brush with remaining oil. Sprinkle with remaining salt and pepper. Cook for 10 minutes.

6 Turn turkey over; cook for 20 minutes. Turn again; cook for 10 minutes or until juices run clear when turkey is pierced with fork. Transfer to plate and cover loosely with foil; let stand for 10 minutes. *(Turkey can be wrapped in plastic wrap and refrigerated for up to 24 hours.)* Slice thinly; serve with Salsa Verde or Basil Tonnato Sauce.

Turkey Breast Spiral with Barley Timbales

Searing the turkey in a 450°F (230°C) oven first seals in flavour and avoids having to find a large enough skillet for the stove top. It also ensures that the turkey breast is glazed to a deep inviting colour, important since we all eat with our eyes before the food even reaches our mouths. The barley timbales offer a textured alternative to rice or mashed potatoes.

2 tbsp	vegetable oil	25 mL
1	onion, chopped	1
3	cloves garlic, minced	3
1½ cups	ricotta cheese	375 mL
1	egg yolk	1
3 tbsp	freshly grated Parmesan cheese	50 mL
1 tsp	salt	5 mL
½ tsp	pepper	2 mL
¼ tsp	nutmeg	1 mL
1	boneless turkey breast (about 3 lb/1.5 kg)	1
1	pkg (10 oz/284 g) fresh spinach, cooked and drained	1
½ cup	diced sweet red pepper	125 mL
¼ tsp	dried thyme	1 mL
2 tsp	all-purpose flour	10 mL
⅓ cup	chicken stock	75 mL
	Barley Timbales (recipe follows)	

1 In small skillet, heat 2 tsp (10 mL) of the oil over medium heat; cook onion and garlic, stirring occasionally, for 3 minutes. Transfer to bowl; mix in ricotta, egg yolk, Parmesan, half each of the salt and pepper, and the nutmeg.

2 Butterfly turkey breast by slicing almost in half horizontally; open like book. Cover with waxed paper; pound lightly until just less than ½ inch (1 cm) thick. Spread with ricotta mixture. Arrange spinach then red pepper over top. Starting at narrow skinless end, roll up. Tie at 3-inch (8 cm) intervals with string. Sprinkle with thyme and remaining salt and pepper.

3 In roasting pan, heat remaining oil in 450°F (230°C) oven for 10 minutes. Place turkey, skin side down, in pan; roast for 10 minutes. Turn roll over; roast for 10 minutes. Reduce heat to 350°F (180°C); roast, basting once, for 25 to 30 minutes or until juices run clear when turkey is pierced. Transfer to platter and tent with foil; let stand for 10 minutes before slicing.

4 Meanwhile, strain pan juices into small saucepan. Whisk in flour; cook over medium-high heat for 30 seconds. Whisk in stock; cook, whisking, until boiling and slightly thickened. Serve over turkey along with Barley Timbales.

Barley Timbales

2½ cups	chicken stock	625 mL
1 cup	pearl or pot barley	250 mL
2 tbsp	butter	25 mL
½ tsp	each salt and pepper	2 mL
¼ tsp	dried thyme	1 mL
4	green onions, chopped	4
1 cup	diced carrots	250 mL
¼ cup	currants	50 mL

1 In saucepan, bring stock, barley, butter, salt, pepper and thyme to boil; reduce heat, cover and simmer for 30 minutes. Stir in onions, carrots and currants; cook, covered, for 20 to 25 minutes or until liquid is absorbed and barley is tender.

2 Pack into timbale moulds, small ramekins or ½-cup (125 mL) dry measures. Let stand for 3 minutes before inverting onto plates.

Makes 8 servings

Per serving (with Barley Timbales): about 563 cal, 49 g pro, 27 g total fat (10 g sat. fat), 31 g carb, 4 g fibre, 172 mg chol. % RDI: 21% calcium, 37% iron, 73% vit A, 27% vit C, 39% folate.

Honey-Glazed Turkey Breast

Choosing a rolled turkey breast means no bones with which to contend and a feast for fans of white meat only. The cut itself is delightfully versatile. Most often marinated to prevent drying out, it can also be pounded flat and rolled around a favourite filling of prosciutto, fresh sage leaves and Fontina cheese or, more simply, ham, basil and Jarlsberg cheese. Or, as is done here, it can be flavoured with a pleasing marinade of lemon juice, sweet mustard and herbs. Slice it thinly for maximum value.

2	cloves garlic, minced	2
⅓ cup	lemon juice	75 mL
¼ cup	sweet mustard	50 mL
¼ cup	extra-virgin olive oil	50 mL
2 tbsp	balsamic or red wine vinegar	25 mL
2 tsp	chopped fresh rosemary (or 2 tsp/10 mL dried)	10 mL
1 tsp	dried thyme	5 mL
1	boneless rolled turkey breast (about 4 lb/2 kg)	1
¼ cup	toasted chopped pecans (optional)	50 mL

1 In bowl, combine garlic, lemon juice, mustard, 3 tbsp (45 mL) of the oil, vinegar, rosemary and thyme.

2 Rinse turkey under cold water; pat dry. Place in large glass baking dish; pour marinade over top, turning to coat. Cover and refrigerate for 24 hours, turning occasionally.

3 Brush marinade from turkey, reserving marinade. In large skillet, heat remaining oil over medium-high heat; brown turkey all over, about 7 minutes per side.

4 Place turkey on greased rack in roasting pan; roast in 325°F (160°C) oven, basting every 30 minutes with reserved marinade and pan drippings, for about 2 hours or until juices run clear when turkey is pierced and meat thermometer registers 170°F (77°C). Transfer to carving board and tent with foil; let stand for 20 minutes. Slice turkey thinly; arrange on warmed serving platter. Garnish with pecans (if using).

Makes 12 servings

Per serving: about 221 cal, 35 g pro, 7 g total fat (1 g sat. fat), 3 g carb, 0 g fibre, 80 mg chol. % RDI: 2% calcium, 12% iron, 2% vit C, 3% folate.

Buying, Storing and Handling Poultry and Beef

- When buying poultry, look for whole birds that appear plump, with meaty breasts or parts that seem plump, and with skin that is smooth, moist and free of bruises and pinfeathers. The bone ends should be pinkish white.
- Always avoid packages that are broken or are leaking.
- If buying frozen meat or poultry, look and feel to make sure it is frozen rock-hard and shows no signs of freezer burn. The packaging should be intact and free of any frozen liquid; liquid could indicate that it was thawed and then refrozen.
- Select beef with a bright to deep red colour and even, ivory-colour marbling. Exposed bones should show no signs of splintering.

- For best storage, store poultry and beef in their original wrapping in the coldest part of the refrigerator for no more than three days. Keep both away from cooked and ready-to-eat foods.
- To freeze, remove the poultry or meat from its wrapping and rewrap in heavy-duty plastic wrap and then foil. Mark carefully and freeze for up to six months. Ground chicken, turkey and beef should be frozen for no longer than three months.
- Thaw poultry pieces and beef in the refrigerator, on a tray or plate to catch any leaking juices. Whole poultry can be thawed by immersing the wrapped bird in cold water and changing the water every 30 minutes to maintain chilling until thawed.

- Always wash your hands before and after working with raw poultry and beef. Utensils and cutting boards must also be thoroughly washed with hot soapy water after contact with either raw beef or poultry.
- Ground beef remains one of the cheapest and most popular sources of high-quality protein. It is available under four different labels:

    Extra Lean – up to 10% fat

    Lean – up to 17% fat

    Medium – up to 23% fat

    Regular – up to 30% fat

Chicken Breasts with Mushroom Sauce

Learning how to debone chicken breasts means extra dollars in your wallet since boneless skinless chicken breasts cost more. It also means you'll have bones at the ready in your freezer to make chicken stock. Use a sharp small paring knife: if it's not sharp enough, you'll tear the meat, and a small knife gives you more flexibility than a large chef's knife against a relatively small, delicate chicken breast.

Ingredients

4	chicken breasts	4
¼ cup	all-purpose flour	50 mL
2 tbsp	light sour cream	25 mL
4 tsp	Dijon mustard	20 mL
1 cup	chicken stock	250 mL
Pinch	each dried thyme, salt and pepper	Pinch
1 tbsp	butter	15 mL
1½ cups	quartered mushrooms	375 mL
3	green onions, cut in 1-inch (2.5 cm) pieces	3
	Chopped fresh parsley	

Makes 4 servings

Per serving: about 232 cal, 35 g pro, 6 g total fat (3 g sat. fat), 7 g carb, 1 g fibre, 92 mg chol. % RDI: 4% calcium, 11% iron, 4% vit A, 3% vit C, 9% folate.

Variation

Apple Caraway Chicken: Decrease mustard to 1 tbsp (15 mL) and add along with 2 tsp (10 mL) cider vinegar. Replace ½ cup (125 mL) of the stock with apple juice. Substitute crushed caraway seeds for thyme and 1 large (unpeeled) tart apple, diced, for the green onions.

Tips

This recipe provides a great alternative to whipping cream when you want a rich, creamy dish. Our method of stabilizing sour cream (which would separate otherwise) with all-purpose flour results in a creamy lower-fat substitute.

Be sure to clean mushrooms by brushing or wiping them gently with a wet paper towel as opposed to rinsing them with water. Mushrooms are like little sponges when run under water, which can interfere with the recipe. As the mushrooms cook, they release all the liquid they have absorbed and turn a sauté into a braise or considerably lengthen the cooking time.

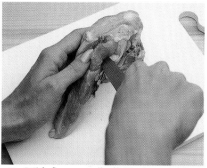

1 With fingers, pull off skin from chicken; trim any fat on edges of breasts. Place chicken on cutting board, bone side down. Using tip of sharp knife, make shallow cut along ridge of breastbone between meat and bone.

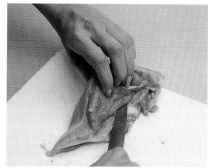

2 Holding knife flat against bone and working with short strokes, cut between meat and bone to within ¼ inch (5 mm) of other edge, lifting meat away with fingers.

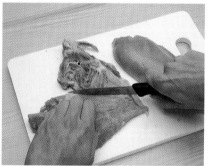

3 Open breast out flat; cut meat neatly away from edge of bone. Whisk together 2 tsp (10 mL) of the flour, sour cream, mustard and 2 tbsp (25 mL) of the stock; set aside for sauce.

4 Spread remaining flour in shallow dish. Sprinkle 1 side of chicken with thyme, salt and pepper; press into flour to coat both sides.

5 In large nonstick skillet, melt butter over medium-low heat until foaming; cook chicken for about 5 minutes per side or until no longer pink inside. To check for doneness, cut small slit in thickest part. Transfer to serving platter; cover and keep warm.

6 Add mushrooms to skillet; cook, stirring, for 3 minutes. Add remaining stock; boil over high heat for 3 minutes. Whisk in sour cream mixture. Add onions; cook, stirring, for about 3 minutes or until thickened. Pour over chicken. Garnish with parsley.

Roasted Herb Chicken with Lemon Wine Sauce

This technique of separating the skin from the meat and then stuffing the formed "pocket" with herbs and other goodies is very popular. It not only transforms a chicken breast into a beautiful marvel, it also infuses the meat with all of the flavour of the stuffing, something that can get lost if you later remove the skin. Be careful to keep one side of the skin attached to the chicken though or you'll end up losing the stuffing.

8	chicken breasts (5 lb/2.2 kg total)	8
2 tbsp	packed fresh tarragon leaves (about 64) or 32 sage leaves	25 mL
2 tbsp	lemon juice	25 mL
2 tbsp	olive oil	25 mL
¼ tsp	salt	1 mL
Sauce:		
½ cup	white wine	125 mL
¼ cup	lemon juice	50 mL
1	shallot, minced	1
1	clove garlic, minced	1
¼ tsp	each granulated sugar and pepper	1 mL
Pinch	salt	Pinch
2	egg yolks	2
⅓ cup	butter, cubed	75 mL

1 Run hand under skin of breasts to form pocket; insert 8 tarragon or 4 sage leaves into each. Arrange, skin side up, on foil-lined rimmed baking sheet. Whisk lemon juice with oil; brush over chicken. Sprinkle with salt. Roast in 425°F (220°C) oven for 30 minutes or until no longer pink inside. Broil for 2 to 3 minutes or until golden.

2 **Sauce:** Meanwhile, in saucepan, bring wine, lemon juice, shallot, garlic, sugar, pepper and salt to boil; boil for 5 minutes or until reduced to ½ cup (125 mL). Strain into heatproof bowl; let cool.

3 Place bowl over saucepan of hot (not boiling) water; whisk in egg yolks and cook, whisking vigorously, for 5 minutes or until pale and thickened. Remove from heat; whisk in butter. Serve with chicken.

Makes 8 servings
Per serving (without skin): about 425 cal, 47 g pro, 24 g total fat (9 g sat. fat), 1 g carb, 0 g fibre, 205 mg chol. % RDI: 3% calcium, 14% iron, 14% vit A, 3% vit C, 5% folate.

Harvest Chicken

This particularly colourful dish has a medley of vegetables stuffed under the skin. When closing up the open side with toothpicks, it's important that the entire side is "sewn" shut so that the stuffing doesn't end up on the baking sheet. For a change of stuffing, try substituting corn for the zucchini, Asiago for the mozzarella and oregano for the basil.

2 tbsp	olive oil	25 mL
3	cloves garlic, minced	3
1	onion, chopped	1
Pinch	hot pepper flakes	Pinch
2 cups	cubed zucchini	500 mL
1 cup	diced sweet red pepper	250 mL
⅓ cup	shredded mozzarella cheese	75 mL
1 tbsp	chopped fresh basil (or 1 tsp/5 mL dried)	15 mL
½ tsp	salt	2 mL
¼ tsp	pepper	1 mL
2	whole boneless chicken breasts	2
	Fresh basil leaves	

1 In large ovenproof skillet, heat half of the oil over medium heat; cook garlic, onion and hot pepper flakes, stirring occasionally, for 3 minutes or until softened.

2 Add zucchini and red pepper; cook, stirring often, for 3 minutes. Remove from heat. Stir in cheese, chopped basil, salt and pepper; let cool slightly.

3 Using fingers, gently loosen skin from thick end of breasts to form pocket, leaving skin attached at edges. Stuff half of the vegetable mixture into each pocket, patting to flatten slightly. Secure skin at edges with toothpicks.

4 In same skillet, heat remaining oil over medium heat; cook chicken, skin side down, for about 3 minutes or until golden brown.

5 Turn chicken skin side up; bake in 375°F (190°C) oven for about 30 minutes or until chicken is no longer pink inside. Halve breasts vertically. Garnish with basil leaves.

Makes 4 servings
Per serving: about 337 cal, 33 g pro, 19 g total fat (5 g sat. fat), 7 g carb, 2 g fibre, 105 mg chol. % RDI: 7% calcium, 8% iron, 16% vit A, 75% vit C, 10% folate.

Chicken Breast Parmesan

Using Parmesan cheese in the bread crumb coating gives these everyday chicken breasts a little boost. Try to use authentic Parmigiano-Reggiano cheese, identified by the stencilling on the rind. This means it has been imported from the Parma district of Italy, where the controls are rigorous and the cheeses are often aged for more than two years, as opposed to the usual 14 months in North America. This extra aging, of course, translates into a deeper, melt-in-your-mouth flavour and texture. It costs more but is well worth the expense since you don't use as much.

⅓ cup	freshly grated Parmesan cheese	75 mL
¼ cup	dry bread crumbs	50 mL
½ tsp	each dried oregano, basil and pepper	2 mL
1	egg	1
2 tbsp	all-purpose flour	25 mL
4	boneless skinless chicken breasts	4
2 tbsp	chopped fresh parsley	25 mL

Sauce:

1 cup	pasta sauce	250 mL
¼ cup	shredded zucchini	50 mL
¼ cup	shredded carrots	50 mL

1 In shallow dish, combine cheese, bread crumbs, oregano, basil and pepper. In separate shallow dish, beat egg lightly. Place flour in third shallow dish.

2 Press chicken into flour to coat all over. Dip into egg; press into crumb mixture, shaking off excess. Arrange on greased baking sheet; bake in 375°F (190°C) oven, turning once, for about 20 minutes or until no longer pink inside. Broil for about 3 minutes or until golden.

3 Sauce: Meanwhile, in saucepan, cook pasta sauce, zucchini and carrots over medium heat for 8 to 10 minutes or until vegetables are tender-crisp; spread on serving platter. Arrange chicken on top. Sprinkle with parsley.

Makes 4 servings
Per serving: about 234 cal, 33 g pro, 5 g total fat (2 g sat. fat), 13 g carb, 1 g fibre, 127 mg chol. % RDI: 12% calcium, 16% iron, 27% vit A, 8% vit C, 9% folate.

Tip

If not using homemade, buy a thick, full-flavoured pasta sauce listing herbs, onions and tomatoes in its ingredients.

Chicken Pot Pie

**Chicken pot pie is supremely comforting, nourishing and now even easier with our
phyllo-topped version. This lesson shows you how to put it all together with chicken thighs
and breasts and a fall smorgasbord of root vegetables.**

Ingredients

2 cups	chicken stock	500 mL
1	bay leaf	1
3 lb	chicken thighs and breasts, skinned	1.5 kg
1	potato, peeled and cut in large cubes	1
2 cups	cubed peeled butternut squash	500 mL
3 tbsp	butter	50 mL
1 cup	pearl onions, peeled and halved	250 mL
3	each carrots and stalks celery, coarsely chopped	3
2 cups	quartered mushrooms	500 mL
¾ tsp	each dried thyme and dry mustard	4 mL
½ tsp	each dried oregano, salt and pepper	2 mL
⅓ cup	all-purpose flour	75 mL
½ cup	18% cream	125 mL
1 cup	frozen peas	250 mL

Pastry:

5	sheets phyllo pastry	5
¼ cup	butter, melted	50 mL

Makes 6 servings

*Per serving: about 495 cal, 37 g pro, 22 g total fat
(12 g sat. fat), 38 g carb, 5 g fibre, 144 mg chol.
% RDI: 9% calcium, 24% iron, 146% vit A,
25% vit C, 22% folate.*

1 In large saucepan, bring stock, 1 cup (250 mL) water and bay leaf to boil. Add chicken; reduce heat, cover and simmer for 15 minutes for breasts, 25 minutes for thighs, or until juices run clear when chicken is pierced. Remove chicken; let cool. Cut meat from bones; cut into bite-size pieces.

2 Return stock to boil. Add potato; cover and simmer for 5 minutes. Add squash; cook, covered, for 10 minutes or just until vegetables are tender. Discard bay leaf. Drain through sieve, reserving 2¼ cups (550 mL) liquid, adding water or boiling to reduce liquid if necessary for correct amount.

3 Meanwhile, in separate large saucepan, melt butter over medium heat; cook onions, carrots, celery and mushrooms, stirring often, for about 10 minutes or until softened and starting to turn golden. Add thyme, mustard, oregano, salt and pepper; cook, stirring, for 1 minute.

4 Sprinkle with flour; cook, stirring, for 1 minute. Gradually whisk in reserved cooking liquid and cream; bring to boil, stirring. Reduce heat and simmer, stirring often, for 5 minutes or until thickened. Stir in chicken, potato mixture and peas. Pour into 8-cup (2 L) oval casserole dish.

5 **Pastry:** Place 1 sheet of phyllo on work surface, keeping remaining phyllo covered with plastic wrap and damp towel to prevent drying out. Brush lightly with butter. Scrunch gently with fingertips to 6- x 5-inch (15 x 12 cm) oval; place on filling. Repeat with remaining phyllo to cover filling.

6 Bake in 425°F (220°C) oven for 25 to 30 minutes or until filling is bubbling and phyllo is golden. Let cool on rack for 5 minutes before serving.

Chicken Couscous Wraps

"Grab it and go" might as well be the rallying cry of sandwich lovers the world over. And grabbing it and going has never been as delicious and easy as when it's a flour tortilla encasing a chicken and couscous filling, made all the more tempting by a jalapeño mayonnaise. Different coloured and flavoured tortillas are as ubiquitous as bagels, and a great standby to keep in your freezer. If you can't find them, they're a snap to make (see tip).

3	jalapeño peppers	3
¼ cup	light mayonnaise	50 mL
1 tbsp	vegetable oil	15 mL
2 tsp	chili powder	10 mL
½ tsp	dried oregano	2 mL
3	boneless skinless chicken breasts	3

Tortillas:

3½ cups	all-purpose flour	875 mL
1½ tsp	baking powder	7 mL
¾ tsp	salt	4 mL
⅓ cup	shortening	75 mL

Filling:

⅔ cup	couscous	150 mL
¼ tsp	salt	1 mL
2 tbsp	vegetable oil	25 mL
2 tbsp	lime juice	25 mL
½ tsp	granulated sugar	2 mL
Pinch	pepper	Pinch
Half	avocado, diced	Half
½ cup	corn kernels	125 mL
1	plum tomato, diced	1

1 Tortillas: In bowl, stir together flour, baking powder and salt; with pastry blender or 2 knives, cut in shortening until crumbly. Stir in 1¼ cups (300 mL) water to make soft dough. Turn out onto lightly floured surface; knead just until dough comes together. Divide into 8 pieces; roll each into ball. Cover and let rest for 30 minutes. Roll out each ball into 10-inch (25 cm) circle.

2 Heat heavy skillet over medium heat. Peel tortilla from work surface by lifting closest edge away from you. Cook, 1 at a time, for 1 to 2 minutes per side or until speckled. Wrap in foil to keep soft, adding to stack as cooked. *(Tortillas can be refrigerated for up to 8 hours or frozen in freezer bag for up to 2 weeks; warm in 350°F/180°C oven for 5 minutes.)*

3 On baking sheet, broil jalapeño peppers, turning occasionally, for 7 to 10 minutes or until blackened; let cool slightly. Remove skins and seeds; chop finely. Stir 1 tsp (5 mL) of the chopped jalapeño into mayonnaise; set aside.

4 Filling: In bowl, mix couscous with salt. Add ⅔ cup (150 mL) boiling water; stir once. Cover and set aside for 10 minutes. Whisk together remaining jalapeño, oil, lime juice, 1 tbsp (15 mL) water, sugar and pepper; stir into couscous. Stir in avocado, corn and tomato.

5 Meanwhile, stir together oil, chili powder and oregano; brush all over chicken. Broil on greased baking sheet for about 5 minutes per side or until no longer pink inside. Cut into thin strips.

6 Spread mayonnaise mixture over each tortilla, leaving 1-inch (2.5 cm) border. Starting just below centre of tortilla, mound couscous filling in 6- x 2-inch (15 x 5 cm) rectangle; top with chicken. Fold bottom border over filling, then sides; roll up.

Makes 4 servings

Per wrap: about 484 cal, 18 g pro, 19 g total fat (3 g sat. fat), 59 g carb, 3 g fibre, 27 mg chol. % RDI: 4% calcium, 22% iron, 7% vit A, 20% vit C, 15% folate.

Tip

To tint tortillas green or pink, stir 1/4 cup (50 mL) pesto or tomato paste into water before adding to flour.

Chicken and Broccoli Stir-Fry

Stir-frying is one of the easiest techniques to master. A wok is great but not essential, as any large skillet or Dutch oven will do the trick. The key to a stir-fry is to have all the ingredients prepared and measured beforehand. Try to cut the vegetables to a uniform size to ensure even cooking. Use high heat and stir constantly. Substituting chicken stock for some of the oil is a good way to cut back on fat.

1	bunch broccoli	1
1	sweet red pepper	1
2	large green onions	2
3	boneless skinless chicken breasts	3
½ cup	chicken stock	125 mL
2 tbsp	soy sauce	25 mL
1 tbsp	cornstarch	15 mL
1 tbsp	oyster sauce	15 mL
1 tbsp	dry sherry	15 mL
1 tsp	sesame oil	5 mL
¼ tsp	Asian chili paste (or dash hot pepper sauce), optional	1 mL
3 tbsp	vegetable oil	50 mL
2	cloves garlic, minced	2
1 tbsp	minced gingerroot	15 mL
¼ cup	halved cashew nuts (optional)	50 mL

1 Cut broccoli into florets; peel and cut stalks on diagonal into ¼-inch (5 mm) thick slices. Core, seed and cut red pepper into 1-inch (2.5 cm) squares. Halve green onions length-wise; cut on diagonal into 2-inch (5 cm) pieces. Cut chicken into 2- x ½-inch (5 x 1 cm) strips. Set each ingredient aside separately.

2 Whisk together ¼ cup (50 mL) of the stock, soy sauce, cornstarch, oyster sauce, sherry, sesame oil, and chili paste (if using); set aside.

3 Heat wok or deep skillet over high heat until drop of water sprinkled on surface sizzles into steam. Pour in half of the oil and swirl wok to evenly coat side of pan; heat for 30 seconds.

4 Add half of the chicken; stir-fry by lifting and tossing chicken for 3 to 4 minutes or until no longer pink inside. Transfer to plate. Repeat with remaining chicken, adding more oil if necessary. Add to plate.

5 Add remaining oil to wok; stir-fry garlic and ginger for 10 seconds or until fragrant. Add broccoli and red pepper; stir-fry for 1 minute. Add onions; stir-fry for 30 seconds. Pour in remaining ¼ cup (50 mL) stock; cover and steam for 2 minutes or until broccoli is tender-crisp, stirring once.

6 Return chicken to wok. Push contents to side of pan. Pour soy mixture into centre of wok; cook, stirring, for 1 to 2 minutes or until thickened. Stir vegetables and chicken into sauce to coat. Sprinkle with cashew nuts (if using). Serve immediately.

Makes 4 servings
Per serving: about 290 cal, 29 g pro, 14 g total fat (1 g sat. fat), 13 g carb, 4 g fibre, 63 mg chol. % RDI: 7% calcium, 14% iron, 28% vit A, 227% vit C, 34% folate.

Variation

Beef Stir-Fry: Substitute 12 oz (375 g) thinly sliced top sirloin grilling steak for chicken; stir-fry for 2 to 3 minutes or until slightly browned but still pink inside. Substitute beef stock for chicken stock.

Spicy Stir-Fry Sauce

Add a little more hot pepper sauce if you're feeling adventurous.

½ cup	chicken stock or water	125 mL
2 tbsp	cornstarch	25 mL
2 tbsp	soy sauce	25 mL
2 tbsp	bottled chili sauce	25 mL
1 tbsp	each sesame oil and cider vinegar	15 mL
1 tbsp	liquid honey	15 mL
Dash	hot pepper sauce	Dash

1 In measuring cup or small bowl, whisk together stock, cornstarch, soy sauce, chili sauce, oil, vinegar, honey and hot pepper sauce. Add to wok after vegetables are tender-crisp and meat is returned to wok. Stir-fry for 1 to 2 minutes or until thickened.

Makes about 1 cup (250 mL)
Per each of 4 servings (sauce only): about 20 cal, 0 g pro, 1 g total fat (0 g sat. fat), 3 g carb, 0 g fibre, 0 mg chol. % RDI: 1% iron.

Orange Stir-Fry Sauce

Frozen orange juice makes a great flavouring that's often better than fresh because it's concentrated.

⅓ cup	thawed orange juice concentrate	75 mL
2 tbsp	each chicken stock and teriyaki sauce	25 mL
1 tbsp	cornstarch	15 mL
1 tbsp	each rice vinegar and Worcestershire sauce	15 mL
2 tsp	granulated sugar	10 mL
1 tsp	sesame oil	5 mL

1 In measuring cup or small bowl, whisk together orange juice concentrate, stock, teriyaki sauce, cornstarch, vinegar, Worcester-shire sauce, sugar and oil. Add to wok after vegetables are tender-crisp and meat is returned to wok. Stir-fry for 1 to 2 minutes or until thickened.

Makes about 2/3 cup (150 mL)
Per each of 4 servings (sauce only): about 28 cal, 1 g pro, 0 g total fat (0 g sat. fat), 6 g carb, 0 g fibre, 0 mg chol. % RDI: 1% iron, 17% vit C, 4% folate.

Salmon Strudels

Few things say Canadian more readily than salmon and wild rice. Combined with flaky phyllo pastry, earthy mushrooms and tender spinach, the patriotic duo is transformed into a heavenly package designed specifically for entertaining occasions. The Test Kitchen itself has served this dynamite entrée for special corporate dinners, always earning high praise and well-satisfied appetites. The strudels can be assembled up to four hours ahead.

Ingredients

2	pkg (each 10 oz/284 g) fresh spinach	2
1 tsp	lemon juice	5 mL
Pinch	nutmeg	Pinch
1	salmon fillet (1½ lb/750 g)	1
8	sheets phyllo pastry	8
⅓ cup	butter, melted	75 mL

Rice:

2 tsp	butter	10 mL
1	onion, chopped	1
¾ cup	sliced mushrooms	175 mL
¾ cup	vegetable stock	175 mL
⅔ cup	water	150 mL
¼ tsp	salt	1 mL
Pinch	pepper	Pinch
¼ cup	wild rice, rinsed	50 mL
⅓ cup	long-grain rice	75 mL

Sauce:

¼ cup	white wine vinegar	50 mL
¼ cup	white wine	50 mL
2 tbsp	finely minced shallots or onion	25 mL
¼ tsp	each salt and pepper	1 mL
⅔ cup	unsalted butter, cut in ½-inch (1 cm) cubes	150 mL
1 tbsp	chopped fresh parsley	15 mL

Makes 4 servings

Per serving: about 940 cal, 42 g pro, 62 g total fat (32 g sat. fat), 55 g carb, 6 g fibre, 215 mg chol. % RDI: 20% calcium, 58% iron, 149% vit A, 25% vit C, 111% folate.

Tip

Remove all the pin bones from the salmon before separating the skin from the flesh. Do this by running the straight, dull edge of a knife across flesh side of fillet. This raises the pin bones, making them easy to extract with tweezers.

1 **Rice:** In saucepan, melt butter over medium heat; cook onion and mushrooms, stirring occasionally, for 5 minutes or until softened. Add stock, water, salt and pepper; bring to boil. Add wild rice; return to boil. Reduce heat, cover and simmer for 35 minutes. Stir in long-grain rice; simmer, covered, for 25 minutes or just until liquid is absorbed and rice is tender. Let cool.

2 Trim spinach; rinse, shaking off excess water. In saucepan, cook spinach, with just the water clinging to leaves, over medium heat for 8 minutes or until wilted; drain in sieve, pressing out moisture. Chop; toss with lemon juice and nutmeg. Cut salmon crosswise into 4 pieces. Separate some skin from flesh. Holding skin, insert knife at 45-degree angle; slide along to remove fillet.

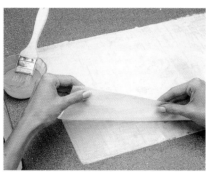

3 Lay 1 sheet of phyllo on work surface, keeping remaining phyllo covered with plastic wrap and damp towel to prevent drying out. Brush with about 2 tsp (10 mL) of the butter. Place second sheet on top; brush with butter.

4 About 1 inch (2.5 cm) from long side of pastry, spoon ½ cup (125 mL) rice mixture lengthwise into 3-inch (8 cm) wide strip, leaving 4-inch (10 cm) border at short sides. Top with one-quarter of the spinach. Top with 1 piece of salmon.

5 Fold 1-inch (2.5 cm) border over filling; fold each side over and roll up. Place, seam side down, on greased baking sheet. Brush with butter. Repeat to form 4 packages. Bake in 425°F (220°C) oven for 15 to 20 minutes or until golden.

6 **Sauce:** Meanwhile, in saucepan, boil vinegar, wine, shallots, salt and pepper for 5 minutes or until reduced to 2 tbsp (25 mL). Reduce heat to low; vigorously whisk in butter, a few cubes at a time, until thickened. Stir in parsley. Serve with salmon.

Grilled Salmon Fillets

As cooking generalizations go, the rule of 10 minutes of cooking time per inch (2.5 cm) of thickness of fish is still a good guideline, although many are choosing to eat their fish slightly undercooked these days. Time is only one indicator of readiness. For thoroughly cooked fish check that the flesh has firmed up, is opaque throughout and flakes easily when tested with a fork. Remember that fish will continue to cook slightly even after it's removed from the heat.

Ingredients

1 lb	salmon or sea bass fillet (with skin)	500 g

Lemon Dill Marinade:

⅓ cup	extra-virgin olive oil	75 mL
1 tsp	grated lemon rind	5 mL
¼ cup	lemon juice	50 mL
2 tbsp	chopped fresh dill (or 2 tsp/10 mL dried dillweed)	25 mL
¼ tsp	each salt and pepper	1 mL

Makes 4 servings

Per serving: about 277 cal, 21 g pro, 21 g total fat (3 g sat. fat), 1 g carb, 0 g fibre, 57 mg chol. % RDI: 1% calcium, 6% iron, 1% vit A, 7% vit C, 11% folate.

Variations

Teriyaki Grilled Salmon Fillets: Marinate fish in mixture of ¼ cup (50 mL) soy sauce, 4 tsp (20 mL) white wine vinegar, 2 tsp (10 mL) granulated sugar, 2 tsp (10 mL) vegetable oil and 1 clove garlic, minced.

Lime Cumin–Grilled Salmon Fillets: Marinate fish in mixture of ¼ cup (50 mL) each olive oil and lime juice, 4 tsp (20 mL) Worcestershire sauce, 1½ tsp (7 mL) ground cumin, 1 tsp (5 mL) grated lime rind, 2 cloves garlic, minced, and ¼ tsp (1 mL) each salt and pepper.

Tip

Be sure to marinate fish no longer than specified, otherwise it will "cook" in the acids of the marinade and become dry during grilling.

1 On cutting board, cut salmon crosswise into 4 pieces. Measure thickest portion of fillet to determine cooking time.

2 **Lemon Dill Marinade:** Whisk together oil, lemon rind and juice, dill, salt and pepper; pour into shallow glass dish. Add fillets; turn to coat evenly. Cover with plastic wrap and marinate in refrigerator for up to 30 minutes, turning occasionally.

3 Reserving marinade, place fillets, skin side down, on greased grill over medium-high heat.

4 Cook fillets, basting frequently and using all the marinade, for 10 minutes per inch (2.5 cm) of thickness.

5 Turn fillets over halfway through cooking by placing 1 metal spatula under fillet and another on top.

6 Cook fillets just until fish flakes easily when tested with fork and flesh is opaque.

Roasted Salmon with Dill Wine Sauce

Cooking a whole fish is just as easy as cooking a fish steak or fillet – except that you get the pleasure of
feeding more people. When choosing a whole fish, buy from a reliable store with a quick turnover.
The fish should be displayed on ice, have firm flesh and clear unclouded eyes and smell fresh.
Don't be afraid to ask to feel or smell the fish. The gills should be bright red or pink and
not dull or brown, and the tail should be flat and not look dried out.

Ingredients

1	whole salmon, cleaned (5 lb/2.2 kg)	1
¼ tsp	each salt and pepper	1 mL
3	lemons, sliced	3
½ cup	each fresh dill and parsley sprigs	125 mL
2 tbsp	butter, melted	25 mL

Dill Wine Sauce:

2 tbsp	butter	25 mL
2 tbsp	all-purpose flour	25 mL
½ cup	each milk, dry white wine and whipping cream	125 mL
¾ tsp	salt	4 mL
¼ tsp	pepper	1 mL
¼ cup	chopped fresh dill	50 mL

Makes 12 servings

Per serving: about 242 cal, 23 g pro, 15 g total fat (6 g sat. fat), 2 g carb, 0 g fibre, 86 mg chol. % RDI: 4% calcium, 9% iron, 10% vit A, 2% vit C, 15% folate.

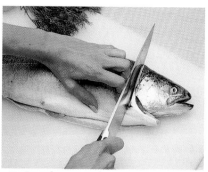

1 Let salmon stand at room temperature for 30 minutes. Using sharp chef's knife, cut off head behind gills (or have fishmonger remove it). Rinse under cold water; pat dry. Season inside and out with salt and pepper. Arrange one-third of the lemon slices in lengthwise row along centre of foil-lined baking sheet. Top with salmon.

2 Fill body cavity with dill, parsley and another third of the lemons. Brush butter over salmon; top with remaining lemons. Measure thickest part of salmon; calculate 12 to 15 minutes of cooking time for every 1 inch (2.5 cm) of thickness. Crumple up foil around fish to hold juices, leaving salmon uncovered.

3 Bake salmon in 450°F (230°C) oven for about 45 minutes or until flesh at thickest part is opaque and flakes easily when tested with fork. Remove from oven and tent with foil; let stand for 5 minutes. With baster or spoon, remove ¼ cup (50 mL) pan juices; set aside.

4 **Dill Wine Sauce:** In saucepan, melt butter over medium heat; stir in flour and cook, stirring, for 1 minute. Gradually whisk in milk, wine, cream, salt and pepper; cook, whisking, for 5 minutes or until thickened. Stir in pan juices; reduce heat and simmer for 5 minutes. Keep warm while carving salmon; stir in dill.

5 Discard lemon on top. Cut along backbone through to bone. Starting at backbone, pull off skin. Cut along midline, parallel to backbone, through to bone. Cut crosswise into 4-inch (10 cm) wide portions.

6 With spatula, lift portions to plates. Gently remove exposed bones from other side of salmon; discard. Repeat cutting along midline as in Step 5, then into portions; ease away from skin. Serve with sauce.

Cooking Lesson: Roasted Salmon with Dill Wine Sauce

Glazed Poached Salmon

Poaching – cooking in a small amount of gently simmering flavoured liquid – is an excellent method for preparing delicate foods such as fish. Poaching is to be distinguished from stewing in that the former usually implies discarding or reserving the poaching liquid, whereas the latter indicates a preference for seasoning the liquid and serving the fish or meat in it. Both poached and steamed fish tend to be pale, so colourful accompaniments should be chosen.

Ingredients

6 cups	water	1.5 L
1½ cups	dry white wine	375 mL
1	onion, chopped	1
7	peppercorns	7
4	sprigs fresh parsley	4
1	stalk celery, coarsely chopped	1
1 tsp	dried thyme (or 2 sprigs fresh)	5 mL
4	salmon or halibut steaks (8 oz/250 g each)	4
	Salt and pepper	
1	pkg (7 g) unflavoured gelatin	1
	Dill sprigs and lemon slices	

Makes 4 servings

*Per serving: about 256 cal, 36 g pro, 11 g total fat
(2 g sat. fat), 0 g carb, 0 g fibre, 95 mg chol.
% RDI: 2% calcium, 11% iron, 2% vit A,
18% folate.*

Variation

Glazed Whole Trout: Substitute 4 cleaned whole rainbow trout (about 8 oz/250 g each) for salmon. After trout has been cooked and chilled, remove skin by carefully pulling skin back from head toward tail. Using small pliers or tweezers, remove bones sticking out along back of fish. Using sharp knife, scrape off any brownish fat.

Tip

Serve fish with a herb mayonnaise. Mix mayonnaise with any combination of the following: chopped fresh watercress, parsley, cucumber, dill, capers and green onion, along with chopped hard-cooked eggs and lemon juice.

1 In deep heavy skillet or flameproof casserole large enough to hold salmon in single layer, combine water, wine, onion, peppercorns, parsley, celery and thyme. Bring to boil; reduce heat and simmer for 20 minutes. Carefully add salmon, adding enough boiling water at side of pan, if necessary, to cover fish.

3 Strain enough of the cooking liquid through double thickness of cheese-cloth to make 2 cups (500 mL). Season with salt and pepper to taste. Measure out ¼ cup (50 mL) into small bowl; sprinkle gelatin over top and let stand for 1 minute.

5 Arrange dill and lemon over salmon; spoon second light coat of glaze over top. Refrigerate until set. Repeat with third coating.

2 Simmer until fish is opaque, about 10 minutes per inch (2.5 cm) of thickness. Let cool in cooking liquid at room temperature for 30 minutes. Refrigerate for 1½ hours or until chilled. Using slotted spoon, carefully transfer salmon to rack on baking sheet. Cover and refrigerate while preparing glaze.

4 In saucepan, bring remaining 1¾ cups (425 mL) strained cooking liquid to boil. Remove from heat; stir in gelatin mixture until dissolved. Place pan in larger bowl of ice water. Let stand, stirring frequently, for 20 to 30 minutes or until syrupy. Spoon some evenly over fish to coat lightly. Refrigerate until set.

6 Using spatula, carefully transfer glazed steaks to serving platter.

Grilled Whitefish

Delicately flavoured and textured, whitefish is a freshwater fish abundant in Canada.
Because it's so delicate, you have to grill it in a fish basket or else run the risk of having it fall apart.
If you don't have a fish basket, improvise by placing the whole fish between two well-greased
wire cake racks and tying them together with thin wire.

Ingredients

1	whole whitefish, cleaned (about 2 lb/1 kg)	1
1 tsp	salt	5 mL
4	slices lemon, halved	4
	Parsley sprigs	

Marinade:

⅓ cup	extra-virgin olive oil	75 mL
¼ cup	lemon juice	50 mL
2 tbsp	Dijon mustard	25 mL
1	clove garlic, minced	1
4 tsp	chopped fresh oregano (or 2 tsp/10 mL dried)	20 mL
Pinch	cayenne pepper	Pinch

Make 4 servings

Per serving: about 305 cal, 28 g pro, 21 g total fat (3 g sat. fat), 1 g carb, 0 g fibre, 85 mg chol. % RDI: 4% calcium, 5% iron, 5% vit A, 5% vit C, 2% folate.

Variations

Soy Ginger–Grilled Whitefish:
Omit salt. Substitute 2 green onions, julienned, for parsley sprigs.

Marinade: In small bowl, whisk together ⅓ cup (75 mL) vegetable oil, ¼ cup (50 mL) rice vinegar, ¼ cup (50 mL) soy sauce, 2 cloves garlic, minced, 2 tbsp (25 mL) liquid honey, 2 tbsp (25 mL) minced gingerroot and 1 tbsp (15 mL) each sesame oil and black bean sauce.

Lime Coriander–Grilled Whitefish: Substitute coriander sprigs for parsley sprigs.

Marinade: In small bowl, whisk together ½ cup (125 mL) chopped fresh coriander, ⅓ cup (75 mL) vegetable oil, ¼ cup (50 mL) lime juice, 2 cloves garlic, minced, 1 small onion, minced, 2 tbsp (25 mL) Worcestershire sauce, 1½ tsp (7 mL) each ground cumin and minced jalapeño pepper.

1 **Marinade:** In small bowl, whisk together oil, lemon juice, mustard, garlic, oregano and cayenne; set aside. Rinse and pat fish dry inside and out. With scissors, cut off all fins and trim tail. Remove head by slicing firmly through backbone just behind gills.

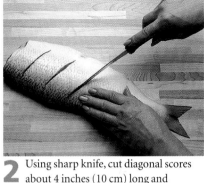

2 Using sharp knife, cut diagonal scores about 4 inches (10 cm) long and 2 inches (4 cm) apart on each side of fish. Sprinkle fish inside and out with salt.

3 Stuff cavity with lemon and parsley; loosely skewer closed. Place fish in shallow glass dish; pour marinade over top and turn to coat evenly. Cover and marinate for 30 minutes at room temperature, turning occasionally.

4 Reserving marinade, place fish in greased fish basket. Place basket on greased grill over medium-high heat.

5 Close lid or tent with foil; cook for 10 minutes per inch (2.5 cm) of thickness or until flesh is opaque and flakes easily when tested with fork, basting occasionally with reserved marinade and turning fish over halfway through cooking time.

6 Carefully transfer fish to serving platter; remove skewers. To serve, cut ¼-inch (5 mm) deep slit along backbone. Cut top fillet crosswise into serving portions; carefully lift away from bones. Discard bones and lemon stuffing; cut lower fillet into serving portions.

Coconut Curry Shrimp with Rice

This ravishing dish takes its inspiration from the splendid curries found in India. Our curry derives its intensity from the spice paste that is cooked in oil to release its flavours. Straining it eliminates the grainy texture that would fight the silky smoothness of the coconut milk. Black mustard seeds are an essential part of this dish, so do try to find them in Indian markets or gourmet shops.

Ingredients

1 cup	chopped onion	250 mL
¾ cup	chopped sweet red pepper	175 mL
2 tbsp	chopped gingerroot	25 mL
3	cloves garlic	3
1 tsp	grated lime rind	5 mL
½ tsp	hot pepper flakes	2 mL
2 tbsp	ground almonds	25 mL
2 tsp	ground coriander	10 mL
¾ tsp	paprika	4 mL
¼ tsp	turmeric	1 mL
1½ tsp	black mustard seeds	7 mL
1 tbsp	vegetable oil	15 mL
1¼ tsp	salt	6 mL
1 cup	coconut milk	250 mL
1 tbsp	lime juice	15 mL
1 lb	shrimp, peeled and deveined	500 g
1⅓ cups	white basmati rice	325 mL
2 tbsp	toasted sliced almonds	25 mL
1 tbsp	chopped fresh coriander	15 mL

Makes 4 servings

*Per serving: about 528 cal, 26 g pro, 21 g total fat
(12 g sat. fat), 60 g carb, 2 g fibre, 129 mg chol.
% RDI: 9% calcium, 34% iron, 15% vit A,
62% vit C, 13% folate.*

Tip

**Coconut milk is available in cans or
powdered form at Asian food shops
and some grocery stores. Do not
confuse sweetened cream of coconut,
used mainly for desserts, with
unsweetened coconut milk.**

1 In blender or food processor, finely chop together onion, red pepper, ginger, garlic, lime rind and hot pepper flakes. Scrape down side of bowl. Add ground almonds, ground coriander, paprika and turmeric; blend until in paste. Set aside.

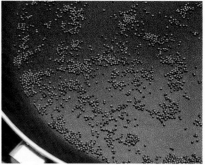

2 In large nonstick skillet, toast mustard seeds over medium-high heat, shaking pan constantly, for about 3 minutes or until seeds turn grey and pop. Remove from pan and set aside.

3 Add oil to skillet, swirling to coat; cook reserved paste over medium heat, stirring with flat wooden spatula and scraping bottom of pan, for 12 minutes or until paste is deep orange and separates into dry clumps.

4 Return mustard seeds to pan. Add 1 cup (250 mL) water and ¾ tsp (4 mL) of the salt; bring to boil. Reduce heat and simmer for 5 minutes. Strain through fine-mesh sieve into bowl, pressing with rubber spatula to extract liquid. Wipe skillet clean. Return strained liquid to skillet.

5 Gently whisk coconut milk and lime juice into skillet until blended; bring to boil. Reduce heat and add shrimp; simmer gently, stirring occasionally, for about 3 minutes or just until shrimp are pink.

6 Meanwhile, in saucepan, bring 2⅔ cups (650 mL) water and remaining ½ tsp (2 mL) salt to boil; stir in rice. Cover and reduce heat to low; simmer for about 20 minutes or until rice is tender and liquid is absorbed. Fluff with fork. To serve, spoon curry over rice. Sprinkle with toasted almonds and fresh coriander.

Paella

Paella gets its name from the broad shallow pan used to cook the classic dish, born in the Valencia region of Spain. Originally a dish that didn't feature seafood at all, it has evolved to encompass many elaborate versions, including this majestic seafood one. Some of its majesty derives from saffron, probably the world's most expensive spice. Spring the extra dollars for the orange-tinted threads since so little is needed. Besides, you're virtually throwing your money away if you purchase the ground variety, which has no flavour in comparison.

Ingredients

8 oz	chorizo sausage	250 g
1¾ lb	chicken legs	875 g
1 tbsp	olive oil	15 mL
¼ tsp	saffron threads	1 mL
3 cups	warm chicken stock	750 mL
1	onion, chopped	1
2	cloves garlic, minced	2
1	can (28 oz/796 mL) tomatoes	1
1	small sweet green pepper, diced	1
1½ cups	short-grain rice	375 mL
½ tsp	each salt and pepper	2 mL
½ cup	frozen peas	125 mL
12 oz	large raw shrimp	375 g
12 oz	mussels	375 g
2	green onions, minced	2
8	lemon wedges	8

Makes 8 servings

Per serving: about 443 cal, 32 g pro, 17 g total fat (5 g sat. fat), 40 g carb, 2 g fibre, 122 mg chol. % RDI: 5% calcium, 24% iron, 10% vit A, 37% vit C, 14% folate.

Tips

You can use clams instead of mussels, omit the seafood altogether and double up the chicken, or replace chorizo with any spicy sausage.

Authentic paella is made with starchy, short-grain rice, which provides good body to the dish.

Chorizo, used extensively in Spanish and Mexican cooking, is a highly seasoned, textured pork sausage spiced with garlic, chili powder and other flavourings. The Spanish version uses smoked pork whereas Mexican chorizo tends to be made with fresh pork.

1 Cut sausage into ½-inch (1 cm) thick slices. Remove skin from chicken; trim off fat. Using sharp heavy knife, cut through each chicken leg at joint to separate thigh from drumstick.

2 In large paella pan or deep wide skillet, heat oil over high heat; cook sausage, stirring, for 2 minutes or until browned. Transfer to platter. Add chicken to pan; cook over medium heat for 7 to 10 minutes per side or until evenly browned. Add to platter.

3 Stir saffron into stock; set aside to soften. Add onion and garlic to pan; cook, stirring often, for 4 minutes or until softened. Add stock mixture, tomatoes and green pepper; bring to boil, breaking up tomatoes with spoon and scraping up any brown bits from bottom of pan.

4 Stir in rice, salt and pepper; reduce heat to low. Add chicken; simmer gently, stirring often, for 20 minutes. Gently stir in peas and sausage.

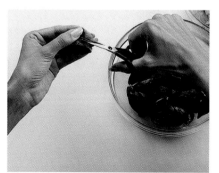

5 Meanwhile, peel and devein shrimp. Scrub mussels under running water; trim off beards with kitchen scissors. Discard any mussels with cracked shells or any that do not close when tapped.

6 Nestle shrimp and mussels in rice until almost covered; cook for 7 to 10 minutes or until rice is tender, shrimp are pink and mussels are open. Discard any mussels that do not open. Garnish with onions and lemon.

Curried Mussels

Add a touch of glamour and sophistication to your entertaining repertoire by serving mussels. The shiny blue-black mussels are at their most delicious in the early winter months and are especially stylish piled high in a large serving bowl. The creamy curry sauce marries beautifully with the meatiness of the mussels.

Ingredients

2 lb	mussels	1 kg
2 tbsp	vegetable oil	25 mL
1	onion, finely chopped	1
2	cloves garlic, minced	2
2 tsp	finely chopped gingerroot	10 mL
1 tbsp	curry powder	15 mL
½ cup	dry white wine or clam juice	125 mL
1 cup	whipping cream	250 mL
	Salt and pepper	
2 tbsp	chopped fresh coriander or green onion	25 mL

Makes 4 servings

Per serving: about 340 cal, 10 g pro, 29 g total fat (14 g sat. fat), 8 g carb, 1 g fibre, 95 mg chol. % RDI: 6% calcium, 21% iron, 23% vit A, 12% vit C, 14% folate.

Variation

Light Herbed Mussels: In large saucepan, melt 2 tbsp (25 mL) butter over medium heat; cook 1 onion or shallot, finely chopped, and 2 cloves garlic, minced, for 2 to 4 minutes or until softened. Add 1½ cups (375 mL) white wine; bring to boil and boil for 4 minutes. Add mussels; cover and boil for 4 minutes or until opened, shaking pan occasionally. Transfer mussels to bowls. To pan, add 2 tbsp (25 mL) chopped green onion, 1 tbsp (15 mL) chopped fresh dill, and salt and pepper to taste; pour over mussels.

Tips

Most mussels sold today are cultivated and are sand- and grit-free. Choose clean, shiny ones with a sweet, fresh smell. Shells should be tightly closed or close when tapped.

To store live mussels, refrigerate for up to 24 hours in open container with well-wrung-out wet towel over top; mussels need air and moisture but must not sit in water.

1 Just before cooking, scrub mussels with stiff brush or nylon pad under cold running water.

2 Remove byssus (beard) attached to shell by pulling up toward rounded end of shell, or by cutting off. Discard any mussels with cracked shells or any that do not close when tapped. Set aside.

3 In large heavy saucepan, heat oil over medium heat; cook onion, garlic and ginger, stirring often, for 3 minutes or until softened. Add curry powder; cook, stirring, for 30 seconds. Pour in wine; bring to simmer over medium-high heat.

4 Add mussels; cover and cook for 5 to 7 minutes or until mussels open, shaking pan occasionally to redistribute mussels. With slotted spoon, remove mussels and keep warm, discarding any that do not open.

5 Bring liquid to boil over high heat; boil, uncovered, for about 3 minutes or until reduced to ½ cup (125 mL). Pour in cream; boil for about 2 minutes or until thick enough to coat spoon. Season with salt and pepper to taste.

6 Transfer mussels to serving dishes. Pour sauce over mussels; sprinkle with coriander. To eat, remove mussels from shells using fork or empty hinged shells as pincers.

Classic Lobster

There's nothing more fun than eating a lobster – twisting off and cracking the claws, cutting through the tail
to expose the tender meat, breaking off the flippers. It's work all right, but what a tasty reward
for your efforts! When buying lobsters, always buy ones that are still moving vigorously,
with tails that curl underneath when picked up and that feel heavy for their size.

Ingredients

4	live lobsters (each 1½ lb/750 g)	4
½ cup	butter, melted, or Light Lemon Chive Dipping Sauce (recipe below)	125 mL

Makes 4 servings

Per serving: about 376 cal, 36 g pro, 24 g total fat (15 g sat. fat), 2 g carb, 0 g fibre, 189 mg chol. % RDI: 10% calcium, 5% iron, 26% vit A, 8% folate.

Light Lemon Chive Dipping Sauce: In bowl, combine ½ cup (125 mL) low-fat plain yogurt, ¼ cup (50 mL) light mayonnaise, 4 tsp (20 mL) chopped fresh chives or green onion, 1 tbsp (15 mL) lemon juice, 1 tsp (5 mL) mustard and pinch cayenne pepper. Makes ¾ cup (175 mL).

Tips

For even cooking, buy lobsters of similar weight. Cook 1 1/4-lb (625 g) lobsters for 11 to 13 minutes; 1 1/2-lb (750 g) for 12 to 14 minutes; 1 3/4-lb (875 g) for 13 to 15 minutes.

If you don't have lobster crackers, use kitchen shears to cut along edge of claws. If you don't have any picks, use small forks to remove meat.

1 Fill large deep pot with enough salted water (1 tbsp/15 mL salt per 4 cups/ 1 L water) to completely cover lobsters; bring to full rolling boil over high heat. Grasp back of each lobster; plunge headfirst into water. Cover and return to boil.

2 Start cooking time when water boils; reduce to bubbly simmer. Cook each lobster for 10 minutes for first pound (500 g) and 1 minute for each additional 4 oz (125 g) or until lobster is bright red and small leg comes away easily when twisted and pulled.

3 Remove meat from lobster, discarding shells and setting meat aside or dipping into butter to eat as you proceed. First, twist off claws at joint at body; separate into claw and arm sections. Break off smaller part of claw and remove meat with lobster pick or nut pick. Using lobster cracker or nutcracker, crack larger part of claw at widest part; lift out meat. Crack arm; pick out meat.

4 Separate tail piece from body by twisting apart. Bend tail backward and break off flippers; pick out meat from flippers.

5 Using kitchen shears or steak knife, cut through shell along underside of tail to expose meat. With fingers or fork, pry meat from shell. Remove and discard intestinal vein (if any).

6 Holding legs and inner section of body, pull off back shell. Remove and eat red coral (if any) and green tomalley (liver). Insert thumbs in inner body and pry apart to separate in half lengthwise; extract any meat. Break off legs; suck out juice and meat.

Pad Thai

Noodles are a Chinese invention but have become so popular in Thailand that street vendors (in river boats, in stalls and on bicycles along the street) serve small bowlfuls as snacks. Essentially, noodles are a way of life. *Pad Thai*, the best known of all the Thai noodle dishes, combines rice stick noodles, egg, tofu and sometimes pork and shrimp. Ketchup, surprisingly, gives the dish its characteristic colour and flavour.

Ingredients

1	pkg (227 g) wide rice stick noodles	1
½ cup	chicken stock	125 mL
¼ cup	granulated sugar	50 mL
¼ cup	fish sauce	50 mL
3 tbsp	lime juice	50 mL
2 tbsp	ketchup	25 mL
¼ tsp	hot pepper flakes	1 mL
8 oz	large raw shrimp	250 g
4 oz	boneless pork loin	125 g
6 oz	firm tofu	175 g
1	sweet red pepper	1
6	green onions	6
¼ cup	vegetable oil	50 mL
1	egg, beaten	1
3	cloves garlic, minced	3
2 cups	bean sprouts	500 mL
½ cup	coriander leaves, coarsely chopped	125 mL
¼ cup	unsalted peanuts, chopped	50 mL

Makes 4 servings

Per serving: about 623 cal, 31 g pro, 25 g total fat (3 g sat. fat), 72 g carb, 3 g fibre, 136 mg chol. % RDI: 14% calcium, 26% iron, 18% vit A, 103% vit C, 41% folate.

Tip

Iron-rich tofu is made from curdled soy milk in a process similar to cheese making. It comes in regular, silken, firm and extra-firm. Use firm tofu in this recipe since the softer varieties will fall apart during cooking.

1 In large bowl, soak noodles in warm water for 15 minutes; drain and set aside. Meanwhile, in small bowl, whisk together stock, sugar, fish sauce, lime juice, ketchup and hot pepper flakes; set aside.

2 Peel shrimp. With small sharp knife, devein shrimp by making shallow cut lengthwise along back to locate dark vein just below surface; pull out vein. Pull off tail. Cut pork across the grain into ¼-inch (5 mm) thick strips. Set aside.

3 Cut tofu into ½-inch (1 cm) cubes. Slice red pepper in half lengthwise; remove seeds and membranes. Cut lengthwise into ¼-inch (5 mm) wide strips, then crosswise into dice. Trim green onions; thinly slice white and green parts diagonally.

4 In wok, heat 1 tsp (5 mL) of the oil over medium heat; cook egg, stirring, for 3 minutes or until scrambled and set. Transfer to plate. Wipe out wok; add 1 tbsp (15 mL) of the oil. Stir-fry garlic, shrimp and pork over medium-high heat for 3 minutes or until shrimp are pink. Add to egg.

5 Heat remaining oil in pan. Stir in tofu and red pepper; cook, stirring occasionally, for 2 minutes or until tofu begins to brown. Gently stir in noodles until beginning to wilt, about 1 minute. Pour in sauce; stir-fry for 3 minutes or until noodles are tender.

6 Return egg mixture to pan. Add bean sprouts, coriander and half of the green onions; stir-fry for 2 to 3 minutes or until heated through. Serve garnished with peanuts and remaining green onions.

Spring Omelette

We all know that dinner can be as easy as cracking a few eggs into a skillet. But why not set your sights
and goals a bit higher and aim for a perfectly formed, delicious omelette? An omelette can encase a variety
of tempting fillings, three of which we highlight in this lesson. They are sure to cement
your budding talent as the omelette maker in your family.

Ingredients

2	eggs	2
2 tsp	water	10 mL
Pinch	each salt and pepper	Pinch
2 tsp	butter	10 mL
	Filling (recipes follow)	

Fillings

Asparagus: Snap off ends of 6 asparagus stalks; cut into 1-inch (2.5 cm) lengths. Steam or boil for 2 to 5 minutes or until tender-crisp; drain. Toss with ¼ cup (50 mL) freshly grated Parmesan cheese, and pepper to taste.

Mushroom: In small skillet, melt 1 tbsp (15 mL) butter over medium heat; cook 1 cup (250 mL) sliced mushrooms and 1 tbsp (15 mL) minced onion for 3 to 5 minutes or until tender. Stir in 2 tbsp (25 mL) whipping cream; cook, stirring, for 1 minute or until thickened. Stir in 1 tbsp (15 mL) chopped fresh parsley. Season with salt and pepper to taste.

Cheddar and Salsa: Combine ¼ cup (50 mL) finely shredded Cheddar or Monterey Jack cheese and 2 tbsp (25 mL) each salsa and chopped green onion.

Makes 1 serving

Per serving (with asparagus filling): about 352 cal, 25 g pro, 25 g total fat (13 g sat. fat), 6 g carb, 1 g fibre, 471 mg chol. % RDI: 37% calcium, 16% iron, 35% vit A, 15% vit C, 75% folate.

Tips

To lighten up an omelette, substitute 2 egg whites for 1 of the eggs.

To make a perfect omelette, use a nonstick pan or one that has been seasoned by heating a thin layer of vegetable oil over medium-high heat for 5 minutes. Let cool and wipe out with paper towel. Do not wash seasoned pan with detergent. Instead, rub it with salt, then wipe out with clean towel.

1 In bowl, combine eggs, water, salt and pepper. With fork, stir briskly just until blended but not frothy. In nonstick skillet with 8-inch (20 cm) diameter bottom, heat butter over medium-high heat until foaming, tilting to coat pan all over.

2 When foam starts to subside and butter just begins to darken, pour egg mixture into middle of pan. Immediately shake pan back and forth while stirring eggs in circular motion with underside of fork for 10 seconds.

3 Cook, shaking pan occasionally and using spatula to push cooked egg to centre and allow uncooked egg to flow underneath (tipping pan if necessary), for 40 to 60 seconds longer or until creamy but not liquid and bottom is light golden.

4 Tilt handle up and shake pan to slide omelette up opposite side of pan.

5 Spoon filling across centre of omelette. Using spatula, lift one-third of the omelette closest to handle; fold over filling.

6 Lift/roll filled part of omelette over remaining uncovered omelette. Slide out omelette, seam side down, onto plate.

5 **Maple Apple Topping:** Meanwhile, in skillet, whisk together maple syrup, orange juice and sugar; bring to boil over medium-high heat. Add butter (if using). Boil for 1 minute.

6 Add apples and raisins; cover and cook, stirring once, for 5 minutes or until apples are tender. Dissolve cornstarch in 1 tbsp (15 mL) water; add to skillet and cook, stirring constantly, for 1 minute or until thickened. Serve warm over strata.

Makes 6 servings

Per serving: about 545 cal, 12 g pro, 16 g total fat (7 g sat. fat), 93 g carb, 4 g fibre, 193 mg chol. % RDI: 18% calcium, 21% iron, 18% vit A, 15% vit C, 20% folate.

Cinnamon Toast Strata with Maple Apple Topping

This breakfast or brunch dish is simplicity itself, but what a terrific presentation and taste sensation! It's cinnamon toast, French toast and bread pudding all rolled into one. The scrumptious maple apple topping stands in for maple syrup or yogurt, which can also be served alongside. Originally developed as the perfect treat for Mother's Day, it's so good that cooks in our Test Kitchen have been known to bake it up on the weekend for no reason at all.

1 tbsp	granulated sugar	15 mL
½ tsp	cinnamon	2 mL
Strata:		
10	slices egg bread	10
¼ cup	butter, softened	50 mL
3 tbsp	granulated sugar	50 mL
½ tsp	cinnamon	2 mL
1½ cups	milk	375 mL
4	eggs	4
Maple Apple Topping:		
⅔ cup	maple syrup	150 mL
½ cup	orange juice	125 mL
¼ cup	packed brown sugar	50 mL
2 tbsp	butter (optional)	25 mL
5	tart apples, peeled, cored and thinly sliced	5
⅓ cup	raisins	75 mL
1 tbsp	cornstarch	15 mL

1 **Strata:** Trim crusts from bread. In small bowl, mix together butter, sugar and cinnamon. Spread on 5 of the bread slices; top with remaining slices. Cut diagonally into quarters to make triangles.

2 Arrange triangles, longest side down, overlapping and curving slightly, around edge of greased deep 10-inch (25 cm) pie plate. Arrange remaining triangles in tight circle in centre. (Or arrange around edge of greased 11- x 7-inch/2 L baking dish, curving slightly to fit; arrange remaining triangles in centre.)

3 Whisk milk with eggs until blended; pour evenly over triangles in dish. Combine sugar with cinnamon; sprinkle over triangles. *(Strata can be prepared to this point, covered with plastic wrap and refrigerated for up to 12 hours.)* Let stand at room temperature for 30 minutes.

4 Bake, uncovered, in 350°F (180°C) oven for about 45 minutes or until puffed and golden. Let stand on rack for 10 minutes.

Variation

Cinnamon Toast Strata with Banana Topping: Use 4 cups (1 L) sliced bananas instead of apples. Reduce brown sugar to 2 tbsp (25 mL). Omit raisins. Reduce cooking time of fruit to 1 minute.

Scrambled Eggs and Smoked Salmon Strata

For an elegant Sunday brunch, pair this savoury variation on a napoleon with a tangy citrus salad and fresh melon wedges.

4	sheets phyllo pastry	4
3 tbsp	butter, melted	50 mL
2 tbsp	freshly grated Parmesan cheese	25 mL

Extra-Easy Hollandaise:

3	egg yolks	3
3 tbsp	water	50 mL
¼ cup	butter, softened	50 mL
2 tsp	lemon juice	10 mL
Pinch	pepper	Pinch

Filling:

1 lb	thin asparagus, trimmed	500 g
12	eggs	12
¼ cup	10% cream	50 mL
Pinch	each salt and pepper	Pinch
1 tbsp	butter	15 mL
6 oz	sliced smoked salmon	175 g

1 Place 1 sheet of phyllo on work surface, keeping remainder covered with plastic wrap and damp towel to prevent drying out. Brush with some of the butter; sprinkle with 2 tsp (10 mL) of the cheese. Top with second sheet. Repeat layering once. Brush top with butter.

2 Cut lengthwise into 4 strips; cut crosswise into 3 strips to make 12 pieces. Place about 1 inch (2.5 cm) apart on greased baking sheets. Bake, 1 sheet at a time, in 375°F (190°C) oven for 5 minutes or until golden. (*Phyllo can be covered and stored at room temperature for up to 24 hours.*)

3 **Extra-Easy Hollandaise:** In saucepan, cook egg yolks with water over medium-low heat, whisking, for 2 to 4 minutes or until thick enough to coat back of spoon. Remove from heat. Whisk in butter, lemon juice and pepper. Keep warm.

4 **Filling:** Cut asparagus into 3-inch (8 cm) lengths. In pot of boiling salted water, cook asparagus for about 3 minutes or until tender-crisp. Drain and plunge into cold water; drain and set aside, separating tips for garnish.

5 In bowl, whisk together eggs, cream, salt and pepper. In large nonstick skillet, melt butter over medium heat; pour in egg mixture.

Cook, stirring with spatula, for 10 to 15 minutes or until thickened and moist but no visible liquid remains.

6 Spoon all but 2 tbsp (25 mL) of the hollandaise onto 6 plates; top each with phyllo square. Spoon three-quarters of the eggs over phyllo. Top with asparagus pieces and half of the salmon. Top each with phyllo square. Top with remaining eggs, then remaining salmon. Top with asparagus tips; drizzle with remaining hollandaise. Serve immediately.

Makes 6 servings

Per serving: about 432 cal, 23 g pro, 32 g total fat (15 g sat. fat), 13 g carb, 1 g fibre, 593 mg chol. % RDI: 11% calcium, 21% iron, 43% vit A, 10% vit C, 57% folate.

Buying and Storing Eggs

- When buying eggs, observe the "best before" date on the carton and always avoid eggs that are cracked, broken or leaking.
- An egg shell's colour is determined by the breed of the hen and has no bearing on either taste or nutritive value.
- Store eggs in the coldest part of the refrigerator as soon as you get them home. Do not store them on the refrigerator door, which is much warmer. Keeping them in their original carton also protects highly porous eggs from absorbing other refrigerator odours.
- Store eggs pointed end down to keep the yolk centred.
- To tell if an egg is fresh, place it in a bowl of cool salted water. If it sinks, it's fresh. If it floats, it's definitely past its prime.
- Let eggs stand at room temperature for 30 minutes before using in recipes for most baked goods (except pastries). If you are in a rush, place eggs in a bowl of warm water (not hot or they could coddle) for five minutes.

Spanish Omelette

This open-faced omelette is a great solution for a light dinner for four in a hurry.

2 tsp	vegetable oil	10 mL
1	onion, chopped	1
1	sweet green pepper, chopped	1
2 cups	grated (unpeeled) potatoes	500 mL
6	eggs	6
2 tbsp	water	25 mL
¼ tsp	each salt and pepper	1 mL

1 In 8-inch (20 cm) nonstick skillet, heat oil over medium-high heat; cook onion, green pepper and potatoes, stirring often, for about 15 minutes or until potatoes are golden brown.

2 Meanwhile, whisk together eggs, water, salt and pepper; stir into vegetable mixture. Cook over medium heat, stirring gently with wooden spatula, for about 30 seconds or until starting to set. Cook, without stirring, for about 2 minutes longer or until bottom is golden.

3 Slide omelette onto large plate; invert pan over plate and invert again to turn omelette. Cook for 1 to 2 minutes or until knife inserted in centre comes out clean. Cut into quarters to serve.

Makes 4 servings

Per serving: about 196 cal, 11 g pro, 10 g total fat (3 g sat. fat), 16 g carb, 2 g fibre, 322 mg chol. % RDI: 5% calcium, 16% iron, 16% vit A, 55% vit C, 20% folate.

Pasta, Grains, Side Dishes

If bread is the staff of life, then surely pastas and grains have earned a similar ranking. It's hard to think of a week, let alone life, without a bowlful of steaming hot pasta blanketed by a sweetly scented tomato sauce or coated with an arresting garlicky dressing. Rice, whether plain or the foundation of a pilaf or a creamy risotto, is a reliable weekly staple. Certainly meal planning would be paralysed without comforting side dishes such as couscous or polenta. Every one of these dishes is among the easiest to make. Once you understand the basics, your imagination and flair can do the rest in the kitchen. Our boxes and tips teach how to pair pasta shapes with appropriate sauces, and also show how to tell if pasta is perfectly cooked – dispelling notions such as throwing it on the ceiling to see if it sticks. Our pasta sauces will open a floodgate of possibilities once you've mastered the two main recipes: one tomato-based and one oil-based. Our recipes for grains illustrate how they are more alike than unalike, not in flavour but in the techniques used to cook them. Feel free to make risotto with barley, a pilaf with couscous and a salad with kasha. With this chapter's lessons and recipes in mind, you'll easily be able to incorporate versatile pasta and grains into almost any meal.

Homemade Pasta

Worth every crank of the pasta machine, freshly made pasta is best paired with delicate sauces made of butter, cheese and cream, typically found in northern Italy. If you don't have a pasta machine, you can still make your own (see tip).

Ingredients

2 cups	all-purpose flour	500 mL
3	eggs	3
¼ tsp	salt	1 mL

Makes about 12 oz (375 g), enough for
4 main-course servings

*Per serving: about 283 cal, 11 g pro, 4 g total fat
(1 g sat. fat), 48 g carb, 2 g fibre, 161 mg chol.
% RDI: 3% calcium, 21% iron, 7% vit A,
37% folate.*

Variations

Spinach Pasta: Cook 4 cups (1 L)
trimmed spinach until wilted. Drain,
let cool and squeeze dry; chop finely to
make about ⅓ cup (75 mL). Reduce eggs
to 2; add spinach to eggs, mixing well.

Roasted Red Pepper Pasta: Broil
1 sweet red pepper, turning several times,
for 20 to 25 minutes or until blackened
and blistered. Let cool. Peel and halve
pepper; discard seeds and membranes
and chop finely. In food processor or
blender, process until smooth to make
about ⅓ cup (75 mL). Reduce eggs to 2;
add purée to eggs, mixing well.

Tips

**You can make your own fresh pasta
even if you don't have a pasta
machine. Prepare dough as outlined
in Step 1. Follow Step 2 but let dough
rest for 1 hour before rolling out
with rolling pin until 1/16 inch
(1.5 mm) thick, rotating dough often
and lightly dusting with flour to
prevent sticking. Follow Step 5.
Roll up dough jelly roll–style into
flat roll about 4 inches (10 cm) wide.
Using sharp knife, cut roll crosswise
into 1/4-inch (5 mm) wide strips.
Unroll strips.**

**Cut pasta can be covered with plastic
wrap and kept at room temperature
for up to 1 hour, refrigerated for
up to 2 days or frozen for up to
2 months.**

1 Mound flour on work surface; make
well in centre. Add eggs and salt to well.
Using fork, beat eggs. Starting from inside
edge and working around well, gradually
incorporate flour into eggs until soft dough
forms. Scoop up any flour left on work
surface, sift and set aside.

2 On clean lightly floured surface, knead
dough for 10 minutes, working in
enough of the sifted flour to make dough
smooth and elastic. Cover with plastic wrap;
let rest for 20 minutes. Divide dough into
thirds to make handling easier; cover.

3 Place 1 piece of dough on lightly
floured surface; roll into 5-inch
(12 cm) long strip. Dust with flour. Feed
through widest setting of pasta machine
rollers 4 times or until edges form smooth
line, folding dough in half and lightly
flouring after each pass through machine.

4 Set machine to next narrowest setting;
run pasta through once without
folding. Repeat running dough through
rollers until next-to-finest setting is reached,
cutting dough in half if awkwardly long.
Lightly flour dough; run through finest
setting. Repeat with remaining dough.

5 Using pasta rack or broomstick
balanced between 2 chairs, hang dough
for 15 to 20 minutes or until leathery but not
dry. If dough dries, remove from rack and
pat with damp cloth.

6 Change setting from rolling to cutting
position. Cut pasta into lengths of up to
10 inches (25 cm). Feed each length through
cutter. In large pot of boiling salted water,
cook pasta for 1 to 2 minutes or until tender.
Drain and toss immediately with desired
sauce or butter.

Spaghetti Bolognese

Look no further than this recipe for the ultimate in meat and tomato sauce. This classic rendition simmers the meat in milk, which keeps it deliciously moist through the long cooking. You can substitute Italian sausage for half of the beef, if you prefer.

Ingredients

3 tbsp	vegetable oil	50 mL
1	onion, chopped	1
2	cloves garlic, minced	2
1	each carrot and stalk celery, finely diced	1
1 lb	ground beef	500 g
1 cup	white wine	250 mL
½ cup	milk	125 mL
1¼ tsp	salt	6 mL
¾ tsp	pepper	4 mL
Pinch	nutmeg	Pinch
1	can (28 oz/796 mL) tomatoes, chopped	1
2 tbsp	tomato paste	25 mL
1	bay leaf	1
12 oz	spaghetti	375 g
	Freshly grated Parmesan cheese	
	Chopped fresh parsley	

Makes 4 servings

Per serving: about 696 cal, 33 g pro, 26 g total fat (7 g sat. fat), 81 g carb, 7 g fibre, 58 mg chol. % RDI: 13% calcium, 36% iron, 61% vit A, 42% vit C, 20% folate.

1 In large heavy saucepan, heat oil over medium-low heat; cook onion, garlic, carrot and celery, stirring occasionally, for about 5 minutes or until softened.

2 Add beef; cook, breaking up meat, for about 10 minutes or just until no longer pink, being careful not to brown. Drain off fat.

3 Pour in wine and increase heat to medium-high; cook, stirring occasionally, until wine is evaporated. Add milk, salt, pepper and nutmeg; cook, stirring, until milk is evaporated.

4 Add tomatoes, tomato paste and bay leaf; bring to boil. Reduce heat to low; cook, stirring occasionally, for about 2 hours or until thickened. Discard bay leaf.

5 Fill large pot (about 24 cups/6 L) with 20 cups (5 L) water and 2 tbsp (25 mL) salt; cover and bring to boil. Add spaghetti; cook for 8 to 10 minutes or until tender but firm. Drain well and return to pot.

6 Add half of the sauce to spaghetti; toss to coat. Place in warmed bowls; top with remaining sauce. Sprinkle with Parmesan cheese and parsley to taste.

Spaghetti with Meatballs

An all-time favourite, spaghetti with meatballs is a family- and crowd-pleaser. We've substituted Italian sausage in the meatballs for some of the ground beef, but they can be used interchangeably. The meatballs and sauce are also delicious on their own tucked into a sliced crusty Italian roll.

1½ lb	spaghetti	750 g
¼ cup	freshly grated Parmesan cheese	50 mL
¼ cup	chopped fresh basil or parsley	50 mL
	Hot pepper flakes (optional)	

Meatballs:

8 oz	sweet Italian sausage	250 g
1½ lb	ground beef	750 g
2	eggs	2
½ cup	dry bread crumbs	125 mL
1 tsp	salt	5 mL
¼ tsp	pepper	1 mL

Sauce:

2 tbsp	olive oil	25 mL
1	large onion, chopped	1
2	cloves garlic, minced	2
1	carrot, diced	1
1	stalk celery, diced	1
3 cups	sliced mushrooms (8 oz/250 g)	750 mL
2	cans (each 28 oz/796 mL) tomatoes	2
	Salt and pepper	

1 **Meatballs:** Remove sausage meat from casings. In bowl, combine sausage meat, beef, eggs, bread crumbs, salt and pepper; form into about forty-eight 1-inch (2.5 cm) balls. Bake on rimmed baking sheets in 400°F (200°C) oven for 15 to 20 minutes or until no longer pink inside; drain off fat.

2 **Sauce:** Meanwhile, in large saucepan, heat oil over medium-high heat; cook onion, garlic, carrot, celery and mushrooms, stirring occasionally, for 10 minutes or until just beginning to brown.

3 Add tomatoes, mashing with fork; cook, stirring occasionally, for about 20 minutes or until thickened. Add meatballs; reduce heat and simmer for 15 minutes. Season with salt and pepper to taste. *(Sauce can be covered and refrigerated for up to 24 hours; reheat.)*

4 In large pot of boiling salted water, cook spaghetti for 8 to 10 minutes or until tender but firm; drain well and arrange on plates. Top each serving with sauce; sprinkle with cheese, basil, and hot pepper flakes (if using).

Makes 8 servings

Per serving: about 689 cal, 35 g pro, 25 g total fat (8 g sat. fat), 82 g carb, 7 g fibre, 111 mg chol. % RDI: 14% calcium, 36% iron, 37% vit A, 35% vit C, 23% folate.

Creamy Tomato Shells

The secret to this recipe is 2% evaporated milk, which provides creaminess in place of whipping cream or cream cheese. As an added bonus, it also supplies a healthy boost of calcium.

1 tbsp	vegetable oil	15 mL
2	cloves garlic, minced	2
1	onion, chopped	1
1 tbsp	dried basil	15 mL
½ tsp	pepper	2 mL
¼ tsp	salt	1 mL
¼ tsp	hot pepper sauce	1 mL

1	can (28 oz/796 mL)	1
	tomatoes	
1 cup	2% evaporated milk	250 mL
5 cups	pasta shells	1.25 L
¼ cup	freshly grated	50 mL
	Parmesan cheese	

1 In saucepan, heat oil over medium heat; cook garlic, onion, basil, pepper, salt and hot pepper sauce, stirring occasionally, for about 5 minutes or until softened.

2 Meanwhile, in blender or food processor, purée tomatoes; add to pan and bring to boil. Reduce heat and boil gently, stirring often, for about 20 minutes or until thickened. Remove from heat; stir in milk.

3 Meanwhile, in large pot of boiling salted water, cook pasta for 8 to 10 minutes or until tender but firm; drain well and return to pot. Add sauce and toss to coat. Serve sprinkled with Parmesan cheese.

Makes 4 servings

Per serving: about 635 cal, 25 g pro, 9 g total fat (3 g sat. fat), 113 g carb, 8 g fibre, 10 mg chol. % RDI: 33% calcium, 25% iron, 17% vit A, 43% vit C, 19% folate.

Roasted Tomato Penne

A clever cooking technique transforms a few choice ingredients into a sauce of depth and intensity. The tomatoes rise to a different level altogether once roasted.

12	large plum tomatoes	12
	(3 lb/1.5 kg)	
10	large cloves garlic	10
1 cup	packed fresh basil leaves	250 mL
½ tsp	salt	2 mL
¼ tsp	pepper	1 mL
⅓ cup	extra-virgin olive oil	75 mL
4 cups	penne or rotini	1 L
	(12 oz/375 g)	
1 cup	crumbled feta cheese	250 mL

1 Slice tomatoes in half lengthwise; place, cut side up, in greased shallow roasting pan.

2 In food processor, coarsely chop together garlic, basil, salt and pepper; with motor running, pour in oil in thin steady stream. Spread over cut sides of tomatoes. Bake in

350°F (180°C) oven for 2 hours or until withered and edges are browned. Chop into ½-inch (1 cm) pieces.

3 Meanwhile, in large pot of boiling salted water, cook penne for 8 to 10 minutes or until tender but firm; drain and return to pot. Add most of the tomatoes; toss to combine. Serve sprinkled with feta and remaining tomatoes.

Makes 4 servings

Per serving: about 635 cal, 19 g pro, 27 g total fat (7 g sat. fat), 82 g carb, 8 g fibre, 28 mg chol. % RDI: 20% calcium, 23% iron, 40% vit A, 83% vit C, 25% folate.

Easy Tomato Sauce

When time is of the essence, this is the sauce to prepare. Cook it while others in the family prepare salad and boil the pasta. Adding a pinch of sugar to canned tomatoes is always a good idea because it helps neutralize their natural acidity. Buy canned plum tomatoes.

2 tbsp	vegetable oil	25 mL
1	large onion, chopped	1
2	cloves garlic, minced	2
¼ cup	finely chopped carrot	50 mL
1	can (28 oz/796 mL)	1
	tomatoes	
1	bay leaf	1
½ tsp	each dried basil and oregano	2 mL
¼ tsp	granulated sugar	1 mL
	Salt and pepper	
¼ cup	chopped fresh parsley	50 mL

1 In large skillet, heat oil over medium heat; cook onion, garlic and carrot, stirring occasionally, for about 5 minutes or until softened.

2 Add tomatoes, mashing with fork into small chunks. Add bay leaf, basil, oregano and sugar; bring to boil. Reduce heat and simmer, uncovered, for 20 to 30 minutes or until thickened. Season with salt and pepper to taste. Stir in parsley. Discard bay leaf.

Makes enough for 4 servings

Per serving: about 122 cal, 3 g pro, 7 g total fat (1 g sat. fat), 14 g carb, 3 g fibre, 0 mg chol. % RDI: 7% calcium, 12% iron, 31% vit A, 40% vit C, 11% folate.

Perfect Pasta

- Start with lots of water. Use a large stock pot or Dutch oven filled with about 20 cups (5 L) of water and 2 tbsp (25 mL) of salt for every 1 lb (500 g) of pasta, which is usually sufficient for four servings. Salting the water is important, otherwise the pasta will taste "naked" next to whatever sauce you put on it. Instead of being absorbed by the pasta, the salt merely seasons it. Salting means the pasta has a stable marriage with the sauce.

- Generally 4 oz (125 g) of dried pasta is considered a serving.

- Stirring the pasta often as it cooks encourages even cooking and helps prevent strands or pieces of pasta from sticking to one another or to the bottom of the pot.

- Avoid cooking more than 1 lb (500 g) of pasta at one time, regardless of how large the pot. It's simply inviting trouble because the pasta will not cook evenly or properly. Use two pots instead.

- There are lots of old wives' tales about how to tell if pasta is cooked (such as throwing the

pasta against the wall to see if it sticks!). The best test is to taste it. Perfectly cooked pasta should be *al dente*, or tender but firm, or firm to the bite, yet have no raw taste remaining.

- There is no need to add oil to the cooking water for pasta or to rinse it once it's cooked (unless you are making a cold pasta salad and want to stop the cooking process). Both the oil and any excess water create a barrier between the pasta and the sauce, causing an unpleasant separateness both on the plate and in your mouth.

- Matching a sauce with the shape of the noodle can be a personal preference, but there are a few guidelines to follow. Long strands of pastas, such as spaghetti and fettuccine, pair best with cream, butter and cheese or plain tomato sauces. Short, curled and twisted pastas pair best with chunky meat-, tomato- or oil-based sauces, because they trap the food seductively inside the curls or twists. Very small pastas, such as macaroni and ditali, are best used in soups.

Lasagna

**Timelessly appealing, lasagna always provides a spectacle as the bubbling casserole is brought to the table,
beautifully golden with melted cheese. You can hear the sighs of delight and anticipation as your diners
press their forks through the crusty cheese, mingling the hot and herby meat and tomato layer with
the silken cheese filling. So set aside a couple of hours for preparation and assembly,
and indulge both you and your family.**

Ingredients

8 oz	lasagna noodles	250 g
1	pkg (10 oz/300 g) frozen chopped spinach, thawed and squeezed dry	1
2 cups	shredded mozzarella cheese	500 mL
¼ cup	freshly grated Parmesan cheese	50 mL

Meat Filling:

8 oz	Italian sausage	250 g
8 oz	ground beef	250 g
1	each onion, carrot and celery, chopped	1
4	cloves garlic, minced	4
1½ tsp	each dried oregano and basil	7 mL
Pinch	hot pepper flakes	Pinch
1	can (28 oz/796 mL) tomatoes	1
1	can (14 oz/398 mL) tomato sauce	1
¼ tsp	pepper	1 mL

Cheese Filling:

2	eggs	2
¼ tsp	each pepper and nutmeg	1 mL
2 cups	cottage cheese	500 mL
1 cup	shredded mozzarella cheese	250 mL
½ cup	freshly grated Parmesan cheese	125 mL

Makes 8 servings

Per serving: about 511 cal, 38 g pro, 24 g total fat (12 g sat. fat), 37 g carb, 4 g fibre, 130 mg chol. % RDI: 47% calcium, 23% iron, 69% vit A, 28% vit C, 28% folate.

Tips

To be sure lasagna is heated through, insert knife into centre of lasagna, then test heat of knife on palm of your hand.

To make lasagna ahead of time, refrigerate it, unbaked, for up to 1 day; let stand at room temperature for 30 minutes before baking.

1 **Meat Filling:** Remove sausage from casing; crumble meat into Dutch oven. Add beef; cook over medium-high heat, breaking up with spoon, for about 5 minutes or until no longer pink. Transfer to plate. Spoon off all but 1 tbsp (15 mL) fat from pan.

2 Cook onion, carrot, celery, garlic, oregano, basil and hot pepper flakes, stirring occasionally, for 3 to 5 minutes or until softened. Add tomatoes, tomato sauce and meat; bring to boil. Reduce heat and simmer, breaking up tomatoes and stirring often, for 20 to 25 minutes or until thickened. Add pepper.

3 **Cheese Filling:** In bowl, beat together eggs, pepper and nutmeg; blend in cottage cheese, mozzarella and Parmesan.

4 In large pot of boiling salted water, cook noodles for 6 to 8 minutes or until almost tender. Drain and place in cold water. Drain and layer between damp tea towels.

5 Spread 1 cup (250 mL) of the meat filling as base in greased 13- x 9-inch (3 L) baking dish. Top with one-third of the noodles in single layer; spread with one-third of the remaining meat filling. Spread with half of the cheese filling, then half of the spinach. Starting with noodles, repeat layers once.

6 Top with remaining noodles; spread with remaining meat filling. Sprinkle with mozzarella and Parmesan. Cover loosely with foil; bake in 375°F (190°C) oven for 20 minutes. Uncover and bake for 20 to 25 minutes or until bubbling and heated through. Let stand for 10 minutes before serving.

Sky-High Roasted Red Pepper Lasagna

This fabulously spirited lasagna salutes the flavour of roasted red peppers by making it the main flavouring element in its sauce. The zest comes from the generous amount of red pepper flakes, but you can decrease it to suit your tastes. Do not use the oven-ready lasagna noodles as the cooking time and amount of liquid have been tested with conventional noodles only.

8 oz	non-ruffled spinach lasagna noodles (12)	250 g
1	pkg (10 oz/284 g) fresh spinach, trimmed	1

Tomato Sauce:

1 tbsp	olive oil	15 mL
1	onion, chopped	1
4	cloves garlic, minced	4
2	carrots, diced	2
3 cups	sliced mushrooms	750 mL
1½ tsp	dried oregano	7 mL
1 tsp	dried thyme	5 mL
½ tsp	salt	2 mL
¼ tsp	each pepper and hot pepper flakes	1 mL
2	cans (each 19 oz/540 mL) tomatoes, chopped	2
1	jar (313 mL) roasted red peppers, chopped	1
¼ cup	tomato paste	50 mL
2 tbsp	white wine vinegar	25 mL

Béchamel Sauce:

¼ cup	butter	50 mL
½ cup	all-purpose flour	125 mL
4 cups	milk	1 L
½ tsp	salt	2 mL
¼ tsp	each pepper and nutmeg	1 mL
1 cup	shredded Asiago or Fontina cheese	250 mL
½ cup	freshly grated Parmesan cheese	125 mL

1 **Tomato Sauce:** In saucepan, heat oil over medium heat; cook onion and garlic, stirring occasionally, for 3 minutes. Add carrots, mushrooms, oregano, thyme, salt, pepper and hot pepper flakes; cook, stirring often, for 8 minutes or until liquid is evaporated.

2 Stir in tomatoes, red peppers, tomato paste and vinegar; bring to boil. Reduce heat and simmer, stirring often, for 1 hour or until reduced to 5 cups (1.25 L) and thick enough to mound on spoon.

3 In large pot of boiling salted water, cook noodles for 8 minutes or until tender but firm. With tongs, transfer to cold water. Drain and layer between damp tea towels. Add spinach to boiling water; cook for 1 minute. Drain in sieve, pressing out liquid; chop coarsely. Set aside.

4 **Béchamel Sauce:** In saucepan, melt butter over medium heat; gradually whisk in flour for about 3 minutes or until in bits. Remove from heat. Whisk in milk, salt, pepper and nutmeg; cook, whisking, for 10 to 15 minutes or until thickened. Whisk in ½ cup (125 mL) of the Asiago and ⅓ cup (75 mL) of the Parmesan until melted.

5 Spread one-quarter of the tomato sauce in 11- x 7-inch (2 L) baking dish. Top with layer of noodles, trimming to fit. Repeat layering. Spread with one-third of the béchamel sauce; top with noodles. Sprinkle with spinach, then remaining Asiago. Top with noodles, one-quarter of the tomato sauce, then noodles and one-third of the béchamel sauce. Repeat final layering to come 1 inch (2.5 cm) above dish. Cover with foil. *(Lasagna can be refrigerated for 24 hours; add 10 minutes to first baking time.)*

6 Bake on baking sheet in 375°F (190°C) oven for 30 minutes. Sprinkle with remaining Parmesan; bake, uncovered, for 30 minutes or until golden. Let stand for 20 minutes before serving.

Makes 6 servings
Per serving: about 555 cal, 24 g pro, 23 g total fat (12 g sat. fat), 67 g carb, 8 g fibre, 55 mg chol. % RDI: 57% calcium, 41% iron, 132% vit A, 98% vit C, 50% folate.

Many-Mushroom Manicotti

This is truly a special-events dish. Associate food director Donna Bartolini, who developed it especially for fashion designer Simon Chang's Christmas buffet, toiled over its steps and flavours until she felt it was just perfect. And perfect it is, with its subtle woodsy flavours set off by the creamy sauce. Though you do have to devote a chunk of time to its preparation and assembly, you'll be rewarded by seeing only scraped-clean plates at the end of the meal.

3 tbsp	butter	50 mL
2	onions, chopped	2
4	cloves garlic, minced	4

1 tsp	dried thyme	5 mL
½ tsp	each salt and pepper	2 mL
1½ lb	button mushrooms, sliced (8 cups/2 L)	750 g
1 lb	exotic mushrooms, stemmed and sliced (8 cups/2 L)	500 g
⅓ cup	dry white wine	75 mL
12	manicotti shells	12
2 cups	shredded mozzarella cheese	500 mL
⅓ cup	finely chopped fresh Italian parsley	75 mL
¼ cup	freshly grated Parmesan cheese	50 mL
4	plum tomatoes, diced	4
1	roasted sweet red pepper, diced	1

Sauce:

3 tbsp	butter	50 mL
3 tbsp	all-purpose flour	50 mL
3 cups	milk	750 mL
½ tsp	salt	2 mL
¼ tsp	pepper	1 mL
3 oz	cream cheese, cubed	90 g

1 In large saucepan, melt butter over medium heat; cook onions, garlic, thyme, salt and pepper, stirring occasionally, for about 20 minutes or until light golden.

2 Add button and exotic mushrooms; cook for about 8 minutes or until liquid is released. Increase heat to high; cook, stirring often, for about 10 minutes longer or until mushrooms are tender and no liquid remains. Stir in wine; cook until no liquid remains. Let cool to room temperature.

3 Meanwhile, in large pot of boiling salted water, cook manicotti shells for 15 minutes or until tender but firm. Drain and cool in cold water. Arrange in single layer on damp tea towel; cover with plastic wrap.

4 **Sauce:** Meanwhile, in heavy saucepan, melt butter over medium heat; whisk in flour and cook, whisking, for 1 minute. Whisking constantly, add milk, ½ cup (125 mL) at a time. Stir in salt and pepper. Cook, stirring, for about 15 minutes or until thickened. Whisk in cream cheese until melted. Remove from heat. Spread ¾ cup (175 mL) in 13- x 9-inch (3 L) baking dish.

5 Stir mozzarella cheese and ¼ cup (50 mL) of the parsley into mushroom mixture; spoon

½ cup (125 mL) into each manicotti shell. Arrange in dish in 2 rows. *(Manicotti and remaining sauce can be covered and refrigerated separately for up to 24 hours; increase baking time by 15 minutes.)*

6 Pour remaining sauce over manicotti, spreading to cover; sprinkle with half of the Parmesan cheese. Bake in 400°F (200°C) oven for 25 minutes or until bubbling at edges and cheese is golden.

7 In bowl, stir together tomatoes, red pepper and remaining parsley; spoon half over centre of each row of manicotti. Sprinkle with remaining Parmesan cheese; bake for 5 to 10 minutes or until light golden. Let stand for 10 minutes before serving.

Makes 6 servings
Per serving: about 554 cal, 24 g pro, 31 g total fat (19 g sat. fat), 48 g carb, 6 g fibre, 93 mg chol. % RDI: 43% calcium, 29% iron, 47% vit A, 80% vit C, 25% folate.

Tip

For the exotic mushrooms, use shiitake, crimini or oyster, or a combination. Or you can simply use a total of 16 cups (4 L) button mushrooms (about 3 lb/1.5 kg) for an equally delicious, if milder, dish.

Crusty Puttanesca

Named in honour of Italy's ladies of the night, puttanesca lives up to its delicious lusty reputation.

1 tsp	olive oil	5 mL
3	cloves garlic, minced	3
1	onion, chopped	1
1½ tsp	each dried basil and oregano	7 mL
1¼ tsp	salt	6 mL
1 tsp	granulated sugar	5 mL
½ tsp	pepper	2 mL
¼ tsp	hot pepper flakes	1 mL
½ cup	chopped pitted oil-cured olives	125 mL
3 tbsp	capers	50 mL
1	eggplant, peeled and cubed	1

2	cans (each 28 oz/796 mL) tomatoes, chopped	2
3 tbsp	tomato paste	50 mL
4 cups	radiatore or fusilli pasta (12 oz/375 g)	1 L
1 cup	shredded part-skim mozzarella cheese	250 mL
¼ cup	freshly grated Parmesan cheese	50 mL

1 In Dutch oven, heat oil over medium heat; cook garlic and onion, stirring, for 3 minutes or just until softened. Stir in basil, oregano, salt, sugar, pepper and hot pepper flakes. Add olives, capers and eggplant; cook for 1 minute.

2 Pour in ½ cup (125 mL) water; cover and cook, stirring occasionally, for about 8 minutes or until eggplant is tender. Stir in tomatoes and tomato paste; bring to boil. Reduce heat and simmer, uncovered and stirring occasionally, for 30 minutes.

3 Meanwhile, in large pot of boiling salted water, cook pasta for 8 to 10 minutes or just until tender but firm; drain well and add to sauce, stirring to coat. Sprinkle with mozzarella, then Parmesan.

4 Bake in 375°F (190°C) oven for about 20 minutes or until cheese is melted and becoming golden. Let stand for 10 minutes before serving.

Makes 6 servings
Per serving: about 417 cal, 18 g pro, 11 g total fat (4 g sat. fat), 64 g carb, 8 g fibre, 13 mg chol. % RDI: 28% calcium, 24% iron, 23% vit A, 52% vit C, 18% folate.

Tip

One of the basic rules for pairing sauces and pasta is the more robust the sauce, the bolder the pasta shape. Radiatore, fusilli and penne rigate work well with a spicy puttanesca.

Two Oil-Based Pasta Sauces

For the simple pleasures of southern Italy's exuberant pasta dishes, start with a great-tasting bottle of extra-virgin olive oil. Choose a full-bodied, flavourful oil that specifies it is both bottled and produced in either Italy, Greece or Spain; then add to the pasta dish as you see fit. Sometimes, you may restrict yourself to the classic *aglio e olio*, which depends on garlic and hot pepper flakes for its appeal. Other times, feel free to add shrimp, as we've done here, some broccoli, olives or sun-dried tomatoes. Pictured, Aglio e Olio with Shrimp.

Ingredients

Aglio e Olio with Shrimp

½ cup	extra-virgin olive oil	125 mL
7	cloves garlic, minced	7
1 tsp	salt	5 mL
Pinch	hot pepper flakes	Pinch
1 lb	large shrimp, peeled and deveined	500 g
12 oz	spaghetti	375 g
⅓ cup	chopped fresh parsley	75 mL

Makes 4 servings

Per serving: about 653 cal, 28 g pro, 30 g total fat (4 g sat. fat), 66 g carb, 4 g fibre, 129 mg chol. % RDI: 5% calcium, 23% iron, 7% vit A, 12% vit C, 14% folate.

Fusilli with Broccoli, Garlic and Anchovies

5 cups	fusilli or orecchiette pasta (12 oz/375 g)	1.25 L
4 cups	broccoli florets	1 L
⅓ cup	extra-virgin olive oil	75 mL
4	cloves garlic, minced	4
1	pkg (50 g) flat anchovy fillets (about 8), chopped	1
¼ tsp	pepper	1 mL
¾ cup	fresh bread crumbs	175 mL
½ cup	freshly grated Parmesan cheese	125 mL

Makes 4 servings

Per serving: about 590 cal, 21 g pro, 25 g total fat (5 g sat. fat), 72 g carb, 5 g fibre, 18 mg chol. % RDI: 22% calcium, 17% iron, 9% vit A, 60% vit C, 20% folate.

1 **Aglio e Olio with Shrimp:** Fill large pot (about 24 cups/6 L) with 20 cups (5 L) water and 2 tbsp (25 mL) salt; cover and bring to boil. Meanwhile, in skillet, heat oil over low heat; cook garlic, salt and hot pepper flakes, stirring occasionally, for about 15 minutes or until garlic is light golden but not browned.

2 Increase heat to medium-high. Add shrimp to skillet; stir-fry for 2 to 3 minutes or until lightly pink and opaque. Fill pasta bowls with hot water to warm.

3 Meanwhile, add pasta to water, stirring to separate strands. Cook for 8 to 10 minutes or until tender but firm; drain and return to pot. Add shrimp mixture and parsley; toss to coat. Empty bowls. Spoon in pasta.

4 **Fusilli with Broccoli, Garlic and Anchovies:** Fill large pot (about 24 cups/6 L) with 20 cups (5 L) water and 2 tbsp (25 mL) salt; bring to boil. Add pasta; cook for 8 minutes. Add broccoli; cook for 2 minutes or until tender-crisp and pasta is tender but firm. Drain well and return to pot.

5 Meanwhile, in skillet, heat oil over medium-low heat; cook garlic, stirring occasionally, for 3 minutes. Stir in anchovies and pepper until anchovies are dissolved. Fill pasta bowls with hot water to warm.

6 Add anchovy mixture, bread crumbs and half of the Parmesan to pasta mixture; toss to coat. Empty bowls; spoon in pasta. Sprinkle with remaining cheese.

Pasta Broccoli Toss

Use this time-saving cooking method whenever you're cooking a vegetable to be served with your pasta: simply add the vegetable to the pasta pot for whatever time it needs to be cooked until tender. Using some of the pasta cooking liquid in the sauce is also a great way to keep pasta moist, especially if you're pairing it with an olive oil–based sauce (and you don't want to use more oil) or a chicken stock–based sauce.

4 cups	gemelli or rotini pasta	1 L
3 cups	small broccoli florets	750 mL
2 tbsp	olive oil	25 mL
1	sweet yellow pepper, chopped	1
1	onion, chopped	1
4	cloves garlic, minced	4
1 tsp	salt	5 mL
½ tsp	each pepper and granulated sugar	2 mL
4	large tomatoes, chopped	4
⅓ cup	shredded basil	75 mL
¼ cup	freshly grated Pecorino Romano cheese	50 mL

1 In large pot of boiling salted water, cook pasta for 6 minutes. Add broccoli; cook for 2 to 3 minutes or until pasta is tender but firm and broccoli is tender-crisp. Reserving ¼ cup (50 mL) of the liquid, drain pasta mixture; return to pot.

2 Meanwhile, in large skillet, heat oil over medium heat; cook yellow pepper, onion and garlic, stirring occasionally, for about 5 minutes or until onion is softened. Stir in reserved liquid, salt, pepper and sugar; bring to boil. Pour over pasta mixture. Add tomatoes, basil and cheese; toss to combine.

Makes 4 servings

Per serving: about 347 cal, 12 g pro, 10 g total fat (2 g sat. fat), 54 g carb, 6 g fibre, 6 mg chol. % RDI: 11% calcium, 16% iron, 24% vit A, 178% vit C, 30% folate.

Rotelle with Prosciutto

Rotelle are wagon wheel–shaped pasta and are the ideal choice for this dish since the shape helps catch pieces of the Swiss chard and prosciutto, making each mouthful that much more exciting. Prosciutto is a ham that has been seasoned, salt-cured and air-dried. Prosciutto is both produced domestically and imported; just make sure it is sliced thinly. In a pinch, use sliced ham. Fresh green beans can also replace the lima beans but need to be cooked for about five minutes.

4 cups	rotelle pasta	1 L
2 cups	frozen lima beans	500 mL
2 tbsp	each olive oil and butter	25 mL
1	onion, chopped	1
4	cloves garlic, minced	4
¼ tsp	hot pepper flakes	1 mL
1 cup	chicken stock	250 mL
1 tbsp	white wine vinegar	15 mL

¾ tsp	salt	4 mL
3 cups	chopped Swiss chard or spinach	750 mL
4 oz	prosciutto, cut in strips	125 g
¼ cup	chopped fresh oregano or parsley	50 mL

1 In large pot of boiling salted water, cook pasta for 2 minutes. Add lima beans; cook for about 10 minutes or until pasta and beans are tender but firm. Drain and return to pot.

2 Meanwhile, in large skillet, heat oil and butter over medium heat; cook onion, garlic and hot pepper flakes, stirring occasionally, for about 5 minutes or until softened.

3 Add stock, vinegar and salt; bring to boil. Add Swiss chard; toss for about 30 seconds or until wilted. Pour over pasta mixture. Add prosciutto and oregano; toss to combine.

Makes 4 servings

Per serving: about 472 cal, 20 g pro, 17 g total fat (6 g sat. fat), 61 g carb, 7 g fibre, 31 mg chol. % RDI: 7% calcium, 27% iron, 16% vit A, 20% vit C, 14% folate.

Penne with Arugula Pesto Dressing

Pesto, originally an uncooked pasta sauce from Genoa made with fresh basil, olive oil, garlic, cheese and pine nuts, is now made with myriad ingredients, including coriander, mint, parsley, walnuts and pecans. Here we've gussied it up by making it with arugula, a dark, peppery green. You can also substitute watercress if arugula is unavailable.

4 cups	penne rigate (12 oz/375 g)	1 L
3 oz	Romano cheese	90 g
3 cups	lightly packed stemmed arugula	750 mL
¼ cup	chopped pecans, toasted	50 mL
¼ cup	extra-virgin olive oil	50 mL
1	clove garlic, minced	1
1	sweet red pepper, diced	1
½ cup	sliced black olives	125 mL
2 tbsp	lemon juice	25 mL
Pinch	pepper	Pinch

1 In large pot of boiling salted water, cook penne for about 8 minutes or until tender but firm. Reserving ⅓ cup (75 mL) of the cooking liquid, drain pasta and transfer to large bowl. Set aside.

2 Meanwhile, using vegetable peeler, cut thin shavings of cheese to make ¼ cup (50 mL); grate remaining cheese. Set aside.

3 In food processor, finely chop together 2 cups (500 mL) of the arugula, pecans and grated cheese. With motor running, drizzle in oil; process for about 2 minutes or until a fine paste. Add garlic; process to blend. Add to pasta along with red pepper, olives, lemon juice and pepper; toss to coat. Cover and refrigerate for at least 30 minutes or until chilled. *(Pasta can be refrigerated for up to 24 hours.)*

4 Add reserved cooking liquid to pasta mixture if necessary to moisten. Just before serving, add remaining arugula and toss to combine. Sprinkle with shaved cheese.

Makes 4 servings

Per serving: about 604 cal, 20 g pro, 28 g total fat (6 g sat. fat), 71 g carb, 6 g fibre, 22 mg chol. % RDI: 30% calcium, 15% iron, 31% vit A, 98% vit C, 30% folate.

Pesto Chicken Pasta Salad

Watch carefully as you toast the pine nuts for this salad; a minute too long and they turn from beautifully fragrant taste sensations to burnt nuts that need to be discarded. Just as roasting spices extracts their essential oils and all the underlying flavour, toasting nuts in a skillet releases their wondrous undertones and renders them a beautiful golden colour.

2 tbsp	pine nuts	25 mL
12	dry-packed sun-dried tomatoes	12
2	boneless skinless chicken breasts	2
⅓ cup	extra-virgin olive oil	75 mL
2 cups	tightly packed fresh basil leaves	500 mL
½ cup	freshly grated Parmesan cheese	125 mL
2	cloves garlic, minced	2
¾ tsp	salt	4 mL
¼ tsp	pepper	1 mL
5½ cups	radiatore pasta (500 g pkg)	1.375 L

1 In skillet, toast pine nuts over medium heat, shaking pan occasionally, for 6 minutes or until golden; remove and set aside. Cover tomatoes with boiling water; let stand for 3 to 5 minutes or until softened. Drain and cut into thin strips; set aside. Cut chicken crosswise into ¼-inch (5 mm) thick strips.

2 In skillet, heat 1 tbsp (15 mL) of the oil over medium-high heat; cook chicken, stirring occasionally, for 5 minutes or until no longer pink inside. Set aside.

3 In food processor, purée basil with remaining oil; transfer to large bowl. Mix in cheese, garlic, salt, pepper, sun-dried tomatoes and chicken.

4 Meanwhile, in large pot of boiling salted water, cook radiatore for 6 minutes or until tender but firm; drain, reserving ½ cup (125 mL) of the cooking liquid. Rinse under cold water; drain again. Add to basil mixture and toss to coat, adding a little of the cooking liquid to moisten if desired. Garnish with pine nuts.

Makes 6 servings

Per serving: about 538 cal, 26 g pro, 19 g total fat (4 g sat. fat), 66 g carb, 5 g fibre, 34 mg chol. % RDI: 15% calcium, 14% iron, 2% vit A, 3% vit C, 14% folate.

More Pasta Tidbits

- Buy pasta made from semolina (coarsely ground granules of the hardest durum wheat). The pasta has a pleasant, firm bite to it and retains its shape well when cooked. The ingredient list should specify either durum semolina or *pasta di semola di grano dura*.
- Dried pasta can be stored in the pantry for up to one year.

Plump Perogies

This Ukrainian specialty is great to have on hand in the freezer for an easy meatless weeknight meal. You can refrigerate uncooked perogies for up to eight hours. Freeze uncooked perogies with the potato filling and the mushroom filling on baking sheets, then pack them in freezer bags and freeze for up to one month. Do not thaw before cooking. Serve with sour cream.

Ingredients

2 tbsp	butter	25 mL
1	onion, sliced	1

Dough:

3 cups	all-purpose flour	750 mL
1½ tsp	salt	7 mL
1	egg	1
¾ cup	water (approx)	175 mL
4 tsp	vegetable oil	20 mL

Filling:

1 tbsp	butter	15 mL
⅓ cup	finely chopped onion	75 mL
1 cup	cold mashed potatoes	250 mL
¾ cup	shredded Cheddar cheese	175 mL
½ tsp	salt	2 mL
¼ tsp	pepper	1 mL

Makes about 36 pieces, enough
for 6 servings

*Per serving: about 412 cal, 12 g pro, 15 g total fat
(7 g sat. fat), 57 g carb, 3 g fibre, 67 mg chol.
% RDI: 12% calcium, 21% iron, 12% vit A,
7% vit C, 36% folate.*

Filling Variations

Cottage Cheese: Combine 1 cup
(250 mL) pressed cottage cheese, 1 egg,
beaten, ½ tsp (2 mL) salt, ¼ tsp (1 mL)
pepper and 1 tbsp (15 mL) chopped
green onion.

Mushroom: In skillet, melt 2 tbsp
(25 mL) butter over medium heat; cook
3 cups (750 mL) chopped mushrooms
and ⅓ cup (75 mL) finely chopped onion,
stirring occasionally, for 7 to 9 minutes
or until moisture is evaporated. Remove
from heat; stir in 1 egg yolk and 1 tbsp
(15 mL) chopped fresh dill. Season with
salt and pepper to taste.

1 Dough: In bowl, combine flour with
salt. Beat together egg, water and oil;
stir into flour mixture to make soft but not
sticky dough that holds together in ball.
If necessary, add 1 tbsp (15 mL) more
water at a time, being careful not to make
dough sticky.

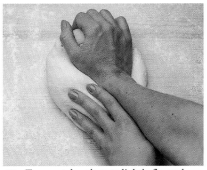

2 Turn out dough onto lightly floured
surface; knead about 10 times or just
until smooth. Halve dough; cover with
plastic wrap. Let rest for 20 minutes.

Filling: Meanwhile, in skillet, heat
butter over medium heat; cook onion,
stirring occasionally, for 3 to 5 minutes
or until tender. Transfer to bowl; mix in
potatoes, cheese, salt and pepper.

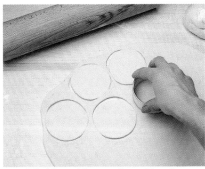

3 Working with 1 portion of dough at a
time, roll out on lightly floured surface
to about 1/16-inch (1.5 mm) thickness. Using
3-inch (8 cm) round cutter, cut out rounds.

4 Place 1 tsp (5 mL) filling on each round.
Lightly moisten edge of 1 half of dough
with water; pinch edges together to seal and
crimp attractively. Place on cloth; cover with
damp cloth to prevent drying out. Repeat
with remaining portion of dough.

5 In large pot of boiling salted water,
cook perogies, in batches, for 1½ to
2 minutes or until they float to top, stirring
gently to prevent perogies from sticking
together or to bottom of pan. With slotted
spoon, transfer to colander to drain.

6 In large heavy skillet, melt butter over
medium heat; cook onion, stirring
occasionally, for about 5 minutes or until
golden. Add perogies; toss to coat and
warm through.

Asparagus Risotto

Risotto is Italy's most significant rice dish and one of its most versatile in accommodating other flavours and ingredients. A technique as well as a dish, risotto is not merely cooked, it is built, as ladle after ladle of stock is gently stirred into the rice until this creamy meal in a bowl is complete. Because the ingredients are right at the forefront, choose only the highest quality: Parmigiano-Reggiano cheese, arborio rice, fragrant chicken stock, dry white wine and, of course, seasonal vegetables.

Ingredients

1 lb	asparagus	500 g
1	sweet yellow or red pepper	1
2	carrots	2
4¾ cups	chicken or vegetable stock	1.175 L
2 tbsp	olive oil	25 mL
1	onion, chopped	1
2	cloves garlic, minced	2
2 tsp	grated lemon rind	10 mL
1 tsp	dried thyme	5 mL
¼ tsp	each salt and pepper	1 mL
1½ cups	arborio rice	375 mL
¾ cup	white wine	175 mL
1 cup	frozen peas	250 mL
½ cup	freshly grated Parmesan cheese	125 mL

Makes 4 servings

Per serving: about 530 cal, 21 g pro, 13 g total fat (4 g sat. fat), 78 g carb, 6 g fibre, 10 mg chol. % RDI: 22% calcium, 23% iron, 106% vit A, 98% vit C, 73% folate.

Variations

Barley Risotto: Substitute 1¾ cups (425 mL) barley for rice. Cut carrots thickly. Increase stock to 6 cups (1.5 L). After stirring in barley, pour in 3½ cups (875 mL) of the stock; bring to boil. Reduce heat and simmer, uncovered and stirring occasionally, for 25 to 30 minutes or until almost all liquid is absorbed. Proceed with Step 4, using remaining stock.

Prosciutto Risotto: Omit carrots. Stir in 5 oz (150 g) diced prosciutto ham along with onion and garlic.

1 Holding asparagus at base and halfway up stalk, bend just until stalk snaps at natural breaking point; reserve bases for another use. Cut stalks into 1-inch (2.5 cm) pieces; set aside.

2 Core and seed yellow pepper; cut lengthwise into 1-inch (2.5 cm) wide strips. Holding about 3 pieces side by side at a time, cut into bite-size chunks. Peel carrots; cut diagonally into thin slices.

3 In saucepan, bring stock just to simmer; reduce heat to low and keep warm. In separate large shallow saucepan, heat oil over medium heat; cook onion and garlic, stirring occasionally, for 3 minutes or until softened. Stir in lemon rind, thyme, salt and pepper. Stir in rice and carrots until grains are well coated.

4 Stir in ½ cup (125 mL) of the warm stock; cook, stirring constantly, until all liquid is absorbed. Stir in wine; cook, stirring, until all wine is absorbed. Add about half of the remaining stock, ½ cup (125 mL) at a time, cooking and stirring until each addition is absorbed before adding next, about 15 minutes total.

5 Stir in asparagus and yellow pepper. Continue stirring and adding remaining stock, ½ cup (125 mL) at a time, for 10 to 15 minutes or until creamy, rice is tender and asparagus is tender-crisp.

6 Stir in peas, cheese and any remaining stock; cook, stirring, for 2 minutes or until risotto is very creamy but still fluid.

Easy Garden Risotto

Although I am a purist, I have to sheepishly admit that this recipe, which requires virtually no stirring, unlike the classic risotto, is delicious. This extremely easy, delectable recipe eliminates the last excuse not to make risotto, a dish you'll fall in love with, whatever method you use.

2 tbsp	olive oil	25 mL
1	large onion, chopped	1
2	cloves garlic, minced	2
1 lb	baby carrots, trimmed	500 g
2 cups	arborio rice or Italian short-grain rice	500 mL
8 cups	chicken or vegetable stock (approx), heated	2 L
1 lb	asparagus	500 g
1 cup	fresh shelled peas	250 mL
1 cup	chopped green onions	250 mL
½ cup	shredded fresh basil	125 mL
½ cup	freshly grated Parmesan cheese	125 mL
1 tbsp	lemon juice	15 mL
	Salt and pepper	

1 In large heavy saucepan, heat oil over medium heat; cook onion, garlic and carrots, stirring occasionally, for about 10 minutes or until onion is tender.

2 Stir in rice and half of the stock; bring to boil, stirring often. Reduce heat to low; simmer for 15 minutes.

3 Meanwhile, trim asparagus; cut into 1-inch (2.5 cm) lengths. Add to pan along with half of the remaining stock; simmer for 10 minutes.

4 Stir in peas and remaining stock; simmer for 10 minutes or until vegetables are tender, mixture is creamy and rice is still slightly firm to the bite.

5 Stir in green onions, basil, Parmesan, lemon juice, and salt and pepper to taste. Serve immediately.

Makes 4 servings

Per serving: about 675 cal, 28 g pro, 15 g total fat (4 g sat. fat), 107 g carb, 9 g fibre, 10 mg chol. % RDI: 26% calcium, 29% iron, 266% vit A, 40% vit C, 88% folate.

Rice Reassurance

- *Long-grain:* Slender, polished white elongated grains of rice that cook into separate fluffy grains.
- *Parboiled (or converted):* Steamed, pressure-treated and packaged rice that cooks into separate fluffy grains.
- *Instant:* Partially or fully cooked rice that is dehydrated and packaged; it cooks quickly but not into grains as separate and fluffy as long-grain or parboiled.
- *Arborio:* A short-grain rice that is used for risotto, it has a fat, roundish grain that is high in starch to yield a moist, creamy texture.
- *Brown:* With the bran and germ still attached, brown rice is the least processed and most nutritious variety. A light tan colour, it's considered a long-grain rice that has a nutty flavour and chewy texture.
- *Basmati:* A long-grain rice native to India, basmati is noted for its aromatic perfume, delicate taste and fluffiness.
- *Wild rice:* Not a rice at all but a grass, wild rice has a chewy texture with an earthy, almost nutty flavour. It needs to be rinsed initially and takes about 45 minutes to cook.

Grain Glossary

- *Amaranth:* High in protein, amaranth kernels are reminiscent of sesame seeds with an added fillip of pepperiness.
- *Barley:* An ancient grain that dates back to the Stone Age, barley is used in soups, cereals, breads and now risottos and salads. At the grocery store, you most commonly find pearl or pot barley, which can be used interchangeably, although the pearl variety has had the tough husk, bran and germ ground away. Both kinds take about 40 minutes to cook.
- *Bulgur:* Hugely popular in Middle Eastern cooking, bulgur is wheat kernels that have been steamed, dried and crushed. Often confused with kasha (cracked wheat), bulgur has a tender, chewy texture and only requires soaking before eating.
- *Couscous:* Not really a grain as much as grains of precooked semolina, couscous is a staple of North African cuisine. It is steamed and served with an aromatic and spicy meat and/or vegetable stew. Instant couscous, ready in five minutes, is widely available.
- *Kasha:* Kasha is the name for roasted buckwheat groats. Buckwheat is actually the hulled and slightly crushed seed (groat) of a plant, not a grain at all, although it is typically grouped with grains. Kasha is available in fine, medium and coarse grinds and should be toasted before steaming to extract all of its flavour.
- *Millet:* Long a staple in African and Asian cuisines, millet is noted for its quick cooking time and its resemblance to couscous. It is great mixed with other grains, such as rice. Store in the refrigerator.
- *Quinoa:* Quick-cooking and high in protein and minerals, quinoa is another ancient grain that was used mostly by the Incas. Quinoa must be stored in the refrigerator since it turns rancid quickly. Toasting it is recommended as this method highlights its nutty flavour.
- *Wheat berries:* Unprocessed whole wheat kernels used in salads, baking and in cereals, wheat berries are noted for their chewy texture. They require soaking and cooking.

Southwestern Rice Pilaf

More than half of the world's population enjoys rice as its main sustenance. It's so adaptable and versatile that it simply defies restrictions. In this Tex-Mex recipe, black beans and pepitas (pumpkin seeds) add flair and whimsy with a dash of elegance. Always rinse canned beans under cold running water to remove excess salt and the liquid in which they have been canned.

1 tbsp	vegetable oil	15 mL
1	large onion, chopped	1
2	cloves garlic, minced	2
1½ cups	long-grain rice	375 mL
½ tsp	each ground cumin and coriander	2 mL
½ tsp	salt	2 mL
¼ tsp	each cayenne pepper and turmeric	1 mL
Pinch	pepper	Pinch
2	carrots, coarsely chopped	2
1	sweet red pepper, diced	1
1	can (19 oz/540 mL) black beans, drained and rinsed	1
3 cups	chicken stock	750 mL
½ cup	pumpkin seeds	125 mL

1 In saucepan, heat oil over medium heat; cook onion and garlic, stirring occasionally, for 5 minutes or until softened. Add rice, cumin, coriander, salt, cayenne, turmeric and pepper; stir for 1 minute.

2 Stir in carrots, red pepper, beans and stock; cover and bring to boil. Reduce heat and simmer for 25 to 30 minutes or until liquid is absorbed. Let stand for 5 minutes. Stir in pumpkin seeds.

Makes 12 servings
Per serving: about 190 cal, 8 g pro, 5 g total fat (1 g sat. fat), 30 g carb, 4 g fibre, 0 mg chol. % RDI: 3% calcium, 14% iron, 34% vit A, 28% vit C, 26% folate.

Confetti Rice Pilaf

Extra steps and extra flavours are the distinguishing hallmarks of a pilaf. Whereas steamed or boiled rice is served plain, a pilaf is characterized by first cooking the seasonings, such as onions, shallots and garlic, in oil or butter. The rice is then stirred in until coated. Other ingredients and stock are then added to the pot and cooked along with the rice until it is fluffy and tender. Our pilaf contains colourful peas, corn and red pepper befitting the name confetti.

1 tbsp	butter	15 mL
1	onion, chopped	1
1	sweet red pepper, diced	1
2	cloves garlic, minced	2
1 cup	parboiled long-grain rice	250 mL
1½ cups	vegetable or chicken stock	375 mL
¼ tsp	each salt and pepper	1 mL
½ cup	frozen peas	125 mL
½ cup	frozen corn kernels	125 mL

1 In heavy saucepan, melt butter over medium heat; cook onion, red pepper and garlic, stirring occasionally, for about 5 minutes or until softened.

2 Stir in rice to coat. Add stock, salt and pepper; bring to boil. Cover, reduce heat and simmer for 15 minutes or until rice is tender and liquid is absorbed.

3 Stir in peas and corn with fork until evenly distributed. Remove from heat. Let stand, covered, for about 5 minutes or until vegetables are hot.

Makes 4 servings
Per serving: about 252 cal, 6 g pro, 4 g total fat (2 g sat. fat), 49 g carb, 3 g fibre, 8 mg chol. % RDI: 4% calcium, 6% iron, 15% vit A, 88% vit C, 13% folate.

Garlicky Mushrooms on Grilled Polenta

Definitions of polenta can be maddeningly elusive. It does no justice to merely explain that it's cooked cornmeal. But how does one identify a dish that can be creamy and fluid as well as dense and firm, that can be prepared quickly or leisurely simmered, that can be hearty and bold yet also delicate and sophisticated? Our elegant appetizer leans toward the richer end of the entertaining scale, but grilling the triangles and topping with a drizzle of emerald green olive oil and a generous sprinkle of fresh herbs is enticingly earthy and easy as well.

Ingredients

2 cups	chicken stock	500 mL
Pinch	pepper	Pinch
1 cup	cornmeal	250 mL
2 tsp	extra-virgin olive oil	10 mL
⅓ cup	freshly grated Parmesan cheese	75 mL
2 tbsp	chopped fresh parsley	25 mL

Garlic Mushroom Topping:

¼ oz	dried porcini mushrooms	7 g
3 tbsp	extra-virgin olive oil	50 mL
5	cloves garlic, minced	5
1½ lb	mixed exotic mushrooms (crimini, oyster, shiitake, portobello), sliced	750 g
1 tsp	each dried rosemary and sage, crumbled	5 mL
½ tsp	salt	2 mL
¼ tsp	pepper	1 mL
1 cup	chicken stock	250 mL
4 tsp	cornstarch	20 mL
¼ cup	Madeira or dry vermouth	50 mL
1 tsp	lemon juice	5 mL

Makes 6 servings

Per serving: about 248 cal, 9 g pro, 11 g total fat (2 g sat. fat), 27 g carb, 3 g fibre, 4 mg chol. % RDI: 9% calcium, 16% iron, 3% vit A, 8% vit C, 13% folate.

Variation

Cheesy Polenta Appetizer: Omit Garlic Mushroom Topping. Reduce cooking time to 8 to 10 minutes. Stir in 4 oz (125 g) Gorgonzola cheese, crumbled, and ⅓ cup (75 mL) freshly grated Parmesan cheese. Spoon into 6 shallow dishes. Sprinkle each with 1 tsp (5 mL) extra-virgin olive oil then chopped fresh basil.

Tip

Polenta is available in fine, medium or coarse meal. If the grind is not specified, it's most likely medium. Use a sturdy spoon for stirring the thick meal.

1 In large saucepan, bring stock, 2 cups (500 mL) water and pepper to boil over high heat; gradually whisk in cornmeal until thickened.

2 Reduce heat to low; cook, stirring often with wooden spoon, for 10 to 15 minutes or until hard to stir and grains are soft.

3 With rubber spatula, scrape into 11- x 7-inch (2 L) baking dish, spreading evenly. Refrigerate, uncovered, for at least 1 hour or until firm or for up to 24 hours.

4 **Garlic Mushroom Topping:** In small bowl, pour 1 cup (250 mL) boiling water over dried porcini mushrooms. Let stand for 15 minutes or until softened. Drain, reserving liquid; slice mushrooms. In large saucepan, heat oil over medium heat; cook garlic, stirring often, for about 3 minutes or until starting to brown.

5 Add fresh and rehydrated mushrooms, rosemary, sage, salt and pepper; cook over medium-high heat for 10 minutes or until starting to brown. Whisk stock with cornstarch; stir into pan along with mushroom liquid and Madeira. Bring to boil; cook, stirring, for 2 minutes or until thickened. Stir in lemon juice.

6 Meanwhile, cut polenta into triangles; brush with oil. Place on greased grill over medium-high heat; cook, turning once, for 8 minutes. (Or microwave at Medium-High/75% for 4 minutes.) Place on plates; spoon topping onto polenta. Sprinkle with cheese and parsley.

Warm Beet Salad over Couscous

Finally grains have risen again to culinary glory. Long a staple in cultures around the world, grains spent many years relegated to the gastronomic sidelines, dismissed as peasant food or, worse, roughage. But no more. The number of grains available is huge, but they are much more alike than unalike, both in cooking and nutrition. We've chosen rice and barley to illustrate the point, cloaking their tastiness in a wintry warm salad of beets, spinach and pancetta. Couscous, while not technically a grain, behaves like one.

Ingredients

4	beets (unpeeled), trimmed	4
2 cups	shredded spinach	500 mL
4	slices pancetta or bacon, chopped	4
1	clove garlic, minced	1
2 tbsp	each lemon juice and balsamic vinegar	25 mL
2 tsp	grainy mustard	10 mL
Pinch	each salt and pepper	Pinch
⅓ cup	extra-virgin olive oil	75 mL

Couscous or Barley or Rice:

1½ cups	chicken stock or water	375 mL
1¼ cups	couscous	300 mL
	OR	
2½ cups	chicken stock	625 mL
1¼ cups	pearl or pot barley	300 mL
	OR	
2⅔ cups	chicken stock	650 mL
1⅓ cups	white, brown or long-grain rice	325 mL

Makes 4 servings

Per serving (with couscous): about 467 cal, 13 g pro, 22 g total fat (4 g sat. fat), 54 g carb, 4 g fibre, 5 mg chol. % RDI: 6% calcium, 18% iron, 22% vit A, 10% vit C, 50% folate.

Tip

Roast enough beets to make this salad and a side dish for the next dinner.

1 Wrap beets in foil. Roast in 425°F (220°C) oven for about 45 minutes or until fork-tender. Let cool enough to handle; peel and cut into cubes. *(Beets can be covered and refrigerated for up to 48 hours.)*

2 **Couscous:** In saucepan, bring stock to boil; add couscous. Add spinach. Remove from heat; cover and let stand for 5 minutes. Fluff with fork.

3 **Or Barley:** In saucepan, bring stock to boil; stir in barley. Cover, reduce heat to low and cook for 35 minutes. Add spinach; cook, covered, for about 5 minutes or until barley is tender and liquid is absorbed.

4 **Or Rice:** In saucepan, bring stock to boil; add rice. Cover, reduce heat to low and cook white rice for 15 minutes or brown rice for 35 minutes. Add spinach; cook, covered, for 5 minutes or until rice is tender and liquid is absorbed.

5 In skillet, cook pancetta over medium heat, stirring, for about 5 minutes or until crisp. Spoon off fat. Add garlic; cook, stirring, for 2 minutes. Add lemon juice, vinegar, mustard, salt and pepper; gradually whisk in oil until thickened and emulsified. Add beets; cook for 2 minutes or until glazed and hot.

6 Place couscous mixture in large serving bowl. Top with beet mixture, scraping all dressing from pan. To serve, toss to combine.

Breads, Rolls, Muffins

A renowned bread baker and author once counselled me that all you have to do is love your bread and it will love you back. I've since marvelled at the wisdom of that advice. Baking bread is not one of those activities that you squeeze in between doing the laundry and organizing the garage, giving the relationship short shrift and hardly a knowing embrace. Instead it's about involving all your senses and getting intimately acquainted with the sensual feel of dough. It's about recognizing the luxurious silkiness that characterizes the dough when it has been sufficiently kneaded. It's about getting to know the right temperature of liquid to jump-start the yeast and what a dough looks like when it has risen long enough. It can even be (according to some bread experts) about what to listen for to indicate a perfectly baked loaf. What it's not about is hard work.

These recipes – from a basic white loaf and traditional braided challah to luscious and gooey cinnamon buns and a festive stollen – will guide you through the steps and give you the skills to make fabulous bread any time of the year.
All you need to supply is the love.

Really Good Basic Bread

When mastering any craft, one has to start at the beginning and build from there. Making excellent bread starts with the foundation of making an excellent plain white loaf and learning all about the cadences of yeast, the vicissitudes of temperature (both inside the oven and out) and the properties of flour. Your tutorial guarantees that every foray into bread making will be a delicious success.

Ingredients

1 tsp	granulated sugar	5 mL
1 cup	warm water	250 mL
1	pkg active dry yeast (or 1 tbsp/15 mL)	1
1 cup	milk	250 mL
2 tbsp	granulated sugar	25 mL
2 tbsp	butter	25 mL
1 tsp	salt	5 mL
5 cups	all-purpose flour (approx)	1.25 L
1	egg yolk	1
1 tbsp	water	15 mL

Makes 2 loaves, 12 slices each

*Per slice: about 117 cal, 3 g pro, 2 g total fat
(1 g sat. fat), 22 g carb, 1 g fibre, 13 mg chol.
% RDI: 2% calcium, 8% iron, 2% vit A,
18% folate.*

Variations

Parker House Buns: Divide dough in half. On lightly floured surface, roll each half into 15- x 8-inch (38 x 20 cm) rectangle. Using 2½ inch (6 cm) round cookie cutter, cut out circles. Brush tops with a little melted butter. Using dull edge of knife, press crease across centre of each round; fold rounds over to form semicircles. Place 2 inches (5 cm) apart on greased baking sheets. Cover, let rise and bake as directed.

Bread Machine Basic Bread: In order, place in pan: ½ cup (125 mL) each water and milk, 1 tbsp (15 mL) each granulated sugar and cubed butter, ½ tsp (2 mL) salt, 3 cups (750 mL) all-purpose flour and 1¼ tsp (6 mL) quick-rising active dry yeast. (Do not let yeast touch liquids.) Choose basic setting or regular/light. Let baked loaf cool on rack.

1 In small bowl, dissolve 1 tsp (5 mL) sugar in water. Sprinkle in yeast; let stand for 10 minutes or until frothy. Meanwhile, in saucepan, heat milk, 2 tbsp (25 mL) sugar, butter and salt over low heat until butter is melted; let cool to lukewarm. In large bowl, combine yeast and milk mixtures.

2 With electric mixer, gradually beat in 3 cups (750 mL) flour until smooth, about 3 minutes. With wooden spoon, stir in enough of the remaining flour to form stiff dough. Turn out onto floured surface. With floured hands, begin kneading by folding dough in half toward you.

3 Beginning at side opposite fold, lean into dough with heels of palms, pressing down and pushing dough away. Turn dough a quarter turn to right. Sprinkle work surface with more flour as needed. Repeat folding, pressing and turning dough for 10 minutes or until smooth and elastic.

4 Place in greased bowl, turning to grease all over. Cover with plastic wrap; let rise in warm draft-free place until doubled in bulk, 1 to 1½ hours. Punch down; turn out onto floured surface. Knead into ball. Cover with tea towel; let rest for 10 minutes.

5 Divide in half; knead each portion into ball. Gently pull into 11- x 8-inch (28 x 20 cm) rectangle. Starting at narrow end, roll into cylinder; pinch along seam to seal. Fit, seam side down, into 2 greased 8- x 4-inch (1.5 L) loaf pans. Cover and let rise until doubled in bulk, about 1 hour.

6 Whisk egg yolk with water; brush over loaves. Bake in 400°F (200°C) oven for about 30 minutes or until loaves are golden brown and bottoms sound hollow when tapped. Remove from pans; let cool on racks.

Crunchy Farmhouse Bread

As you familiarize yourself with bread making, it will get easier and easier to incorporate different textures and flours into your repertoire. Whether it's by textbook or by trial and error, you will soon learn the effect different flours and grains have on yeast, leavening and density. Try this bread for a tasty introduction to the varied world of crunchy multigrain loaves.

½ tsp	granulated sugar	2 mL
1 cup	warm water	250 mL
2 tsp	active dry yeast	10 mL
2 tbsp	liquid honey	25 mL
2 tbsp	butter, melted	25 mL
1	egg, beaten	1
2½ cups	all-purpose flour (approx)	625 mL
¾ cup	whole wheat flour	175 mL
¼ cup	quick-cooking rolled oats	50 mL
¼ cup	each cornmeal and natural bran	50 mL
¼ cup	millet or sesame seeds	50 mL
1 tsp	salt	5 mL

1 In large bowl, dissolve sugar in water. Sprinkle in yeast; let stand for 10 minutes or until frothy. Whisk in honey, butter and egg. With wooden spoon, stir in 2 cups (500 mL) of the all-purpose flour, whole wheat flour, oats, cornmeal, bran, millet and salt until smooth. Gradually stir in enough of the remaining flour to form slightly sticky dough.

2 Turn out dough onto lightly floured surface; knead for 8 to 10 minutes or until smooth and elastic, dusting with as much of the remaining flour as necessary to prevent sticking. Place in greased bowl, turning to grease all over. Cover with plastic wrap; let rise in warm draft-free place until doubled in bulk, about 1½ hours.

3 Punch down dough; turn out onto lightly floured surface. Knead into round loaf, stretching dough down all around and pinching underneath to shape. Dust top with flour; place on greased baking sheet. Cover with tea towel; let rise until doubled in bulk, 45 to 60 minutes.

4 Using serrated knife, slash shallow grid pattern on top of loaf. Bake in 375°F (190°C) oven for 45 minutes or until golden brown and loaf sounds hollow when tapped on bottom. Remove from pan; let cool on rack.

Makes 1 loaf, 24 slices

Per slice: about 113 cal, 3 g pro, 2 g total fat (1 g sat. fat), 21 g carb, 2 g fibre, 12 mg chol. % RDI: 1% calcium, 8% iron, 1% vit A, 10% folate.

Variation

Bread Machine Crunchy Farmhouse Bread: Choose whole grain setting. Let baked loaf cool on rack.

Buttermilk Loaf

Buttermilk, a low-fat milk despite its moniker, imparts a tangy flavour that complements the nuttiness of the whole wheat flour in this loaf. Buttermilk loaves traditionally sport a fine, even texture, making the bread ideal for sandwiches.

1⅓ cups	buttermilk	325 mL
2 tbsp	butter	25 mL
1 tbsp	liquid honey	15 mL
1	egg, beaten	1
2¼ cups	all-purpose flour (approx)	550 mL
1½ cups	whole wheat flour	375 mL
1¼ tsp	rapid or quick-rising instant yeast	6 mL
¾ tsp	salt	4 mL
2 tsp	milk	10 mL

1 In saucepan, heat buttermilk, butter and honey until butter starts to melt; let cool for 5 minutes. Whisk in egg.

2 In large bowl, stir together 1¾ cups (425 mL) of the all-purpose flour, whole wheat flour, yeast and salt. With wooden spoon, stir in buttermilk mixture until smooth. Gradually stir in enough of the remaining flour to form slightly sticky dough.

3 Turn out dough onto lightly floured surface; knead for 8 to 10 minutes or until smooth and elastic, dusting with as much of the remaining flour as necessary to prevent sticking. Place in greased bowl, turning to grease all over. Cover with plastic wrap; let rise in warm draft-free place until doubled in bulk, 1 to 1½ hours.

4 Punch down dough; turn out onto floured surface. Press into 10- x 9-inch (25 x 23 cm) rectangle. Starting at narrow end, roll up into cylinder; pinch along bottom to smooth and seal. Fit, seam side down, into greased 9- x 5-inch (2 L) loaf pan. Cover with towel; let rise until ½ inch (1 cm) above pan, 1 to 1½ hours.

5 Brush top of loaf with milk. Bake in 350°F (180°C) oven for 45 to 55 minutes or until golden brown and loaf sounds hollow when tapped on bottom. Remove from pan; let cool on rack.

Makes 1 loaf, 12 slices
Per slice: about 177 cal, 6 g pro, 3 g total fat
(2 g sat. fat), 32 g carb, 3 g fibre, 24 mg chol.
% RDI: 4% calcium, 12% iron, 3% vit A, 10% folate.

Variation

Bread Machine Buttermilk Loaf:
Omit milk. Choose basic setting. Let baked loaf cool on rack. (If using bread flour, loaf rises very high and may touch lid. To avoid this, measure volume of machine pan. If less than 14 cups/3.5 L, omit egg and reduce white flour to 2 cups/500 mL.)

Old-Fashioned Mashed Potato Rolls

Because this recipe uses quick-rising (instant) yeast, the first rise is only 10 minutes instead of the usual 60. In fact, these buns are quick enough to make for dinner without a lot of advance planning. The caveat to that, of course, is to have the foresight to make enough mashed potatoes the night before to ensure leftovers!

1¼ cups	milk	300 mL
½ cup	mashed potatoes	125 mL
½ cup	shortening	125 mL
4½ cups	all-purpose or white bread flour (approx)	1.125 L
¼ cup	granulated sugar	50 mL
2 tsp	quick-rising (instant) dry yeast	10 mL
1½ tsp	salt	7 mL
1	egg, lightly beaten	1
2 tbsp	butter, melted (optional)	25 mL

1 In small saucepan, heat together milk, potatoes and shortening, stirring occasionally, until 120°F (50°C).

2 Meanwhile, in large bowl, stir together 3½ cups (875 mL) of the flour, sugar, yeast and salt; stir in milk mixture and egg. With wooden spoon, gradually stir in enough of the remaining flour to form soft dough, mixing with hands if necessary. Turn out onto lightly floured surface; knead for 8 to 10 minutes or

until smooth and elastic. Cover with tea towel; let rest for 10 minutes.

3 Lightly grease 24 large muffin cups. Cut dough into 8 pieces; cut each into 9 to make 72 pieces. Using hands, press and pinch each into ball. Arrange 3 balls in cloverleaf pattern in each cup. Cover with tea towels; let rise in warm draft-free place until doubled in bulk, 30 to 60 minutes.

4 Brush with butter (if using). Bake in 400°F (200°C) oven for 10 to 12 minutes or until golden brown. Serve warm. (*Rolls can be individually wrapped in plastic wrap and frozen in airtight container for up to 3 weeks.*)

Makes 24 rolls
Per roll: about 144 cal, 3 g pro, 5 g total fat
(1 g sat. fat), 22 g carb, 1 g fibre, 10 mg chol.
% RDI: 2% calcium, 7% iron, 1% vit A, 7% folate.

Variation

Bread Machine Old-Fashioned Potato Rolls (for dough only):
If desired, substitute bread machine yeast for quick-rising (instant) dry yeast. Use 4½ cups (1.125 L) all-purpose flour. In order, place in pan: mashed potatoes, milk, egg, shortening, sugar, salt, all of the flour and yeast. (Do not let yeast touch liquids.) Choose dough setting. Remove from machine; shape and bake as directed.

All About Yeast

- Active dry yeast can be a tricky wonder. If the water is too cold, the yeast won't froth and increase as expected. If it is too hot, the yeast will surely die on the spot. A little hotter than warm is the perfect temperature, generally about 110°F (43°C). If the yeast does not froth or swell within the first five minutes, start again with newly purchased yeast that is within the "best before" date.
- Stirring a small amount of sugar into the warm water helps yeast grow. Salt inhibits rising, so avoid adding any to the water. Fat also slows yeast growth, which is why rich doughs such as brioche take longer to double in volume.
- Quick-rising (instant) yeast is a more active strain of yeast that makes dough rise up to 50 per cent faster than active dry yeast. Its

particle size is finer than that of regular dry yeast, so it dissolves more readily and feeds quicker on the sugars in the dry ingredient mixture with which it is generally combined. The temperature of the liquid added is higher or hotter than for active dry yeast, 120° to 130°F (50° to 55°C).
- Bread machine yeast is a finely granulated, highly active dry yeast that is activated quickly to accommodate the reduced times often associated with bread machines.
- Cubes of fresh yeast are also available in the refrigerator section of some supermarkets. They need to be dissolved in a small amount of warm sweetened water.
- Always store yeast in the refrigerator and use before the "best before" date to ensure success.

Tip

If you prefer larger rolls, cut the dough into only 54 pieces to make 18 rolls.

Challah

Challah – a braided egg-rich bread – is traditionally served at the Jewish Sabbath meal on Friday nights. After the ceremonial candles are lit, a prayer is said over the bread, which is then sliced or pulled apart so that everyone can enjoy a piece. The bread resonates with even deeper meaning at the Jewish New Year, when it is traditionally sweetened not only with honey but also with raisins and shaped into a crown to usher in what is hoped will be a resoundingly sweet year.

Ingredients

2 tsp	granulated sugar	10 mL
½ cup	warm water	125 mL
1	pkg active dry yeast (or 1 tbsp/15 mL)	1
3½ cups	all-purpose flour (approx)	875 mL
1 tsp	salt	5 mL
¼ cup	liquid honey	50 mL
2	eggs, lightly beaten	2
2	egg yolks	2
¼ cup	butter, melted (or vegetable oil)	50 mL
¾ cup	golden raisins	175 mL

Topping:

1	egg yolk, lightly beaten	1
1 tbsp	sesame seeds	15 mL

Makes 1 loaf, 16 slices

Per slice: about 191 cal, 5 g pro, 5 g total fat (2 g sat. fat), 32 g carb, 2 g fibre, 76 mg chol. % RDI: 2% calcium, 11% iron, 6% vit A, 13% folate.

Variation

Bread Machine Challah (for dough only): Replace active dry yeast with 2½ tsp (12 mL) quick-rising (instant) dry yeast. In order, place in pan: water, honey, sugar, butter, eggs, egg yolks, salt, flour and yeast. (Do not let yeast touch liquids.) Choose dough setting. Remove from pan; knead in raisins, if desired. Let rest for 5 minutes. Proceed with Step 3 or 4.

1 In small bowl, dissolve sugar in water. Sprinkle in yeast; let stand for 10 minutes or until frothy. In large bowl, stir 3 cups (750 mL) flour with salt. With wooden spoon, stir in yeast mixture, honey, eggs, egg yolks and butter. Turn out onto floured surface; knead for 10 minutes or until smooth and elastic, dusting with enough of the remaining flour to prevent sticking.

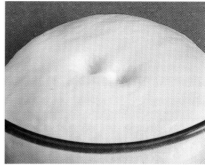

2 Place dough in large greased bowl, turning to grease all over. Cover with plastic wrap; let rise in warm draft-free place until doubled in bulk and indentation remains when dough is poked with 2 fingers, about 1 hour. Punch down dough; knead in raisins. Let rest for 5 minutes.

3 **To make crown:** Roll into 30-inch (76 cm) long rope. Holding 1 end in place, wind remaining rope around end to form fairly tight spiral that is slightly higher in centre. Transfer to lightly greased baking sheet.

4 **To make braid:** Divide into quarters; roll into 18-inch (45 cm) long ropes. Place side by side on greased baking sheet; pinch 1 end together. At pinched end, move second rope from left over rope on right. Move far right rope over 2 ropes on left.

5 Move far left rope over 2 ropes on right. Repeat until braid is complete; tuck ends under braid. Cover crown loaf or braid loaf loosely with plastic wrap. Let rise in warm draft-free place until doubled in bulk, about 1 hour.

6 **Topping:** Stir egg yolk with 1 tsp (5 mL) water; brush over loaf. Sprinkle with sesame seeds. Bake in 350°F (180°C) oven for 35 to 45 minutes or until golden brown and loaf sounds hollow when tapped on bottom. Let cool on rack.

Montreal-Style Bagels

There are so many different kinds of bagels available these days that it's hard to get two people to agree on what constitutes the best-tasting or best-textured bagel. Indeed, contests have been run for people to determine which is the very best bagel in their city. These bagels salute the city of Montreal, where the custom of immersing them in a sweetened poaching liquid results in a slightly chewy, slightly sweet, dense bagel for which its citizens have an undying fondness, often imploring friends to send them dozens once they've moved to other locales.

Ingredients

1 tsp	granulated sugar	5 mL
1 cup	warm water	250 mL
1	pkg active dry yeast	1
	(or 1 tbsp/15 mL)	
2	eggs	2
1 tbsp	vegetable oil	15 mL
3½ cups	all-purpose flour	875 mL
	(approx)	
2 tbsp	granulated sugar	25 mL
2 tsp	salt	10 mL

Poaching Liquid:

16 cups	water	4 L
2 tbsp	granulated sugar	25 mL

Glaze:

½ cup	sesame or poppy seeds	125 mL
1	egg, beaten	1

Makes 12 bagels

*Per bagel: about 209 cal, 7 g pro, 6 g total fat
(1 g sat. fat), 31 g carb, 1 g fibre, 54 mg chol.
% RDI: 2% calcium, 16% iron, 2% vit A,
32% folate.*

Variation

Whole Wheat Cinnamon Raisin
Bagels: In dough, substitute 1 cup
(250 mL) whole wheat flour for 1 cup
(250 mL) of the all-purpose flour.
Increase 2 tbsp (25 mL) sugar to ¼ cup
(50 mL). Stir in 2 tsp (10 mL) cinnamon
along with eggs. After punching down
dough, thoroughly knead in 1 cup
(250 mL) raisins. Omit sesame seeds.

Tips

**Unless the ends of the dough are
pinched together very firmly, they
will come apart in the water.**

**The bagels can be wrapped well and
frozen for up to 2 weeks.**

1 In large bowl, dissolve 1 tsp (5 mL)
sugar in water. Sprinkle in yeast; let
stand for 10 minutes or until frothy. Whisk
in eggs and oil. With wooden spoon, beat in
2 cups (500 mL) of the flour, sugar and salt
until smooth. Gradually stir in enough of
the remaining flour to make soft but not
sticky dough.

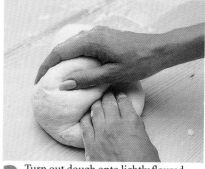

2 Turn out dough onto lightly floured
surface; knead for 8 to 10 minutes or
until smooth and elastic, dusting with
enough of the remaining flour to prevent
sticking. Place in greased bowl, turning to
grease all over. Cover with plastic wrap; let
rise in warm draft-free place until doubled in
bulk, 1 to 1½ hours.

3 Punch down dough; turn out onto
lightly floured surface. Knead several
times. Divide into 12 portions; roll each into
12-inch (30 cm) rope, covering pieces with
tea towel as you work.

4 Bring ends of each rope together, overlapping by about 1 inch (2.5 cm) and
stretching overlap around other end to meet
underneath; pinch firmly to seal. Place on
lightly floured baking sheet; cover with tea
towel and let rise for 15 minutes.

5 **Poaching Liquid:** In wide saucepan,
bring water to boil; add sugar. Slip
bagels into water, 3 or 4 at a time; cook over
medium heat for 1 minute. Turn and cook
for 1 minute. Using slotted spatula, transfer
bagels to well-greased baking sheets.

6 **Glaze:** Place sesame seeds in dish. Brush
egg over bagels. Using hands, dip egg
side into seeds; return to baking sheets. Bake
in 400°F (200°C) oven for 20 to 25 minutes
or until tops are golden. Transfer to rack and
let cool.

Herbed Focaccia

Focaccia has become a member of our sandwich and bread lexicon. It's used as a stylish addition to the breadbasket, as a wrapper for a great vegetable sandwich or as a scooper for an antipasto spread. Recognizable by its dimpled topping intended to hold tantalizing puddles of olive oil and herbs, focaccia can also, with the addition of some sugar and cut-up grapes or dried fruit, become a delicious ending to a meal. Making a sponge before adding all the flour and flavourings encourages the yeast to develop and gives the bread a better texture.

Ingredients

1 tsp	granulated sugar	5 mL
1 cup	warm water	250 mL
1	pkg active dry yeast	1
	(or 1 tbsp/15 mL)	
2½ cups	all-purpose flour	625 mL
	(approx)	
2 tbsp	olive oil	25 mL
1 tsp	salt	5 mL
½ tsp	each dried sage, rosemary	2 mL
	and marjoram	
2 tbsp	cornmeal	25 mL

Topping:

3 tbsp	olive oil	50 mL
1	onion, thinly sliced	1
½ tsp	dried rosemary	2 mL

Makes 6 servings

*Per serving: about 314 cal, 6 g pro, 12 g total fat
(2 g sat. fat), 45 g carb, 2 g fibre, 0 mg chol. % RDI:
2% calcium, 18% iron, 2% vit C, 47% folate.*

Variations

Sweet Pepper and Thyme
Focaccia: Brush dough with 1 tbsp
(15 mL) olive oil. Scatter 1 small sweet
red pepper, thinly sliced, over top.
|Sprinkle with fresh thyme sprigs
(or ½ tsp/2 mL dried thyme). Bake
as directed.

Sea Salt Focaccia: Brush dough with
1 tbsp (15 mL) olive oil; sprinkle with
¼ tsp (1 mL) coarse sea salt, and pinch
coarsely ground pepper if desired.
Bake as directed.

1 In small bowl, dissolve sugar in
water. Sprinkle in yeast; let stand for
10 minutes or until frothy. In large bowl and
with electric mixer, combine yeast mixture
with 1 cup (250 mL) of the flour; beat for
2 minutes or until smooth. Cover lightly
with plastic wrap; let stand until doubled,
spongy and bubbly, about 30 minutes.

2 Stir in oil, salt, sage, rosemary,
marjoram and 1 cup (250 mL) of the
flour. Turn out onto lightly floured surface;
knead for 5 minutes, adding enough of the
remaining flour to make soft dough. Place
in greased bowl, turning to grease all over.
Cover with plastic wrap; let rise in warm
draft-free place until doubled in bulk,
about 1 hour.

3 Gently punch down dough; turn out
onto lightly floured surface. Divide in
half; cover with tea towel and let rest for
5 minutes.

4 Roll out each half into rough 8-inch
(20 cm) circle ½ inch (1 cm) thick, or
roll each half into 3 smaller circles. Sprinkle
cornmeal over baking sheet; place rounds
on top. Cover with tea towel; let rise until
doubled in height, about 30 minutes.

5 **Topping:** Meanwhile, in small skillet,
heat oil over medium-low heat; cook
onion and rosemary, stirring occasionally,
for 7 to 10 minutes or until softened and
golden. Let cool.

6 Press fingers into dough almost to
bottom to give dimpled effect. Top with
onion mixture. Bake in 400°F (200°C) oven
for about 20 minutes or until golden and
hollow sounding when tapped on bottom.
Let cool on rack.

Perfect Pizzas

There are no rules for pizza toppings except to combine your favourite sauce with your favourite vegetables and meats. Pizza Bianca, for example, has no tomato sauce at all, just a drizzle of olive oil, some onions and herbs. If you like, you can even substitute whole wheat flour for some of the all-purpose flour. Let creativity, a hearty appetite and the season be your organizing principles and you'll be sure to end up with a beautiful and delicious repast. Sprinkling cornmeal on the pan prevents the dough from sticking and adds texture to the crust.

3	zucchini	3
	Vegetable oil	
2	sweet peppers	2
	Cornmeal	
3 cups	shredded mozzarella cheese	750 mL
8	black olives, halved	8
½ cup	shredded fresh basil	125 mL

Tomato Sauce:

2 tbsp	olive oil	25 mL
1	onion, minced	1
2	cloves garlic, minced	2
3½ cups	chopped tomatoes	875 mL
3 tbsp	tomato paste	50 mL
1 tbsp	chopped fresh basil	15 mL
½ tsp	granulated sugar	2 mL
¼ tsp	each salt and pepper	1 mL
Pinch	hot pepper flakes	Pinch

Pizza Dough:

2 tsp	granulated sugar	10 mL
1 cup	warm water	250 mL
1	pkg active dry yeast (or 1 tbsp/15 mL)	1
2¼ cups	unbleached all-purpose flour (approx)	550 mL
¼ cup	cornmeal or rye flour	50 mL
1 tbsp	olive oil	15 mL
1 tsp	salt	5 mL

1 Tomato Sauce: In large skillet, heat oil over medium heat; cook onion and garlic, stirring occasionally, for 3 to 5 minutes or until softened. Add tomatoes, tomato paste, basil, sugar, salt, pepper and hot pepper flakes; bring to boil. Reduce heat to medium-low; simmer, stirring occasionally, for 30 to 35 minutes or until reduced to 2½ cups (625 mL). (*Sauce can be refrigerated in airtight container for up to 3 days or frozen for up to 3 months.*)

2 Pizza Dough: In large bowl (or 2-cup/ 500 mL measure if using food processor), dissolve sugar in water. Sprinkle in yeast; let stand for 10 minutes or until frothy. With electric mixer, gradually beat in 1 cup (250 mL) of the flour, cornmeal, oil and salt until smooth, about 3 minutes. Mix in enough of the remaining flour to make slightly stiff dough.

3 Turn out dough onto lightly floured surface; knead for about 10 minutes or until smooth and elastic, adding more flour if very sticky. Form into ball. (Or, in food processor, blend all of the flour, cornmeal, oil and salt. With machine running, gradually add yeast mixture; process until in ball. Process for 45 to 60 seconds or until soft. Knead on floured surface 8 times; form into ball.)

4 Place in greased bowl, turning to grease all over. Cover with plastic wrap; let rise in warm draft-free place until doubled in bulk, 1 to 1½ hours. Punch down dough and halve. Cut zucchini diagonally into ¼-inch (5 mm) thick slices; lightly brush with oil. Grill or broil for 4 to 7 minutes or until tender. Slice peppers into rings.

5 For each pizza, roll out half of the dough on lightly floured surface into 13-inch (33 cm) circle. Dust 12-inch (30 cm) pizza pan with cornmeal; place dough on pan. Using fingertips, fold excess dough under, pressing to form slightly raised border. Lightly brush dough with oil.

6 Sprinkle one-quarter of the cheese over dough; spread with half of the sauce. Sprinkle with one-quarter of the cheese; top with half of the zucchini, peppers and olives. Bake on lowest rack of 500°F (260°C) oven for 10 to 12 minutes or until crust is golden. Sprinkle with half of the basil. Repeat for second pizza.

Makes 2 pizzas, enough for 4 to 6 servings
Per each of 6 servings: about 538 cal, 21 g pro, 24 g total fat (10 g sat. fat), 62 g carb, 7 g fibre, 51 mg chol. % RDI: 35% calcium, 29% iron, 55% vit A, 217% vit C, 70% folate.

Tips

After punching down dough, you can refrigerate it for up to 2 days or freeze in greased plastic bag for up to 2 months, then thaw in refrigerator for 8 hours.

For fresh tomatoes, you can substitute 1 can (28 oz/796 mL) tomatoes (undrained), crushed, and 1 tbsp (15 mL) extra tomato paste.

For a crispy crust, place inverted baking sheet on bottom rack of oven while it's preheating, then place pizza pan right on top.

Provençale Olive Fougasse

Fougasse hails from Provence in the south of France, where it is typically enjoyed alfresco with a glass of wine or a plate of hors d'oeuvres. Satisfyingly chewy, the ladder- or tree-shaped bread is handsomely studded with either olives, fresh herbs and cheese or anchovies.

¼ tsp	granulated sugar	1 mL
1¼ cups	warm water	300 mL
2½ tsp	active dry yeast	12 mL
3 tbsp	extra-virgin olive oil	50 mL
3¼ cups	all-purpose flour (approx)	800 mL
¾ tsp	salt	4 mL
½ cup	chopped pitted black olives	125 mL
2 tbsp	milk	25 mL

1 In large bowl, dissolve sugar in water. Sprinkle in yeast; let stand for 10 minutes or until frothy. Stir in oil. Stir in 3 cups (750 mL) of the flour and salt to form moist dough.

2 Turn out dough onto lightly floured surface. Knead for about 8 minutes or until smooth and elastic yet still slightly moist, dusting with as much of the remaining flour as necessary to prevent sticking. Cover with tea towel; let rest for 5 minutes.

3 Flatten dough into disc; sprinkle with olives. Fold dough over; knead for 3 minutes or until olives are evenly distributed. Form into ball. Place in greased bowl, turning to grease all over. Cover with plastic wrap; let rise in warm draft-free place until doubled in bulk, about 45 minutes.

4 Punch down dough; turn out onto lightly floured surface. Stretch into 12- x 8-inch (30 x 20 cm) rectangle. Leaving 1-inch (2.5 cm) border all around, cut centre of rectangle completely through to work surface into 2 rows of 4 diagonal slashes each. Cut 1-inch (2.5 cm) notches into edge of dough between slashes. Gently lift onto greased 17- x 11-inch (45 x 28 cm) baking sheet. Pull slashes open by at least 1 inch (2.5 cm). Cover and let rise in warm draft-free place for 20 minutes.

5 Brush with milk. Bake in 450°F (230°C) oven for about 20 minutes or until golden and bread sounds hollow when tapped on bottom. Let cool on rack.

Makes 1 loaf, 10 servings

Per serving: about 195 cal, 5 g pro, 5 g total fat (1 g sat. fat), 32 g carb, 2 g fibre, 0 mg chol. % RDI: 1% calcium, 14% iron, 32% folate.

Bread Machine Basics

- Read your manual carefully. Every bread machine is different. Make sure you select the appropriate setting or cycle on your machine.
- Add the ingredients to the pan in the order recommended in your manual. Generally, this will be wet ingredients first (such as water, milk, butter, eggs, oil, honey or yogurt), followed by sugar and salt. The next addition is flour, with the yeast being sprinkled on last to avoid any contact either with the liquids or with the salt.
- Situate your machine away from the counter edge. Occasionally, a machine will move during the knead cycle.
- Do not open the machine once the proof cycle has begun.
- If a baked loaf sticks to the pan, rap a top corner of the pan against the countertop to loosen the bread or run a plastic spatula around the edge to ease the loaf out. Do not use a paring knife; this may damage the pan's nonstick coating.
- If the blade sticks to the pan after the loaf has been removed, soak it in warm water for 15 minutes and then remove. If the crust of

your bread is too dark, change your bread machine setting to sweet bread.

Many recipes for conventionally made breads can be adapted for bread machine use, as long as you follow a few basic principles outlined below:

- Using the manufacturer's manual, determine the amount of flour that can be used in your bread machine. Do not exceed this amount or you may damage the machine.
- For best results, have all of your ingredients at room temperature.
- For each 1 cup (250 mL) of flour, you will need approximately ⅓ cup (75 mL) liquid, at least 1 tsp (5 mL) sugar, honey or other sweetener, ¼ tsp (1 mL) salt and ½ tsp (2 mL) bread machine or quick-rising (instant) dry yeast. Do not be tempted to leave out either the sweetener or the salt; both are essential for successful yeast development.
- If fat is called for in a recipe, calculate at least 1 tsp (5 mL) for each 1 cup (250 mL) of flour.
- Remove the bread pan from the bread machine before starting to add any ingredients. Always add ingredients to the pan in the order suggested.

- Peek into the pan as the machine starts to knead the ingredients. If the dough is too firm and dry or the machine sounds as though it is straining, add a few drops of liquid to soften the dough; conversely, if the dough appears too sticky, add only enough flour to make it smooth.
- Bread flours specially formulated for use in bread machines come in rye, multigrain, whole wheat, white, 60% whole wheat and unbleached. These flours have a higher protein count than regular flours, which results in higher, airier, softer loaves.
- You can substitute equal amounts of bread flour for standard flours of the same grain. However, be warned that this sometimes creates breads that rise higher and causes them to stick to the lid.
- There is a dry yeast specially formulated for use in bread machines; however, it can be used interchangeably with active dry, quick-rising or any other instant yeast.

Cinnamon Buns

These cinnamon buns are just about as close to the perfect bun as you can get: a feather-light, soft and buttery dough, a gooey caramelized coating of sweet brown sugar and fragrant cinnamon and a satisfying bite of crunchy pecans. Make the super-easy dough the night before and as it comes to room temperature in the morning before being rolled out, prepare the filling.

Ingredients

¼ cup	granulated sugar	50 mL
½ cup	warm water	125 mL
1	pkg active dry yeast	1
	(or 1 tbsp/15 mL)	
½ cup	milk	125 mL
¼ cup	butter	50 mL
1 tsp	salt	5 mL
2	eggs, beaten	2
4 cups	all-purpose flour (approx)	1 L

Filling:

1 cup	butter	250 mL
1½ cups	packed brown sugar	375 mL
1 cup	coarsely chopped pecans	250 mL
1 tbsp	cinnamon	15 mL

Makes 15 buns

Per bun: about 421 cal, 6 g pro, 22 g total fat (10 g sat. fat), 52 g carb, 2 g fibre, 71 mg chol. % RDI: 5% calcium, 17% iron, 16% vit A, 27% folate.

Variation

Chelsea Buns: Omit pecans. Sprinkle 1 cup (250 mL) raisins or currants over sugar-coated dough before rolling up.

Tips

Use a serrated knife to slice the roll of dough into pieces; this prevents it from being torn and squeezed out of shape.

Although it could be considered overkill, you can drizzle icing over the buns. Whisk together 1 cup (250 mL) unsifted icing sugar and 3 tbsp (50 mL) milk or water until smooth; drizzle over buns once they've cooled a bit (or else the icing will simply melt).

1 Dissolve 1 tsp (5 mL) of the sugar in warm water. Sprinkle in yeast; let stand for 10 minutes or until frothy. Meanwhile, in small saucepan, heat together milk, remaining sugar, butter and salt until butter is melted; let cool to lukewarm. In large bowl, combine eggs, milk mixture and yeast mixture.

3 Place in greased bowl, turning to grease all over. Cover with plastic wrap (or greased waxed paper and tea towel); let rise in warm draft-free place for 1 to 1½ hours (or in refrigerator for 8 hours) or until doubled in bulk and impression remains when fingertips are pressed into dough. Punch down dough.

5 On floured surface, roll dough to 18 x 14 inches (45 x 35 cm). Brush with all but 2 tbsp (25 mL) melted butter, leaving ½-inch (1 cm) border; sprinkle with sugar mixture. Starting at long side, roll up tightly. Brush with remaining butter. Cut into 15 pieces; place in pan. Cover and let rise until doubled in bulk, about 1 hour.

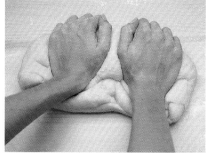

2 With mixer, gradually beat in 1½ cups (375 mL) flour for 2 minutes or until smooth. With wooden spoon, stir in enough of the remaining flour to make soft slightly sticky dough. Turn out onto floured surface; knead for about 10 minutes or until smooth and elastic, dusting with enough of the remaining flour to prevent sticking.

4 **Filling:** In saucepan over medium heat, melt ¾ cup (175 mL) of the butter with ¾ cup (175 mL) of the sugar; whisk until smooth. Pour into greased 13- x 9-inch (3 L) baking dish. Sprinkle with half of the pecans. Melt remaining butter. Combine remaining sugar, pecans and cinnamon.

6 Bake in 375°F (190°C) oven for 25 to 30 minutes or until crusts are golden and tops sound hollow when tapped. Let stand in pan for 3 minutes. Invert onto serving platter, scraping off any remaining filling in pan to drizzle over buns.

Panettone

Rich with egg yolks and unsalted butter, studded with the fruit of the season and fragrant with vanilla and citrus, panettone epitomizes the festiveness and generosity of Christmastime. Traditionally made in a special tubular mould, our version simplifies the ritual by using 2-lb (1 kg) coffee tins. The first and second risings are longer than that of a lighter bread because of the dough's density and weight.

Ingredients

¾ cup	golden raisins	175 mL
½ cup	candied mixed peel	125 mL
½ cup	candied citron	125 mL
8¾ cups	all-purpose flour (approx)	2.175 L
¾ cup	milk	175 mL
1 cup	granulated sugar	250 mL
2 tbsp	active dry yeast	25 mL
6	eggs	6
6	egg yolks	6
1 tbsp	each grated orange and lemon rind	15 mL
1 tbsp	vanilla	15 mL
1½ tsp	salt	7 mL
1½ cups	unsalted butter, softened	375 mL

Makes 2 loaves, 24 slices each

*Per slice: about 192 cal, 4 g pro, 7 g total fat
(4 g sat. fat), 27 g carb, 1 g fibre, 70 mg chol.
% RDI: 2% calcium, 9% iron, 8% vit A, 20% folate.*

Variations

Small Panettone: Use 10- to
28-oz (284 to 796 mL) cans. Make ball
of dough small enough to fill can just
under halfway. Let rise as in recipe; bake
for 30 to 40 minutes.

Chocolate Fig Panettone:
Omit peel, citron and lemon rind.
Reduce raisins to ½ cup (125 mL).
Add ¾ cup (175 mL) each chopped
dried figs and chocolate chips, and
1 tbsp (15 mL) rum (optional).

1 In bowl, combine raisins, peel and citron; toss with 2 tbsp (25 mL) of the flour. Set aside. In saucepan, heat milk with 1 tsp (5 mL) of the sugar to lukewarm (110 to 112°F/ 43 to 44°C); remove from heat. Sprinkle in yeast; let stand for 10 minutes or until frothy.

3 Gradually stir in remaining flour to make soft, somewhat lumpy dough. Turn out onto lightly floured surface; knead for 8 minutes or until soft, smooth and elastic, using up to ⅓ cup (75 mL) more flour if needed. Lightly dust with flour; cover with tea towel and let rest for 5 minutes.

5 Grease two 2-lb (1 kg) coffee cans or panettone moulds. If using cans, line bottoms and sides with parchment paper to extend 1 inch (2.5 cm) above top; wrap outsides and bottoms with double thickness of foil. Punch down dough; divide in half. Roll each into ball; place, seam side down, in can. Cover and let rise in warm draft-free place until doubled in bulk, about 1½ hours.

2 Whisk together eggs, egg yolks, orange and lemon rinds and vanilla; stir into milk mixture. In large bowl, stir together 4 cups (1 L) of the flour, remaining sugar and salt; stir in egg mixture. Add butter all at once; stir until blended.

4 Flatten into 15-inch (38 cm) circle; top with raisin mixture. Fold dough over mixture; pinch to seal. Knead for 2 to 3 minutes to distribute mixture. Place in large greased bowl, turning to grease all over. Cover with plastic wrap; let rise in warm draft-free place until doubled in bulk, 1½ to 2 hours.

6 With sharp knife, cut X on top of each loaf. Place on baking sheet; bake on lowest rack of 350°F (180°C) oven for about 1 hour or until knife inserted in centre comes out clean, covering tops lightly with foil if browning too quickly. Let cool in cans on rack for 1 hour. Remove from cans by gently pulling paper; let loaves cool completely on rack.

Christmas Stollen

Originally from Dresden, Germany, stollen is traditionally served at Christmastime. The shape and folds of the bread are said to represent the folds in the blanket of the infant Jesus. The rich, buttery dough is akin to a classic brioche but has less sugar and a coarser texture. It is also liberally studded with dried fruit and flavoured with cinnamon, nutmeg and cardamom. It's important to let the dough rest for five minutes so that it is not too springy for kneading in the dried fruit.

Ingredients

1¼ cups	milk	300 mL
½ cup	granulated sugar	125 mL
2	pkg active dry yeast (or 2 tbsp/25 mL)	2
2	eggs, beaten	2
5 cups	all-purpose flour (approx)	1.25 L
1½ tsp	salt	7 mL
Pinch	each cinnamon, nutmeg and cardamom	Pinch
¾ cup	unsalted butter, softened	175 mL
1 cup	raisins	250 mL
½ cup	mixed candied peel	125 mL
½ cup	candied cherries, chopped	125 mL
½ cup	toasted slivered almonds	125 mL
1 tsp	grated lemon rind	5 mL
1	egg white, lightly beaten	1
¼ cup	butter, melted	50 mL
	Icing sugar	

Makes 2 loaves, 12 slices each

Per slice: about 256 cal, 5 g pro, 10 g total fat
(5 g sat. fat), 38 g carb, 2 g fibre, 40 mg chol.
% RDI: 3% calcium, 11% iron, 9% vit A, 2% vit C,
24% folate.

Tip

Loaves can be stored in plastic bags at room temperature for up to 3 days or wrapped tightly in plastic wrap and frozen for up to 1 month.

1 In saucepan, heat milk with 1 tsp (5 mL) of the sugar to lukewarm (110 to 112°F/ 43 to 44°C). Sprinkle in yeast; let stand for 10 minutes or until frothy. Stir in eggs. In large bowl, stir together 3 cups (750 mL) of the flour, remaining sugar, salt, cinnamon, nutmeg and cardamom; stir in milk mixture. Add softened butter, stirring until blended.

3 Flatten dough into rectangle; sprinkle two-thirds with half of the raisin mixture. Fold over in thirds; knead for about 4 minutes to distribute mixture. Cover; let rest for 5 minutes. Repeat with remaining raisin mixture. Place in greased bowl, turning to grease all over; cover with plastic wrap and let rise in warm draft-free place until doubled in bulk, about 1½ hours.

5 Brush egg white over each; fold bottom half of dough up to top, aligning raised borders side by side. Place on 2 greased 17- x 11-inch (45 x 29 cm) baking sheets. Cover; let rise in warm draft-free place until doubled in bulk, about 1 hour.

2 Stir in remaining flour to make soft yet lumpy dough. Turn out onto floured surface; knead for 10 to 12 minutes or until smooth and elastic, adding up to 3 tbsp (50 mL) more flour. Dust with flour; cover with towel and let rest for 5 minutes. In small bowl, stir together raisins, candied peel, cherries, almonds and lemon rind.

4 Punch down dough; divide in half. On floured surface, shape each half into 8-inch (20 cm) long log. With long side closest, roll out each log to ½-inch (1 cm) thickness, leaving 1-inch (2.5 cm) border unrolled at top and bottom.

6 Bake in 350°F (180°C) oven for about 45 minutes or until loaves sound hollow when tapped on bottoms. Transfer to rack; brush all over with melted butter. Let cool. Dust all over with icing sugar.

The Ultimate Bran Muffin

The Test Kitchen spent several days developing this "ultimate" recipe, working tirelessly to achieve just the right texture, just the right amount of fibre and certainly just the right flavour. It was no mean feat! At first, the tops of the muffins were too smooth. Then they flattened too much. Just when we had both those problems solved, the texture became a little too dry. After playing with various amounts of molasses, honey and brown sugar, our persistence paid off and these muffins are truly delicious as well as being good for you.

Ingredients

¾ cup	All-Bran or 100% Bran cereal	175 mL
1⅓ cups	buttermilk	325 mL
¾ cup	natural bran	175 mL
2 cups	all-purpose flour	500 mL
¾ cup	whole wheat flour	175 mL
½ cup	packed dark brown sugar	125 mL
4 tsp	baking powder	20 mL
2 tsp	baking soda	10 mL
¼ tsp	each cinnamon and salt	1 mL
1¼ cups	raisins	300 mL
¾ cup	fancy molasses	150 mL
⅓ cup	vegetable oil	75 mL
1	egg	1
1½ tsp	vanilla	7 mL

Makes 12 muffins

*Per muffin: about 326 cal, 6 g pro, 7 g total fat
(1 g sat. fat), 63 g carb, 5 g fibre, 19 mg chol. % RDI:
12% calcium, 26% iron, 1% vit A, 2% vit C,
15% folate.*

Variations

Smooth-Top Fruit Muffins:
Increase baking powder to 5 tsp (25 mL);
substitute ¾ cup (175 mL) each chopped
dried apricots and figs or dates for
the raisins.

Yogurt Bran Muffins: Substitute
plain yogurt for buttermilk.

Tips

**With muffins, it's important not to
overstir while combining the dry
ingredients with the wet; over-
stirring will toughen the texture.
Stir *just* until the dry ingredients
are moistened.**

**Because these muffins are rather
large, greasing the top of the pan
ensures that the muffin tops will
not stick to the pan.**

**Either golden or Thompson raisins
are delicious in these muffins.**

**Store whole wheat flour and natural
bran in the freezer.**

1 Grease muffin cups, greasing flat top of pan as well; set aside. In bowl, stir cereal into buttermilk; stir in natural bran. Let stand for 10 minutes.

To measure all-purpose and whole wheat flours, spoon into dry measure until overflowing; sweep off excess with blunt edge of knife. Dump into large bowl. To measure brown sugar, pack into dry measure until level with top. Add to flour, breaking up lumps with fingers.

2 With measuring spoons, scoop out baking powder, baking soda, cinnamon and salt, sweeping off excess with blunt edge of knife. Stir into flour mixture. Stir in raisins.

3 With liquid measuring cup, measure molasses and oil. Pour into bran mixture along with egg and vanilla; whisk to combine. Make well in centre of dry ingredients; pour in bran mixture and stir with wooden spoon just until dry ingredients are moistened.

4 With ice-cream scoop or large spoon, divide batter among prepared muffin cups, filling to top.

5 Bake in 375°F (190°C) oven for about 25 minutes or until golden and tops are firm to the touch.

6 Let cool in pan on rack for 2 minutes. Remove from pan and let cool on rack.

Honey Oat Muffins

Healthy muffins suffer from an undeserved reputation of being earnest: in other words, if it's good for you, it can't possibly taste good. Well, these muffins – tasty, moist *and* full of fibre – dispel that notion deliciously.

1½ cups	all-purpose flour	375 mL
1¼ cups	quick-cooking rolled oats	300 mL
1 cup	raisins	250 mL
½ cup	natural bran	125 mL
1½ tsp	cinnamon	7 mL
1 tsp	each baking powder and baking soda	5 mL
½ tsp	salt	2 mL
1½ cups	buttermilk	375 mL
½ cup	liquid honey	125 mL
1	egg	1
¼ cup	vegetable oil	50 mL
1½ tsp	vanilla	7 mL

1 In large bowl, stir together flour, 1 cup (250 mL) of the oats, raisins, bran, cinnamon, baking powder, baking soda and salt. Whisk together buttermilk, honey, egg, oil and vanilla; pour over dry ingredients and stir just until moistened.

2 Spoon into greased or paper-lined muffin cups. Sprinkle with remaining oats. Bake in 375°F (190°C) oven for 20 to 25 minutes or until golden and tops are firm to the touch. *(Muffins can be wrapped individually and frozen for up to 1 month.)*

Makes 12 muffins

Per muffin: about 240 cal, 5 g pro, 6 g total fat (1 g sat. fat), 44 g carb, 3 g fibre, 19 mg chol. % RDI: 6% calcium, 13% iron, 1% vit A, 2% vit C, 10% folate.

Tip

For hot-from-the-oven muffins first thing in the morning, measure and mix wet and dry ingredients in separate bowls the night before. Cover bowls; refrigerate wet ingredients. In the morning, stir together, spoon into muffin cups and bake.

Peaches and Cream Muffins

In baking, remember that sugar is a very important ingredient, not only imparting sweetness but also affecting the amount of liquid, tenderness and colouring. Altering the required amount of sugar haphazardly will change the end result.

2 cups	all-purpose flour	500 mL
¾ cup	granulated sugar	175 mL
2 tsp	baking powder	10 mL
¾ tsp	each nutmeg and cinnamon	4 mL
½ tsp	each baking soda and salt	2 mL
1 cup	sour cream	250 mL
2	eggs	2
¼ cup	butter, melted	50 mL
1 tsp	vanilla	5 mL
1 cup	chopped peeled peaches	250 mL
¼ cup	sliced almonds	50 mL

1 In large bowl, combine flour, sugar, baking powder, nutmeg, cinnamon, baking soda and salt. Whisk together sour cream, eggs, butter and vanilla; pour over dry ingredients. Pour peaches over top; stir just until dry ingredients are moistened.

2 Spoon into greased or paper-lined muffin cups; sprinkle with almonds. Bake in 400°F (200°C) oven for about 20 minutes or until golden and tops are firm to the touch.

Makes 12 muffins

Per muffin: about 222 cal, 4 g pro, 9 g total fat (5 g sat. fat), 32 g carb, 1 g fibre, 54 mg chol. % RDI: 5% calcium, 9% iron, 8% vit A, 2% vit C, 13% folate.

Raspberry Oatmeal Muffins

Muffins are typically baked at a higher temperature to cook them quickly and keep them moist. Like nearly everything else, muffins are best the day they're made. This is especially true if the muffins contain 1/4 cup (50 mL) or less of butter or oil.

1¼ cups	all-purpose flour	300 mL
1 cup	rolled oats (not instant)	250 mL
⅓ cup	packed brown sugar	75 mL
1 tsp	cinnamon	5 mL
1 tsp	each baking powder and baking soda	5 mL
1 cup	buttermilk	250 mL
⅓ cup	vegetable oil	75 mL
2 tbsp	fancy molasses	25 mL
1	egg	1
1 tsp	vanilla	5 mL
1½ cups	fresh raspberries	375 mL

1 In large bowl, combine flour, oats, brown sugar, cinnamon, baking powder and baking soda. Whisk together buttermilk, oil, molasses, egg and vanilla; pour over dry ingredients. Sprinkle with raspberries; gently stir just until dry ingredients are moistened.

2 Spoon into greased or paper-lined muffin cups. Bake in 375°F (190°C) oven for about 20 minutes or until tops are firm to the touch.

Makes 10 muffins

Per muffin: about 219 cal, 5 g pro, 9 g total fat (1 g sat. fat), 31 g carb, 2 g fibre, 22 mg chol. % RDI: 6% calcium, 11% iron, 1% vit A, 7% vit C, 11% folate.

Fibreful Muffins

With skim milk powder providing a calcium boost and nuts, raisins and natural bran providing a hefty dose of fibre, these muffins are a great way to start a nutritious day. One recipe of muffin mix will make four batches of muffins. If you're out of bananas, replace them and the water with 1 cup (250 mL) plain yogurt.

3 cups	Fibre Muffin Mix (recipe follows)	750 mL
1	egg	1

¾ cup	mashed bananas or unsweetened applesauce	175 mL
¼ cup	water	50 mL
2 tbsp	vegetable oil	25 mL

1 Place muffin mix in bowl. Whisk together egg, bananas, water and oil; pour over mix and stir just until moistened.

2 Spoon into greased or paper-lined muffin cups. Bake in 375°F (190°C) oven for about 30 minutes or until tops are firm to the touch.

Makes 6 muffins

Per muffin: about 370 cal, 9 g pro, 9 g total fat (1 g sat. fat), 68 g carb, 6 g fibre, 37 mg chol. % RDI: 14% calcium, 21% iron, 2% vit A, 3% vit C, 10% folate.

Fibre Muffin Mix

6 cups	all-purpose flour	1.5 L
2 cups	granulated sugar	500 mL
2 cups	natural bran	500 mL
2 cups	raisins	500 mL
1¾ cups	skim milk powder	425 mL
1¼ cups	All-Bran cereal	300 mL
1 cup	chopped almonds or unsalted peanuts	250 mL
¼ cup	baking powder	50 mL
1 tbsp	salt	15 mL
2 tsp	nutmeg	10 mL
1 tsp	baking soda	5 mL

1 In bowl, combine flour, sugar, natural bran, raisins, skim milk powder, cereal, almonds, baking powder, salt, nutmeg and baking soda. Refrigerate in airtight container for up to 4 weeks. Stir well to use.

Makes 12 cups (3 L)

Per ½ cup (125 mL): about 290 cal, 8 g pro, 4 g total fat (0 g sat. fat), 61 g carb, 5 g fibre, 1 mg chol. % RDI: 14% calcium, 20% iron, 20% folate.

> **Tip**
>
> **Invest in two boxes of baking soda: one for keeping odours at bay in your fridge, and one just for baking.**

Irish Soda Bread

Although no longer baked in the traditional cast-iron pot over an open hearth, soda bread is still as scrumptious and simple to make as ever. And it's always a boon to know that you can make a satisfying and earthy loaf in less than an hour. This Test Kitchen version features all-purpose and whole wheat flours, which give the bread a nuttiness that marries deliciously with the tang of buttermilk. For a dramatic touch, add 1 tsp (5 mL) caraway seeds, crushed, and/or 1 cup (250 mL) raisins.

Ingredients

2 cups	all-purpose flour	500 mL
1 cup	whole wheat flour	250 mL
2 tbsp	flax or sesame seeds	25 mL
2 tbsp	granulated sugar	25 mL
1 tsp	each baking soda and salt	5 mL
1½ cups	buttermilk	375 mL
¼ cup	vegetable oil	50 mL

Topping:

1 tbsp	all-purpose flour	15 mL

Makes 8 servings

Per serving: about 271 cal, 7 g pro, 9 g total fat
(1 g sat. fat), 42 g carb, 3 g fibre, 2 mg chol. % RDI:
6% calcium, 16% iron, 9% folate.

Variations

Honey Apricot Soda Bread:
Omit sugar and flax seeds. Increase
all-purpose flour to 2¼ cups (550 mL).
Add ½ cup (125 mL) each chopped dried
apricots and raisins to dry ingredients.
Add ⅓ cup (75 mL) liquid honey to
liquid ingredients. For topping, omit
flour. After baking, let stand on rack for
15 minutes. Mix ½ cup (125 mL) icing
sugar with 2 tbsp (25 mL) orange juice;
drizzle over loaf.

Cheese and Onion Soda Bread:
Omit flax seeds and topping. Add 1 cup
(250 mL) shredded old Cheddar cheese,
¼ cup (50 mL) chopped green onion and
pinch cayenne pepper to dry ingredients.

Tip

If you can't get buttermilk, substitute your own soured milk: for each
1 cup (250 mL) buttermilk, substitute
1 cup (250 mL) milk stirred with
1 tbsp (15 mL) vinegar or lemon juice.
Let stand for 10 minutes to thicken.

1 In large bowl, whisk together all-
purpose flour, whole wheat flour, flax
seeds, sugar, baking soda and salt.

2 In small bowl, whisk together buttermilk and oil. Add to dry ingredients all
at once; stir with fork until soft dough forms.

3 Turn out dough onto lightly floured
surface. With floured hands, press
dough into ball; knead lightly 10 times.
Place on greased baking sheet; gently pat
out dough into 6-inch (15 cm) circle.

4 **Topping:** Sprinkle flour over loaf.

5 With sharp knife, score large X on top
of loaf.

6 Bake in 375°F (190°C) oven for about
45 minutes or until golden and tester
inserted in centre comes out clean.

Currant Scones

How do you achieve those light, tender, flaky scones everyone yearns for? Well, in reality, scones and biscuits are rather easy to make and quite forgiving. Technique is the important thing, as opposed to the precise amount of each ingredient. The speed with which you work – mixing just until the dry ingredients are moistened and kneading gently and efficiently – will do the utmost in preventing the dough from getting too tough and will go the furthest in ensuring that you achieve the quintessential scone.

Ingredients

2¼ cups	all-purpose flour	550 mL
2 tbsp	granulated sugar	25 mL
2½ tsp	baking powder	12 mL
½ tsp	baking soda	2 mL
½ tsp	salt	2 mL
½ cup	cold butter, cubed	125 mL
½ cup	currants	125 mL
1 cup	buttermilk	250 mL
1	egg, lightly beaten	1

Makes about 12 scones

*Per scone: about 193 cal, 4 g pro, 9 g total fat
(5 g sat. fat), 26 g carb, 1 g fibre, 39 mg chol.
% RDI: 5% calcium, 9% iron, 8% vit A, 13% folate.*

Variations

Dried Fruit and Lemon Scones:
Substitute ½ cup (125 mL) raisins,
dried blueberries, dried cranberries,
chopped dried cherries (not glacé),
apricots or prunes for the currants.
Add 2 tsp (10 mL) grated lemon rind
to dry mixture.

Oat Scones: Substitute ½ cup
(125 mL) rolled oats (not instant)
for ½ cup (125 mL) of the flour. Add
1 tsp (5 mL) cinnamon to dry mixture.
Substitute raisins for currants.

Cheese Scones: Omit sugar and
currants. Add ¼ tsp (1 mL) cayenne
pepper to dry mixture. Add 1 cup
(250 mL) shredded old Cheddar
cheese after butter has been cut in.

Tip

**Use ungreased baking sheets for
scones, biscuits and shortbread.
The high proportion of fat in the
dough makes greasing unnecessary,
and greasing could even cause frying
of the underside.**

1 In large bowl, stir together flour, sugar,
baking powder, baking soda and salt.
Using pastry blender or 2 knives, cut in
butter until mixture resembles coarse
crumbs. Stir in currants.

2 Add buttermilk all at once, stirring with
fork to make soft, slightly sticky dough.

3 With lightly floured hands, press dough
into ball. Turn out onto lightly floured
surface; knead gently 10 times.

4 Gently pat dough into ¾-inch (2 cm)
thick round.

5 Using 2½ inch (6 cm) floured cookie
cutter, cut out rounds. Place on
ungreased baking sheet. Gather up scraps
and repat dough once; cut out more rounds.

6 Brush tops of scones with egg. Bake
in 425°F (220°C) oven for 12 to
15 minutes or until golden. Transfer to
racks and let cool.

Waffles with Cherry Berry Sauce

Sweetheart waffles with no added fat! What a sweetheart deal! With no sacrifice in flavour or texture, these waffles cook up fluffy and soft with a subtle nuance of vanilla. As with any waffle recipe, the batter is easily convertible into pancakes should your kitchen lack a waffle iron. Feel free to substitute butter for the oil when greasing the waffle iron. But don't be tempted to forgo the greasing altogether – you'll be dismayed at how the waffles stick and at the unsightly mess to clean up.

Ingredients

1½ cups	all-purpose flour	375 mL
2 tbsp	granulated sugar	25 mL
2 tsp	baking powder	10 mL
¼ tsp	salt	1 mL
3	eggs, separated	3
1½ cups	milk	375 mL
1 tsp	vanilla	5 mL
2 tbsp	vegetable oil	25 mL

Cherry Berry Sauce:

1½ cups	frozen sour cherries, thawed	375 mL
1 cup	each frozen strawberries and raspberries, thawed	250 mL
¼ cup	frozen blueberries, thawed	50 mL
¼ cup	granulated sugar	50 mL
¼ cup	water	50 mL
2 tbsp	cornstarch	25 mL
1 tsp	vanilla	5 mL

Makes 8 servings

*Per serving: about 245 cal, 7 g pro, 7 g total fat
(1 g sat. fat), 39 g carb, 2 g fibre, 84 mg chol.
% RDI: 10% calcium, 12% iron, 9% vit A,
15% vit C, 9% folate.*

Variation

Waffles with Apple Cinnamon
Sauce: Add ½ tsp (2 mL) cinnamon
to dry ingredients for waffles.

Apple Cinnamon Sauce: In
saucepan, melt 2 tbsp (25 mL) butter
with ¼ cup (50 mL) packed brown sugar
over medium-high heat. Add 4 cups (1 L)
thickly sliced apples and ½ tsp (2 mL)
cinnamon. Cover and cook, stirring
once, for 5 minutes or until tender.

Tip

**Leftover waffles can be wrapped
individually in plastic wrap and
frozen for up to 3 months. Reheat
in toaster oven.**

1 **Cherry Berry Sauce:** In saucepan, bring cherries, strawberries, raspberries, blueberries, sugar, water and cornstarch to boil over medium-high heat, stirring gently; cook for about 1 minute or until thickened. Stir in vanilla. Keep warm.

2 In large bowl, whisk together flour, 1 tbsp (15 mL) of the sugar, baking powder and salt.

3 In separate bowl, whisk together egg yolks, milk and vanilla.

4 Pour over flour mixture; whisk until well combined and smooth.

5 In clean bowl, beat egg whites until soft peaks form. Sprinkle with remaining sugar; beat until stiff peaks form. Fold one-quarter into batter; fold in remaining whites.

6 Heat waffle iron. For each waffle, brush iron lightly with some of the oil; pour in generous ½ cup (125 mL) batter. Close lid and cook for 4 to 5 minutes or until steam stops and waffle is crisp and golden. Serve warm with sauce.

Desserts, Cakes, Pastries, Cookies, Candies

I started my professional career as a pastry chef and I still adore making (and eating!) all kinds of desserts. Baking is a wonderful pleasure and much easier than many people think. Baking, it's true, is unlike cooking, in that you can't simply throw in a pinch of baking powder or soda as you can a spice and expect the recipe to work. Baking is more precise than that. Still, once you've baked your way through a few of our lessons, you'll be more comfortable letting your own creativity shine through. For example, the first time you make pastry, the feel of its tender flakiness will be unknown to you. However, by the second or third time, you'll know exactly what to look for and what to avoid (such as a hot kitchen). You'll even begin to feel comfortable substituting ground nuts for some of the flour, or adding flavourings such as grated lemon or orange rind. Similarly, the first time you make a cake with chilled (instead of room-temperature) eggs will also be your last because you'll be able to identify the slightly curdled batter that makes a cake denser than desirable. Our lessons are designed for the utmost "teachability," with the goal of making you a confident baker who is ready to meet every new recipe with a plateful of knowledge.

Pecan Pie with Perfect Pastry

Golden, buttery, flaky pastry. Sheer delight – but sheer terror to some bakers. However, there's no need to be intimidated by the prospect of making pie or tart pastry. Like so many desserts, it's straightforward and simple. Be patient. Don't cram pastry making between other chores. And don't defeat yourself right off the bat by making it on the most humid day of the summer, which guarantees problems. Work in a cool kitchen and make sure all your ingredients are very cold: cold butter, cold eggs and cold water.

Ingredients

3⅓ cups	sifted cake-and-pastry flour	825 mL
½ tsp	salt	2 mL
½ cup	cold butter, cubed	125 mL
½ cup	shortening or cold lard, cubed	125 mL
1	egg	1
3 tbsp	ice water (approx)	50 mL
2 tsp	white vinegar	10 mL

Filling:

3	eggs	3
¾ cup	packed brown sugar	175 mL
¾ cup	corn syrup	175 mL
2 tbsp	butter, melted	25 mL
1 tsp	vanilla	5 mL
1½ cups	pecan halves	375 mL

Glaze:

2 tbsp	corn syrup, warmed	25 mL

Makes 8 servings

Per serving: about 552 cal, 6 g pro, 30 g total fat (10 g sat. fat), 68 g carb, 2 g fibre, 123 mg chol. % RDI: 5% calcium, 29% iron, 12% vit A, 18% folate.

Variations

Butter Pastry: Omit shortening; increase butter to 1 cup (250 mL).

All-Purpose Flour Pastry: Substitute 3 cups (750 mL) all-purpose flour for the cake-and-pastry flour.

Tips

Measuring your ingredients accurately (see box, page 176) can make the difference between feathery, flaky pastry and a leaden mass. Try to work quickly but gently. Handling the dough too much will overwork it and make it tough. Add liquid as directed: too much liquid makes pastry soggy and encourages shrinking.

When rolling, slightly elevate your rolling pin as you near the edges of the pastry to make sure that the edge does not become thinner than the centre. Thin edges will bake faster than other parts and turn brittle.

1 In large bowl, combine flour and salt. Using pastry blender or 2 knives, cut in butter and shortening until mixture resembles coarse crumbs with a few larger pieces. Using fork, beat together egg, water and vinegar.

2 Add to flour mixture, 1 tbsp (15 mL) at a time, stirring briskly with fork until dough holds together when pressed. Add more water, a few drops at a time, if necessary. Press into ball; divide in half and flatten into discs. Wrap in plastic wrap and refrigerate 1 disc for at least 20 minutes or until chilled. Freeze remaining disc for up to 3 months for another use.

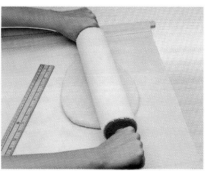

3 On lightly floured pastry cloth or work surface and using stockinette-covered or floured rolling pin, roll out dough from centre toward edge to ⅛-inch (3 mm) thickness.

4 Loosely roll pastry around rolling pin; unroll into 9-inch (23 cm) pie plate. Trim edge evenly, leaving 1-inch (2.5 cm) overhang. Tuck pastry overhang under to make double layer around rim.

5 To flute crust, place index finger and thumb about ¾ inch (2 cm) apart on outside edge of pastry rim. With other index finger, push pastry toward outside to form scalloped edge, pressing to anchor to rim of pie plate. Refrigerate while making filling.

6 **Filling:** In bowl, combine eggs, sugar, corn syrup, butter and vanilla; stir in pecans. Pour into pie shell. Bake in bottom third of 375°F (190°C) oven for 40 to 45 minutes or until filling is just firm to the touch, shielding edge with foil if necessary.

Glaze: Brush filling with corn syrup; let cool. Cut with serrated knife.

Tarte Tatin

This wonderful French creation is everything anyone can ask for in a dessert. A buttery, flaky, tender pastry sets off and illuminates the deep, rich caramelized apple topping, whose juices seep back into the pastry for a luscious mingling of flavours. Use Northern Spy or Golden Delicious apples because they retain their shape when cooked. And be sure to chill the dough for the specified amount of time, both to facilitate rolling out and to avoid shrinkage when the cold pastry meets the hot skillet.

1 cup	all-purpose flour	250 mL
1 tbsp	granulated sugar	15 mL
¼ tsp	salt	1 mL
½ cup	cold unsalted butter, cubed	125 mL
1 tsp	white vinegar	5 mL
	Ice water	
Filling:		
8	Northern Spy apples (about 4 lb/2 kg)	8
2 tbsp	lemon juice	25 mL
¼ cup	unsalted butter	50 mL
¾ cup	granulated sugar	175 mL

1 In large bowl, stir together flour, sugar and salt. Using pastry blender or 2 knives, cut in butter until mixture resembles coarse crumbs with a few larger pieces.

2 In liquid measure, stir vinegar with enough ice water to make ¼ cup (50 mL). Drizzle over flour mixture, stirring with fork until dough holds together when pressed, adding a few more drops of water if necessary. Press into ball; flatten into disc. Wrap in plastic wrap and refrigerate for at least 30 minutes or for up to 3 days.

Filling: Meanwhile, peel, quarter and core apples; cut in half lengthwise. In bowl, toss apples with lemon juice.

3 In 8-inch (20 cm) cast-iron skillet, melt butter over medium-high heat. Add sugar; cook, stirring with wooden spoon, for 3 to 5 minutes or until starting to bubble. Remove from heat. Discarding any juice, arrange layer of apples, flat side down, in concentric circles in syrup in pan. Layer remaining apples over top to cover first layer evenly.

4 Cook over medium heat, basting with syrup that bubbles up, for about 15 minutes or until apples begin to soften and syrup starts to thicken. Cover and cook for 5 minutes or until apples in top layer are just tender. Remove from heat; let cool for 5 minutes.

5 Meanwhile, on lightly floured surface, roll out dough to 10-inch (25 cm) circle; cut 4 small steam vents at centre. Loosely roll pastry around rolling pin; unroll over apples. Using sharp knife, trim off pastry extending over rim of pan; press pastry edge down between apples and pan.

6 Bake in 425°F (220°C) oven for about 25 minutes or until pastry is golden brown. Let stand for 4 minutes. Invert heatproof serving plate over pastry. Wearing oven mitts, grasp plate and pan; turn over to unmould tart onto plate. With tongs, quickly arrange apples stuck in pan over top. Serve warm.

Makes 8 servings

Per serving: about 362 cal, 2 g pro, 18 g total fat (11 g sat. fat), 51 g carb, 3 g fibre, 47 mg chol. % RDI: 1% calcium, 6% iron, 17% vit A, 8% vit C, 8% folate.

Easiest-Ever Apple Pie

This unconventional pastry can't be beat for both flavour and ease. It uses a creamed method (as opposed to a cutting-in method) so there is never any worry about whether the butter is sufficiently pea-size or cold enough. It is also quite "short," which means a relatively high proportion of fat to flour. In other words, it's very buttery.

¾ cup	shortening	175 mL
3 tbsp	butter, softened	50 mL
2¼ cups	all-purpose flour	550 mL
¾ tsp	salt	4 mL
½ cup	ice water	125 mL
Filling:		
8 cups	thinly sliced peeled tart apples (2¼ lb/1.125 kg)	2 L
2 tbsp	lemon juice	25 mL

½ cup	granulated sugar	125 mL
3 tbsp	all-purpose flour	50 mL
½ tsp	cinnamon	2 mL

Glaze:

1	egg yolk	1
2 tsp	granulated sugar	10 mL

1 In bowl, beat shortening with butter until smooth; stir in flour and salt until coarse and ragged looking. Pour in water all at once; stir until loose dough forms. With floured hands, gather into 2 balls. On well-floured surface, gently knead each into ¾-inch (2 cm) thick disc. Wrap and refrigerate for at least 1 hour or until chilled.

2 On well-floured pastry cloth or work surface and using well-floured rolling pin, roll out 1 piece of dough from centre, lifting pin at edge to maintain even thickness. Turn rolling pin clockwise 90 degrees. Repeat rolling out and turning dough until in 13-inch (33 cm) circle.

3 Loosely roll pastry around rolling pin; unroll into 9-inch (23 cm) pie plate. Using sharp knife, trim edge even with pie plate.

Filling: In large bowl, toss apples with lemon juice. Stir together sugar, flour and cinnamon; sprinkle over apples and toss until coated. Scrape into pie shell. Brush pastry rim with water.

4 Roll out remaining dough to same-size circle. Using rolling pin, drape over apples, without stretching pastry. Trim, leaving ¾-inch (2 cm) overhang. Gently lift bottom pastry rim and fold overhang under rim; press together to seal. Tilt sealed pastry rim up from pie plate at 45-degree angle.

5 With hand on outside of tilted pastry rim and using thumb and bent index finger, gently twist rim to form scalloped edge. With decora-tive cutter or tip of sharp knife, cut steam vents in centre of pastry.

6 **Glaze:** Whisk yolk with 1 tbsp (15 mL) water; brush over pastry. Sprinkle with sugar. Bake in bottom third of 425°F (220°C) oven for 15 minutes. Reduce heat to 350°F (180°C); bake for 40 minutes or until golden, filling is bubbly and apples are soft when pierced with knife through vent. Let cool on rack.

Makes 8 servings

Per serving: about 467 cal, 5 g pro, 24 g total fat (8 g sat. fat), 59 g carb, 4 g fibre, 40 mg chol. % RDI: 1% calcium, 12% iron, 6% vit A, 7% vit C, 20% folate.

Tips

Unbaked pastry can be refrigerated for up to 5 days or frozen for up to 2 weeks.

Tart baking apples include Mutsu and Northern Spy; sweet-tart Idared is also a good choice.

Harvest Pumpkin Pie

Blind baking, the prebaking of a pie shell, is a terrific technique to learn since it is the foundation of many tarts and cream pies. The unbaked pie shell can generally be prepared up to two days in advance, then prebaked on the day the pie is needed. Chilling the unbaked shell helps set its shape and avoid shrinkage while baking. Make sure that the pie weights cover the entire bottom of the shell and that they are pressed evenly against the sides in order to retain the pie's shape.

	Pastry for 9-inch (23 cm) single-crust pie	
2	eggs	2
1½ cups	cooked pumpkin purée	375 mL
1 cup	packed dark brown sugar	250 mL
¾ cup	18% cream	175 mL
1 tsp	cinnamon	5 mL
½ tsp	each ground cloves, ginger and nutmeg	2 mL
½ tsp	salt	2 mL
2 tbsp	sour cream	25 mL
1½ tsp	milk	7 mL

1 On floured pastry cloth or work surface and using stockinette-covered or floured rolling pin, roll out pastry and fit into 9-inch (23 cm) pie plate. Trim pastry, leaving 1-inch (2.5 cm) overhang; fold under and flute edge. With fork, prick shell all over. Place in freezer for 30 minutes.

2 Line pastry shell with parchment paper or foil; fill evenly with pie weights or dried beans. Bake in bottom third of 400°F (200°C) oven for 10 minutes. Remove weights and foil; bake for about 10 minutes longer or until pastry is set.

3 Meanwhile, in large bowl, beat eggs lightly. Blend in pumpkin, sugar, cream, cinnamon, cloves, ginger, nutmeg and salt; pour into pastry shell.

4 Combine sour cream with milk; pour into funnel with narrow tube, blocking opening with finger. Remove finger and quickly drizzle mixture in spiral pattern over filling.

5 Beginning at centre, pull tip of knife shallowly through filling and sour cream mixture at 8 evenly spaced intervals. Beginning at outside, pull knife through middle of inter-vals toward centre to create web pattern.

6 Bake in bottom third of 350°F (180°C) oven for about 1 hour or until filling is set and point of knife inserted in centre comes out clean. Let cool on rack.

Makes 6 to 8 servings

Per each of 8 servings: about 297 cal, 4 g pro, 14 g total fat (5 g sat. fat), 41 g carb, 1 g fibre, 69 mg chol. % RDI: 7% calcium, 14% iron, 13% vit A, 3% vit C, 6% folate.

Tip

If desired, omit sour cream and milk. Top with 1/2 cup (125 mL) whipping cream whipped with 2 tbsp (25 mL) pure maple syrup.

Gooey Butter Tarts

As Canadian as they come, this classic treat has devotees that fall into two camps: those who prefer a runny filling and those who opt for a firmer texture. Whatever side you happen to be on, these tarts are great any time of day, be it for dessert, with tea or as a rich snack.

Ingredients

1½ cups	all-purpose flour	375 mL
¼ tsp	salt	1 mL
¼ cup	cold butter, cubed	50 mL
¼ cup	shortening, cubed	50 mL
1	egg yolk	1
1 tsp	vinegar	5 mL
	Ice water	

Filling:

½ cup	packed brown sugar	125 mL
½ cup	corn syrup	125 mL
1	egg	1
2 tbsp	butter, softened	25 mL
1 tsp	each vanilla and vinegar	5 mL
Pinch	salt	Pinch
¼ cup	currants, raisins, chopped pecans or shredded coconut	50 mL

Makes 12 tarts

Per tart: about 240 cal, 3 g pro, 11 g total fat (5 g sat. fat), 33 g carb, 1 g fibre, 52 mg chol. % RDI: 2% calcium, 11% iron, 7% vit A, 3% folate.

Variations

Chocolate Gooey Butter Tarts:
Drizzle cooled tarts with 2 oz (60 g) melted semisweet or white chocolate.

Not-So-Gooey Butter Tarts:
Increase brown sugar to ¾ cup (175 mL); decrease corn syrup to ¼ cup (50 mL).

Tip

Because sugar filling hardens quickly and sticks to the pan, be sure to remove tarts from pan as directed.

1 In large bowl, stir flour with salt. With pastry blender or 2 knives, cut in butter and shortening until mixture resembles coarse crumbs with a few larger pieces. In liquid measure, whisk egg yolk with vinegar; add enough ice water to make ⅓ cup (75 mL).

2 Gradually sprinkle egg mixture over flour mixture, stirring briskly with fork until pastry holds together. Press into disc; wrap in plastic wrap. Refrigerate for at least 1 hour or until chilled or for up to 3 days.

3 **Filling:** In bowl, vigorously whisk together brown sugar, corn syrup, egg, butter, vanilla, vinegar and salt. Set aside.

4 On lightly floured surface, roll out dough to ⅛-inch (3 mm) thickness. Using 4-inch (10 cm) round cookie cutter (or empty 28 oz/796 mL can), cut out 12 circles, rerolling scraps once if necessary.

5 Fit circles into 2¾- x 1¼-inch (7 x 3 cm) muffin cups. Divide currants among pastry shells. Spoon in filling until three-quarters full.

6 Bake in bottom third of 450°F (230°C) oven for about 12 minutes or until filling is puffed and bubbly and pastry is golden. Let stand on rack for 1 minute. Run metal spatula around tarts to loosen; carefully slide spatula under tarts and transfer to rack to let cool.

Cherry Chocolate Baklava

Baklava is one of those perennially favourite treats, though whether it could claim as many devotees in 15th-century Greece or Turkey, where it was first made, is anybody's guess. Its trademark sugar syrup (originally scented with orange or rose flower water) and crisp, buttery phyllo layers are updated by the harmonious addition of bittersweet chocolate and tart dried cherries.

Ingredients

1 cup	dried cherries or raisins	250 mL
2¼ cups	toasted chopped pecans	550 mL
2 tbsp	granulated sugar	25 mL
1 tsp	cinnamon	5 mL
6 oz	bittersweet chocolate, chopped	175 g
⅔ cup	butter, melted	150 mL
12	sheets phyllo pastry	12

Syrup:

1 cup	granulated sugar	250 mL
½ cup	liquid honey	125 mL
⅓ cup	water	75 mL
1	strip (2 inches/5 cm) lemon rind	15 mL
1 tbsp	lemon juice	15 mL
2	whole cloves	2

Makes 24 servings

*Per serving: about 270 cal, 3 g pro, 17 g total fat
(6 g sat. fat), 32 g carb, 2 g fibre, 14 mg chol.
% RDI: 2% calcium, 8% iron, 5% vit A, 2% vit C,
3% folate.*

Variation

Walnut Baklava: Omit cherries and
chocolate. Substitute 3¼ cups (800 mL)
toasted chopped walnuts for pecans.
Increase sugar to ⅓ cup (75 mL). Add
¼ tsp (1 mL) ground cloves. Prepare
syrup as directed.

Tips

**For maximum flavour and freshness,
use California walnuts. Store nuts
in freezer in airtight container.**

**To prevent phyllo from cracking,
be sure it is completely thawed in
refrigerator for 24 hours before
unwrapping and unrolling sheets.**

**Baked baklava can be covered with
plastic wrap and stored at room
temperature for up to 1 day.**

1 In bowl, combine cherries with 1 cup
(250 mL) water; let stand for 5 minutes.
Drain and pat dry; chop coarsely.

Meanwhile, in food processor, grind
together pecans, sugar and cinnamon until
coarse; transfer to bowl. Stir in cherries and
chocolate; set aside.

3 Layer with 5 more sheets, brushing
each with butter. Place in pan; sprinkle
with 1 cup (250 mL) pecan mixture. Stack 4
sheets, brushing each with butter; place on
pecan mixture. Sprinkle with 1 cup (250 mL)
pecan mixture. Stack 4 sheets, brushing each
with butter; place on pecan mixture.

5 Using tip of sharp knife and without
cutting all the way through to filling, cut
phyllo diagonally from 1 corner to opposite
corner; make parallel cuts, 1½ inches (4 cm)
apart, to edge. Repeat in opposite direction
to form diamonds. Bake in 350°F (180°C)
oven for 40 to 45 minutes or until golden.

2 Lightly brush 13- x 9-inch (3.5 L) cake
pan with some of the butter; set aside.
Cut phyllo in half into 14- x 8-inch (35 x
20 cm) sheets. Place 1 sheet on work surface,
keeping remainder covered with plastic wrap
and damp towel to prevent drying out. Brush
sheet with some of the butter.

4 Sprinkle with 1 cup (250 mL) pecan
mixture. Stack 4 sheets, brushing
each with butter; place on pecan mixture.
Sprinkle with remaining pecan mixture.
Stack remaining sheets, brushing each with
butter. Place on top.

6 **Syrup:** In small saucepan, whisk together sugar, honey, water, lemon rind and
juice and cloves. Bring to boil over medium-
high heat; cook, stirring, for 1 minute. Discard rind and cloves. Pour over hot baklava.
Let cool on rack. Cut into diamond shapes.

Peach Ice Cream

Whatever the flavouring – be it fresh fruit purée, chocolate or irreplaceable vanilla – and whatever the season, homemade ice cream can't be beat. Fresh egg yolks cook to a silky custard that serves as the base for our ice creams, which when combined with light and whipping creams churn to a velvety smooth consistency. Because of the freshness of the ingredients, homemade ice creams are best eaten within three days.

Ingredients

6	large peaches	6
	(1½ lb/750 g)	
¼ cup	granulated sugar	50 mL

Custard:

3	egg yolks	3
⅓ cup	granulated sugar	75 mL
1 cup	18% cream	250 mL
½ cup	whipping cream	125 mL
1½ tsp	vanilla	7 mL

Makes about 3 cups (750 mL)

Per each of six ½-cup (125 mL) servings: about 285 cal, 4 g pro, 17 g total fat (10 g sat. fat), 32 g carb, 2 g fibre, 161 mg chol. % RDI: 6% calcium, 3% iron, 23% vit A, 10% vit C, 6% folate.

Variation

Red Plum Ice Cream: Omit peach mixture. In saucepan, combine 3 cups (750 mL) sliced (unpeeled) red plums (about 5), ¼ cup (50 mL) water and 2 tbsp (25 mL) granulated sugar; simmer over low heat for 20 minutes or until tender. Purée, then chill; fold into custard.

1 Custard: In bowl, whisk egg yolks with sugar for 2 minutes or until pale and thickened; set aside. In heavy saucepan, heat 18% cream over medium-high heat just until bubbles form around edge; gradually whisk into yolk mixture.

2 Rinse saucepan clean. Return egg mixture to pan; cook over low heat, stirring constantly, for about 12 minutes or until thick enough to coat back of wooden spoon.

3 Strain through sieve into large bowl. Stir in whipping cream and vanilla. Let cool to room temperature. Place waxed paper directly on surface; refrigerate for at least 2 hours or for up to 24 hours.

4 Peel and slice peaches. In bowl, combine peaches with sugar; let stand for about 20 minutes or until juicy. In food processor or blender, purée peaches to make about 2 cups (500 mL). Fold into chilled custard.

5 If using electric ice-cream maker, or one that uses salt and ice, follow manufacturer's instructions. If using ice-cream maker like one in photo, fit chilled metal canister, then paddle, into container. Pour in custard. Replace lid and crank about 4 turns every 4 or 5 minutes for about 20 minutes or until thickened. Transfer to chilled airtight container; store in freezer. Transfer to refrigerator 30 minutes before serving.

6 If not using ice-cream maker, pour custard into shallow metal pan; cover and freeze for about 3 hours or until almost firm. Break up mixture and transfer to food processor; purée until smooth. Pour into chilled airtight container; freeze for 1 hour or until firm. Transfer to refrigerator 30 minutes before serving.

Chocolate Soufflé

Soufflés are one of the coming-of-age dishes: once you've made one and gotten it to the table before it's had a chance to deflate, you know you've earned your stripes as a serious cook. Keep these pointers in mind for perennial success: soufflés rely on a blast of heat, so be sure your oven is heated to the correct temperature. Use a designated soufflé dish because the straight sides force the expanding soufflé upward, creating its famous drama and height. Be sure to bake the soufflé on the bottom rack not only for the requisite blast of heat but also to allow for plenty of room for it to rise.

Ingredients

2 oz	unsweetened chocolate	60 g
2 tbsp	butter	25 mL
4	eggs, separated	4
¼ tsp	cream of tartar	1 mL
⅔ cup	granulated sugar	150 mL
2 tbsp	hazelnut liqueur, rum or strong coffee	25 mL
1 tbsp	icing sugar or unsweetened cocoa powder	15 mL
½ cup	whipping cream, whipped (optional)	125 mL

Makes 6 servings

Per serving: about 234 cal, 5 g pro, 12 g total fat (6 g sat. fat), 29 g carb, 2 g fibre, 153 mg chol. % RDI: 2% calcium, 8% iron, 10% vit A, 6% folate.

Variation

Mini Chocolate Soufflés: Use six 3½-inch (150 mL) ramekins instead of soufflé dish; use 12- x 6-inch (30 x 15 cm) piece of foil for each, buttering 2-inch (5 cm) strip. Reduce baking time to about 25 minutes.

Tip

The principle of folding is to combine a lighter mixture with a heavier one, without losing any volume. Always fold lighter components (beaten egg whites) into the heavier ones (beaten egg yolks or melted chocolate). This is usually done in steps, again to avoid deflation.

1 Fold 24-inch (60 cm) long piece of foil in half lengthwise; generously butter 3-inch (8 cm) strip lengthwise along 1 edge. Wrap around outside of 6- to 7-inch (1.175 to 1.5 L) soufflé dish (one that has side perpendicular to base) with buttered strip facing in and extending above rim; secure with string.

2 Chop chocolate coarsely. In bowl over saucepan of hot (not boiling) water, melt chocolate with butter, stirring occasionally.

3 In separate bowl, beat egg whites with cream of tartar until soft peaks form. Gradually beat in ⅓ cup (75 mL) of the granulated sugar, 2 tbsp (25 mL) at a time, until stiff peaks form. Set aside.

4 In another bowl, beat egg yolks with remaining granulated sugar for about 5 minutes or until thickened and mixture falls in ribbon when beaters are lifted. Add chocolate mixture and liqueur; beat until thoroughly blended.

5 Fold one-quarter of the egg whites into chocolate mixture; gently fold in remaining egg whites. Scrape into prepared dish. *(Soufflé can be prepared to this point and refrigerated for up to 1 hour.)*

6 Place dish on baking sheet. Bake in bottom third of 375°F (190°C) oven for about 35 minutes or until puffed and almost firm to the touch. Cut string; remove foil. Dust with icing sugar. Serve immediately. Pass whipped cream separately (if using).

Chocolate Angel Food Cake

This is a recipe that you will make over and over – for sure! Gossamer light, ethereal and delicate angel food cake is a treat sure to please everyone, including those who want a sweet fix while watching their cholesterol and fat intakes.

¾ cup	sifted cake-and-pastry flour	175 mL
1½ cups	granulated sugar	375 mL
¼ cup	unsweetened cocoa powder	50 mL
1½ cups	egg whites (about 11 eggs), at room temperature	375 mL
1 tbsp	lemon juice	15 mL
1 tsp	cream of tartar	5 mL
½ tsp	salt	2 mL
1 tsp	vanilla	5 mL
½ tsp	almond extract	2 mL

1 In bowl, sift together flour, ¾ cup (175 mL) of the sugar and cocoa; sift again. Set aside. In large bowl (not plastic), beat egg whites until foamy. Add lemon juice, cream of tartar and salt; beat until soft peaks form.

2 Gradually beat in remaining sugar, 2 tbsp (25 mL) at a time, beating until glossy and stiff peaks form.

3 One-quarter at a time, sift flour mixture over egg whites, gently folding in each addition until well blended. Gently fold in vanilla and almond extract. Pour into ungreased 10-inch (4 L) tube pan.

4 Run spatula through batter to eliminate any large air pockets. Smooth top with spatula. Bake in 350°F (180°C) oven for 40 to 45 minutes or until cake springs back when lightly touched.

5 Turn pan upside down and let hang on legs attached to pan or on inverted funnel, or bottle, until completely cool. Remove from pan. *(Cake can be stored in airtight container for up to 2 days or frozen for up to 1 month.)*

Makes 12 servings
Per serving: about 144 cal, 4 g pro, 1 g total fat (0 g sat. fat), 32 g carb, 1 g fibre, 0 mg chol. % RDI: 1% calcium, 5% iron, 4% folate.

Variations

Classic Angel Food Cake: Increase sifted cake-and-pastry flour to 1 cup (250 mL). Omit cocoa powder.

Citrus Angel Food Cake: Prepare Classic Angel Food Cake. Fold in 1 tbsp (15 mL) each grated lemon and lime rind along with vanilla. Omit almond extract.

Tip

Learning how to read a recipe properly can make the difference between sweet success and disappointing failure. Be mindful of where a comma is placed in the ingredient list, especially for dessert recipes. For example, sifted cake-and-pastry flour means you measure the flour *after* it has been sifted; however, cake-and-pastry flour, sifted, means you measure the flour and then sift it. This slight variation can mean up to 2 tbsp (25 mL) more or less flour, an anathema to careful bakers. The same applies to cocoa powder and icing sugar.

Orange Pecan Meringue Cake

There are two basic types of meringues, soft and hard. Softer meringues, containing less sugar, are most often used to top pies and bars, as in a lemon meringue pie. This recipe utilizes the latter; the higher proportion of sugar means the meringue discs will harden enough to withstand the softening effect of the whipped cream filling. Adding cornstarch to the meringue layers helps to absorb any other moisture, keeping them firm and textured.

2¼ cups	toasted pecans or walnuts	550 mL
1½ cups	granulated sugar	375 mL
2 tbsp	cornstarch	25 mL
9	egg whites	9
1 tsp	vanilla	5 mL

Orange Cream:

2 cups	whipping cream	500 mL
¾ cup	sifted icing sugar	175 mL
2 tbsp	orange liqueur or orange juice	25 mL
1 tbsp	grated orange rind	15 mL

Garnish:

Orange or kumquat slices
Mint or orange leaves

1 Line 2 baking sheets with parchment paper or greased and floured foil. Using 8-inch (20 cm) cake pan as guide, draw 2 circles on each paper; set aside. In food processor, grind together 1½ cups (375 mL) of the pecans, ½ cup (125 mL) of the sugar and cornstarch just until finely ground.

2 In bowl and with electric beaters, beat egg whites until soft peaks form. Gradually beat in remaining sugar, about 2 tbsp (25 mL) at a time, until stiff glossy peaks form. Add vanilla. Sprinkle with half of the nut mixture; using rubber spatula, fold into egg whites. Repeat with remaining nut mixture.

3 Divide meringue among circles on baking sheets; spread evenly to fill circles. Bake in top and bottom thirds of 275°F (140°C) oven for 60 to 75 minutes or until tops are firm to the touch, switching and rotating sheets halfway through baking.

4 With sharp knife and same cake pan as guide, trim meringues into even circles while still hot. Slide long metal spatula under

meringues to loosen; carefully transfer to wire rack and let cool completely. *(Meringues can be stored in airtight container in cool dry place for up to 5 days.)*

5 Orange Cream: In bowl and with electric beaters, whip together cream, sugar and orange liqueur; stir in orange rind. Centre 1 meringue layer on serving plate. Place strips of waxed paper underneath meringue to protect plate from splatters.

6 Sandwich meringues with two-thirds of the orange cream. Spread remaining cream over top and side. Chop remaining pecans; press onto side of cake. Refrigerate for at least 1 hour or for up to 8 hours. Remove waxed paper. Garnish with orange and mint. To serve, slice with serrated knife.

Makes 10 servings
Per serving: about 480 cal, 6 g pro, 31 g total fat (12 g sat. fat), 46 g carb, 1 g fibre, 61 mg chol. % RDI: 4% calcium, 4% iron, 18% vit A, 3% vit C, 5% folate.

Variations

Mocha Cream: Dissolve 2 tbsp (25 mL) instant coffee granules in 1 tbsp (15 mL) hot water; let cool. Whip together 2 cups (500 mL) whipping cream, 1 cup (250 mL) sifted icing sugar and coffee mixture. Garnish with candied coffee beans.

Chocolate Cream: Whip together 2 cups (500 mL) whipping cream, 1 cup (250 mL) sifted icing sugar, ½ cup (125 mL) sifted unsweetened cocoa powder and 1 tsp (5 mL) vanilla. Garnish with chocolate curls.

Tips

For the most even baking of these meringues, place the oven racks as close to the centre of the oven as possible.

To toast nuts, spread pecans or walnuts on rimmed baking sheet and toast in 350°F (180°C) oven for about 10 minutes or until fragrant.

Egg White Magic

- Use only large eggs, as we do in all *Canadian Living* recipes.
- Eggs separate most easily when they're cold. However, the whites beat to their highest volume when at room temperature, so let them come to room temperature before using. To speed this process, cover the unshelled eggs with warm (not hot) water for five minutes.
- To avoid contaminating a bowlful of egg whites with egg yolk (which, because of fat content, can prevent the whites from beating to their potential), crack one egg at a time, separating the white into a small ramekin before transferring it to the larger mixing bowl.
- Avoid plastic and aluminum bowls when beating egg whites. Use only copper, stainless steel or glass.
- Adding a small pinch of acid, such as cream of tartar, lemon juice or vinegar, at the very beginning of beating will help egg whites achieve their maximum volume.
- Be careful to beat egg whites only until they're stiff but not dry. Overbeaten egg whites can collapse or separate into clumps that will not fold smoothly into the rest of the batter.
- Egg whites beaten without sugar will not reach as firm a peak as those beaten with sugar.
- Soft peaks are achieved when they flop when the beater is raised slowly; stiff peaks will stand up and remain standing.

Crème Brûlée

It's amazing how five simple ingredients can be transformed into a heavenly concoction that is creamy, sweet and satisfyingly crunchy. Essentially a baked custard, crème brûlée relies on a water bath (*bain-marie*) to ensure gentle, even cooking, the secret to its luxurious silkiness. Nowadays, most food professionals use a blowtorch to caramelize the topping, but the broiler works just as well.

Ingredients

3 cups	whipping cream	750 mL
8	egg yolks	8
⅓ cup	granulated sugar	75 mL
1½ tsp	vanilla	7 mL
½ cup	packed brown sugar, sifted	125 mL

Makes 8 servings

Per serving: about 439 cal, 5 g pro, 36 g total fat (21 g sat. fat), 25 g carb, 0 g fibre, 335 mg chol. % RDI: 9% calcium, 6% iron, 39% vit A, 10% folate.

Variations

Ginger Crème Brûlée: Add 2 tbsp (25 mL) finely chopped preserved ginger to uncooked custard mixture.

Orange Crème Brûlée: Add 2 tbsp (25 mL) grated orange rind to cold cream before heating. Strain hot cream and discard rind. Substitute 2 tbsp (25 mL) orange liqueur or orange juice for the vanilla.

Tips

When making custard desserts, such as crème brûlée, crème caramel and flan, don't overbeat the eggs: this will make the custard too foamy and cause bubbles to appear on the surface as it bakes.

Don't overbake a custard-based dessert because it may separate and turn watery. Custards are considered done when they're still a little jiggly in the centre; they will firm up as they cool. Also, watch carefully when the topping is broiled. Caramel is a mysterious and wonderful thing but can burn exceptionally quickly.

1 In saucepan, heat cream over medium-high heat until steaming hot. In bowl, whisk egg yolks with granulated sugar; very gradually whisk in cream. Whisk in vanilla.

2 Skim off foam. Divide mixture among eight ¾-cup (175 mL) ramekins or custard cups.

3 Place ramekins in 2 large shallow pans. Gently pour boiling water into pans to come halfway up sides of ramekins.

4 Bake in 350°F (180°C) oven for 30 to 35 minutes or until edges are set but centres still quiver and small knife inserted into centres comes out creamy. Remove from water; let cool on racks. Cover and refrigerate for at least 2 hours or until chilled and set, or for up to 2 days.

5 Fill 2 shallow pans with enough ice cubes to surround ramekins; nestle chilled custards among cubes. Pat surface of each custard dry; sprinkle evenly with brown sugar.

6 Broil 6 inches (15 cm) from heat for 2 to 6 minutes or until sugar bubbles and turns dark brown, rearranging pans and removing each ramekin when ready. Chill, uncovered, for 10 minutes.

Pumpkin Brûlé Cheesecake

I could go on ad nauseam about cheesecake, one of the most popular desserts and one that I and the
Test Kitchen staff love to make. I can't count how many cheesecakes we've tested and developed over the years.
One thing is for sure: they are all creamy, delicious and with nary a crack. This cheesecake is particularly
attractive due to the showstopping caramel shards arranged on top.

Ingredients

1 cup	gingersnap cookie crumbs (about 9 large cookies)	250 mL
½ cup	finely chopped pecans	125 mL
¼ cup	butter, melted	50 mL
2	pkg (each 250 g) cream cheese, softened	2
¾ cup	granulated sugar	175 mL
3	eggs	3
½ cup	sour cream	125 mL
1½ cups	pumpkin purée	375 mL
1 tsp	each cinnamon and vanilla	5 mL
½ tsp	each ground ginger and nutmeg	2 mL
Pinch	ground cloves	Pinch
⅓ cup	packed brown sugar	75 mL

Makes 12 servings

Per serving: about 384 cal, 6 g pro, 26 g total fat (13 g sat. fat), 34 g carb, 1 g fibre, 117 mg chol. % RDI: 7% calcium, 13% iron, 86% vit A, 2% vit C, 8% folate.

Tips

Cheesecakes require gentle heating, so the Test Kitchen always uses a *bain-marie* (water bath) to ensure even, moist cooking.

Even baking is also ensured by baking in a low, 325°F (160°C) oven, not opening the oven at all during the first 30 minutes of baking, and bringing the cake slowly to room temperature once baked. This means letting the cheesecake gently cool down in the oven for 1 hour, then letting it come to room temperature before chilling it overnight.

1 Grease 9-inch (2.5 L) springform pan; line side with parchment or waxed paper. Centre pan on square of heavy-duty foil; press to side of pan.

2 In bowl, combine cookie crumbs, pecans and butter; press evenly over bottom of pan. Bake in 350°F (180°C) oven for 10 minutes or until firm to the touch. Let cool on rack.

3 Meanwhile, in large bowl, beat cream cheese with granulated sugar until smooth. Beat in eggs, 1 at a time; beat in sour cream. Beat in pumpkin, cinnamon, vanilla, ginger, nutmeg and cloves; pour over crust, smoothing top.

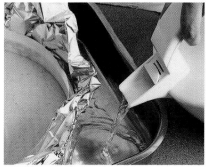

4 Place pan in roasting pan; pour enough hot water into roasting pan to come 1 inch (2.5 cm) up side. Bake in 350°F (180°C) oven for about 50 minutes or until edge is puffed and centre is just set.

5 Turn oven off; let cool in water bath in oven, with door closed, for 1 hour. Remove pan from water. Remove foil; let cool completely in pan on rack. Cover and refrigerate for at least 4 hours or until chilled, or for up to 24 hours. Score into 12 servings.

On greased foil-lined baking sheet, trace 9-inch (23 cm) circle; with spatula, spread brown sugar evenly over circle.

6 With oven door ajar and watching closely, broil sugar for 2 to 3 minutes or until bubbling and starting to darken, rotating pan to melt evenly. With greased knife, immediately cut into 12 triangles; let harden. To serve, break along cuts; with tips at centre, stand long edge of each at 45-degree angle on scored lines.

Chocolate Layer Cake

This cake is fabulous for any occasion. You might even find yourself creating one just for pure enjoyment.
Cake-and-pastry flour is used to give the cake a lighter and smaller-crumbed texture than one made with
all-purpose flour. Folding in beaten egg whites also contributes to the cake's lightness. But don't be fooled
by these techniques. The cake, paired as it is with a decadent icing, is chocolaty to the core,
sure to satisfy even the most brazen of chocoholics.

Ingredients

¾ cup	unsalted butter, softened	175 mL
1½ cups	granulated sugar	375 mL
7	eggs, separated	7
1½ tsp	vanilla	7 mL
1½ cups	sifted cake-and-pastry flour	375 mL
⅔ cup	unsweetened cocoa powder	150 mL
1½ tsp	baking soda	7 mL
¾ cup	buttermilk	175 mL

Chocolate Icing:

1½ cups	unsalted butter, softened	375 mL
½ cup	whipping cream	125 mL
1 tbsp	vanilla	15 mL
3 cups	icing sugar	750 mL
6 oz	unsweetened chocolate, melted and cooled	175 g

Makes 16 servings

Per serving: about 545 cal, 6 g pro, 37 g total fat (22 g sat. fat), 53 g carb, 3 g fibre, 174 mg chol. % RDI: 5% calcium, 16% iron, 31% vit A, 10% folate.

Variation

Mocha Fudge Cake: For icing, dissolve 2 tbsp (25 mL) espresso powder or coffee granules in vanilla.

Tip

Before icing cake, layers can be wrapped in plastic wrap and refrigerated for up to 1 day, or overwrapped in foil and frozen in rigid airtight container for up to 2 months.

1 Grease three 9-inch (1.5 L) round cake pans. Cut three 9-inch (23 cm) rounds of parchment or waxed paper; place in pans, then turn greased side up. In bowl and with electric beaters, beat butter with ¾ cup (175 mL) of the sugar until fluffy. Beat in egg yolks, 1 at a time, beating well after each. Beat in vanilla.

2 In separate bowl, sift together flour, cocoa and baking soda. Using wooden spoon, stir into butter mixture alternately with buttermilk, making 3 additions of flour mixture and 2 of buttermilk.

3 In separate bowl and with clean beaters, beat egg whites until soft peaks form; gradually beat in remaining sugar, 2 tbsp (25 mL) at a time, until stiff peaks form. With spatula, fold one-quarter of the egg white mixture into batter; fold in remaining egg whites in 2 additions.

4 Divide batter among pans and smooth tops. Bake in 350°F (180°C) oven for 25 to 30 minutes or until cake tester inserted in centre comes out clean and top springs back when lightly touched. Let cool in pans on rack for 30 minutes. Remove from pans; let cool completely, paper side down, on rack.

5 **Chocolate Icing:** In bowl and with electric beaters, beat butter until fluffy; gradually beat in cream. Beat in vanilla. Beat in icing sugar, 1 cup (250 mL) at a time. Beat in melted chocolate until fluffy and smooth.

6 Peel paper from bottom of 1 cake layer and place on cake plate; spread 1 cup (250 mL) icing over top. Repeat with next layer. Removing paper, place third layer on top. Spread remaining icing over top and side of cake.

Chocolate Garnishes

Showstopping success can be yours with a bowlful of chocolate and a little ingenuity.

8 oz	semisweet chocolate, melted	250 g

Makes enough for 8-inch (20 cm) cake

Sheet Method

Pour chocolate onto 15- x 10-inch (38 x 25 cm) rimmed baking sheet. With offset palette knife or rubber spatula, spread evenly over pan. Refrigerate until set, about 15 minutes. Place baking sheet on damp towel; let stand for 3 minutes.

Short curls: Brace pan against body. Holding bowl of teaspoon at 90-degree angle to pan and working toward yourself, scrape chocolate into curls, refrigerating pan if chocolate begins to soften. Using toothpick or spatula, transfer curls to waxed paper–lined baking sheet.

Pencil-thin curls: Brace pan against body. At opposite side of pan, hold large chef's knife at 90-degree angle to pan; hold top of blade steady with other hand. Pull knife toward you, scraping chocolate into pencil-thin curls.

Long curls: Let pan stand for 5 minutes; brace opposite side with hand. Holding stainless steel spatula or pastry scraper upside down at 45-degree angle, push spatula away from yourself, scraping chocolate into long curls.

Cutouts: Spread chocolate over *half* of waxed paper–lined baking sheet; refrigerate for 15 minutes. Let stand for 5 minutes. Using cookie cutter or sharp knife, cut out patterns. Lift off with knife; peel off paper, if necessary.

Block Method

Pour chocolate into foil-lined 5¾- x 3¼-inch (625 mL) loaf pan. Refrigerate for 2 hours or until set; unmould. Let stand for 20 minutes.

Long thin curls: Holding block with piece of foil, coarsely grate 1 long side of chocolate into long thin curls.

Chocolate Banana Cake

Chocolate and banana are a match made in culinary heaven. This cake renews their vows in a modern rendition that sees both white and dark chocolate sharing the spotlight. Chill the cream well before whipping, and make sure the cream and white chocolate are the same temperature before folding together.

4	bananas, sliced	4
	Melted chocolate	

Cake:

¾ cup	butter, softened	175 mL
1 cup	granulated sugar	250 mL
3	eggs	3
1½ tsp	vanilla	7 mL
½ cup	sour cream	125 mL
3 cups	sifted cake-and-pastry flour	750 mL
1½ tsp	baking soda	7 mL
4 oz	semisweet chocolate, chopped	125 g
1½ cups	mashed bananas	375 mL

White Chocolate Icing:

3 cups	whipping cream	750 mL
10 oz	white chocolate, chopped	300 g
1 tsp	vanilla	5 mL

Dark Chocolate Ganache:

½ cup	whipping cream	125 mL
4 oz	semisweet chocolate, chopped	125 g

1 Cake: In bowl, beat butter with sugar until fluffy. Beat in eggs, 1 at a time; beat in vanilla. Beat in sour cream. In separate bowl, stir together flour, baking soda and chocolate; using wooden spoon, stir into butter mixture alternately with bananas, making 3 additions of flour mixture and 2 of bananas. Scrape into 2 greased 8½-inch (2.25 L) springform pans, smoothing tops.

2 Bake in 350°F (180°C) oven for 35 to 40 minutes or until tops spring back when touched. Let cool on rack for 20 minutes. Remove sides of pans; let cool completely.

White Chocolate Icing: In saucepan, bring half of the cream to boil; pour over chocolate in bowl, whisking until melted. Add vanilla. Refrigerate for about 1 hour or until chilled, whisking often.

3 Beat chocolate mixture at medium speed just until ridges hold shape. In separate bowl, whip remaining cream; fold into chocolate mixture. With serrated knife, slice cakes in half horizontally. Place 1 top layer, cut side up, on plate. Spread ¾ cup (175 mL) icing over top; cover with single layer of bananas, leaving ½-inch (1 cm) border. Cover with 1 bottom cake layer, cut side down; repeat with icing and bananas.

4 Repeat with remaining top layer, cut side up, and some of the icing and bananas. Top with remaining cake layer, cut side down.

5 Using palette knife, cover cake smoothly with remaining icing. Refrigerate until firm, about 1½ hours.

Dark Chocolate Ganache: Meanwhile, bring cream to boil; pour over chocolate in small bowl, whisking until melted. Let cool for 20 minutes or until at room temperature.

6 Pour over centre of cake, spreading to edge with palette knife if necessary and letting some flow down side. Refrigerate for 40 minutes or until firm or for up to 1 day. To serve, drizzle melted chocolate over remaining bananas; let set. Arrange on cake.

Makes 14 to 16 servings

Per each of 16 servings: about 611 cal, 6 g pro, 39 g total fat (24 g sat. fat), 63 g carb, 2 g fibre, 133 mg chol. % RDI: 9% calcium, 15% iron, 29% vit A, 7% vit C, 16% folate.

White Chocolate Carousel Cake

This impressive cake belies its humble and simple assembly. Try to buy berries that are uniform in size. If the white chocolate looks a bit grainy after melting, whisk in a little more hot water or liqueur until smooth and satiny. Buy only white chocolate that contains cocoa butter in the ingredient list.

3	eggs	3
½ cup	granulated sugar	125 mL
½ tsp	vanilla	2 mL
½ cup	all-purpose flour	125 mL
¼ tsp	baking powder	1 mL
Pinch	salt	Pinch
3 tbsp	butter, melted	50 mL

White Chocolate Mousse:

10 oz	white chocolate, finely chopped	300 g
3 tbsp	orange liqueur	50 mL
3 cups	strawberries, hulled	750 mL
1½ cups	whipping cream	375 mL

Garnish:

⅓ cup	apricot jam	75 mL
¼ cup	sliced toasted almonds	50 mL
	Gold and silver candy-coated almonds	
	Candied violets	

1 In bowl and with electric mixer, beat eggs until foamy; gradually beat in sugar. Beat for 5 to 8 minutes or until batter falls in ribbons when beaters are lifted. Beat in vanilla. Stir together flour, baking powder and salt; sift half over egg mixture and fold in. Fold in remaining flour mixture.

2 Transfer one-quarter of the batter to small bowl; gradually fold in butter. Gradually fold back into batter. Scrape into greased 8½-inch (2.25 L) springform pan. Bake in 325°F (160°C) oven for 40 minutes or until cake springs back when lightly pressed. Let cool in pan for 20 minutes. Turn out onto rack; let cool completely.

3 White Chocolate Mousse: In bowl over saucepan of hot (not boiling) water, melt together chocolate, liqueur and 2 tbsp (25 mL) water; let cool to room temperature. Place springform ring on platter. Cut 28- x 4-inch (71 x 10 cm) strip of waxed paper; fit around inside of ring. Trim top of cake if rounded; fit cake back into pan.

4 Cut 12 large berries in half; arrange with tips up and cut sides against waxed-paper collar on top of cake. Arrange remaining whole berries, tips up, to cover top of cake, making sure they are lower than top of halved berries.

5 In bowl, whip cream; fold in white chocolate mixture in 3 additions. Pour over strawberries, spreading to cover berries and swirling attractively. Cover lightly with plastic wrap; refrigerate for at least 4 hours or for up to 24 hours.

6 Garnish: Gently remove springform ring; peel off paper. In small saucepan, melt jam with 1 tbsp (15 mL) water; strain and brush over side of sponge cake only. Press toasted almonds into jam to adhere. Garnish top with candy-coated almonds and violets.

Makes 12 servings

Per serving: about 376 cal, 5 g pro, 23 g total fat (13 g sat. fat), 39 g carb, 1 g fibre, 100 mg chol. % RDI: 8% calcium, 6% iron, 17% vit A, 35% vit C, 9% folate.

Very Berry Chiffon Pie

A real stunner, this pie maximizes the flavour of seasonal berries. The berries' natural sweetness is a terrific foil for the chocolate, and the filling is lightened up by the addition of drained yogurt instead of more cream. The crumb crust is crunchy and textured with an extra hit of chocolate spread on top. Using chocolate wafer crumbs for the crust also means you can avoid making regular pastry in the heat of summer.

Ingredients

35	chocolate wafer cookies (three-quarters of 200 g pkg)	35
¼ cup	butter, melted	50 mL
3 oz	bittersweet chocolate, melted	90 g

Filling:

⅔ cup	plain yogurt	150 mL
5 cups	strawberries	1.25 L
¾ cup	granulated sugar	175 mL
1½ cups	raspberries	375 mL
¼ cup	lemon juice	50 mL
2 tbsp	orange juice	25 mL
2 tsp	unflavoured gelatin	10 mL
⅔ cup	whipping cream	150 mL

Topping:

3 oz	bittersweet chocolate, melted	90 g

Makes 10 servings

Per serving: about 349 cal, 5 g pro, 20 g total fat (11 g sat. fat), 44 g carb, 4 g fibre, 34 mg chol. % RDI: 6% calcium, 15% iron, 11% vit A, 82% vit C, 11% folate.

Variation

Raspberry Blackberry Chiffon Pie: Increase raspberries to 2½ cups (625 mL). Substitute 1½ cups (375 mL) blackberries, coarsely chopped, for the strawberries. Increase sugar to 1 cup (250 mL). Increase setting time to 4 hours.

Topping: Reduce chocolate to 1 oz (30 g); drizzle all of it over tart. Garnish with ½ cup (125 mL) more raspberries.

1 Filling: Line sieve with double thickness of cheesecloth; set over bowl. Spoon in yogurt; cover and refrigerate to drain for at least 2 hours or for up to 8 hours or until yogurt measures ⅓ cup (75 mL). Discard drained liquid. Meanwhile, in food processor, grind cookies to make fine crumbs.

2 Add butter and 1 tbsp (15 mL) water to crumbs; blend until moistened. Pat onto bottom and side of 9-inch (23 cm) tart pan with removable bottom or pie plate. Bake in 350°F (180°C) oven for 10 minutes. Let cool on rack. With spatula, spread chocolate gently over base without disturbing crumbs.

3 Set aside 10 of the strawberries with hulls. Hull and cut remaining strawberries into quarters, or sixths if large. In food processor, purée together sugar and ½ cup (125 mL) each of the strawberries and raspberries. Press through fine sieve into bowl to remove seeds. Stir in remaining raspberries and quartered strawberries; set aside.

4 In saucepan, stir lemon juice with orange juice. Sprinkle gelatin over top; let stand for 5 minutes to soften. Warm over low heat, stirring, until liquefied and clear. Stir into berry mixture. Cover and refrigerate for 20 to 30 minutes or until partially set.

5 In separate bowl, whip cream; set aside. Fold drained yogurt into berry mixture; fold in whipped cream. Spoon into baked pie shell. Cover loosely with plastic wrap; refrigerate for at least 2 hours or until set or for up to 24 hours.

6 Topping: Dip tip of each reserved strawberry into chocolate; let stand on waxed paper–lined plate until set. With fork, drizzle any remaining chocolate over pie. Arrange strawberries around edge.

Bûche de Noël

What would Christmas be without a traditional Yule log cake? Some might answer a whole lot easier, but then they'd certainly pay the price in festive cheer – especially when the bûche de Noël is as simple and arresting as this one. Making a sheet cake is a snap, especially when you keep in mind that they need to be baked at a higher temperature and for a shorter period than a conventional round cake. The egg white–based buttercream is foolproof and can be made up to three months ahead and stored in the freezer. Bring to room temperature completely before whipping up again to use as icing.

Ingredients

6	egg yolks	6
¾ cup	granulated sugar	175 mL
1 tsp	vanilla	5 mL
3	egg whites	3
¼ tsp	cream of tartar	1 mL
½ cup	all-purpose flour	125 mL
¼ tsp	salt	1 mL
3 tbsp	icing sugar	50 mL

Buttercream:

4 oz	bittersweet chocolate, coarsely chopped	125 g
2	egg whites	2
½ cup	granulated sugar	125 mL
⅔ cup	unsalted butter, softened	150 mL

Sugar Syrup:

3 tbsp	granulated sugar	50 mL

Makes 8 to 10 servings

Per each of 10 servings: about 360 cal, 6 g pro, 20 g total fat (11 g sat. fat), 43 g carb, 1 g fibre, 162 mg chol. % RDI: 2% calcium, 9% iron, 17% vit A, 9% folate.

Variation

Mocha Bûche de Noël: Use ⅓ cup (75 mL) unsweetened cocoa powder instead of ⅓ cup (75 mL) flour in cake.

Buttercream: Increase recipe by half. Substitute 2 tbsp (25 mL) instant coffee granules dissolved in 1 tbsp (15 mL) water for chocolate.

Sugar Syrup: Use 2 tbsp (25 mL) coffee liqueur instead of 2 tbsp (25 mL) water.

Tip

Cake can be frozen, wrapped in plastic wrap and stored in rigid airtight container for up to 1 month.

1 In bowl, beat yolks with ½ cup (125 mL) of the sugar for 3 minutes or until pale and thickened; blend in vanilla. In separate bowl, beat whites with cream of tartar until soft peaks form; gradually beat in remaining sugar until stiff peaks form. Combine flour and salt; fold into yolk mixture alternately with whites, making 3 additions of whites and 2 of flour.

3 **Buttercream:** In bowl set over saucepan of hot (not boiling) water, melt chocolate; let cool. In heatproof bowl over pan of boiling water, whisk whites with sugar for 2 minutes or until candy thermometer registers 110°F (43°C) or finger can remain in mixture for 10 seconds. Remove from heat. Beat for 5 minutes or until very cool.

5 Starting 1 inch (2.5 cm) from end and angling to bottom edge, cut off piece; set aside. Trim other end on parallel angle. Reserve 3 tbsp (50 mL) buttercream; spread remaining buttercream over roll. With fork, make shallow lengthwise ridges for bark.

2 Spread on parchment paper–lined 15- x 10-inch (40 x 25 cm) jelly roll pan. Bake in 375°F (190°C) oven for 12 to 15 minutes or until top springs back when touched. Dust tea towel with icing sugar. With knife, loosen edges of cake; invert onto towel. Carefully remove pan and paper; trim edges with serrated knife. Starting at long edge, immediately roll up cake in towel; let cool on rack.

4 Beat in butter, one-quarter at a time, until satiny. Beat in chocolate.

Sugar Syrup: In saucepan, bring sugar and ¼ cup (50 mL) water to boil, stirring until dissolved; let cool. Unroll cake. Brush with syrup; spread with 1 cup (250 mL) buttercream. Using towel as support, roll up cake without towel. Place, seam side down, on platter.

6 Place reserved cake piece cut side down; spread with reserved buttercream. Place on log to resemble knot. Refrigerate for at least 1 hour or for up to 24 hours. Let stand at room temperature for 15 minutes.

Panforte

Siena, Italy, is home to the world's most delicious panforte, which literally translates as "strong bread." It is really a candylike cake densely studded with dried fruits and nuts and liberally seasoned with spices and honey. Traditional at Christmastime, this *dolce,* or Italian sweet, contains only enough flour to hold the fruit and nuts together.

1 cup	hazelnuts	250 mL
1 cup	whole blanched almonds	250 mL
¾ cup	chopped candied mixed peel	175 mL
¾ cup	chopped candied citron	175 mL
½ cup	all-purpose flour	125 mL
1 tsp	each grated orange and lemon rind	5 mL
¾ tsp	each cinnamon and white pepper	4 mL
¼ tsp	each ground nutmeg and coriander	1 mL
Pinch	ground cloves	Pinch
⅔ cup	granulated sugar	150 mL
⅔ cup	liquid honey	150 mL

1 Grease 8½-inch (2.25 L) springform pan. Line bottom and side with parchment paper; lightly grease paper. Set aside.

2 Spread hazelnuts and almonds on rimmed baking sheet; bake in 350°F (180°C) oven for 8 to 10 minutes or until fragrant and lightly browned. Transfer to terry-cloth tea towel; rub off as much of the hazelnut skins as possible.

3 Coarsely chop nuts; place in large bowl. Add candied peel, candied citron, flour, orange and lemon rinds, cinnamon, pepper, nutmeg, coriander and cloves; stir to mix. Set aside.

4 In small heavy saucepan, stir sugar with honey. Bring to boil over medium heat; cook for about 3 minutes or until at hard-ball

stage of 265°F (129°C), or until ½ tsp (2 mL) syrup dropped into cold water forms hard but pliable ball.

5 Quickly stir into nut mixture, mixing well. Immediately scrape into prepared pan, spreading evenly with spatula. Bake in 325°F (160°C) oven for about 45 minutes or until slightly raised, golden brown and edge is firm. (Panforte will still be soft at centre.)

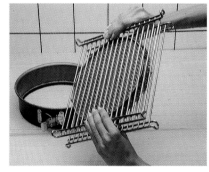

6 Let cool in pan on rack until centre is firm to the touch, about 45 minutes. Remove side of pan; invert onto second rack. Remove pan base; peel off paper. Invert panforte back onto first rack; let cool completely. Wrap in foil; let stand for 24 hours. *(Foil-wrapped panforte can be stored in airtight container for up to 2 weeks.)*

Makes 20 servings
Per serving: about 206 cal, 3 g pro, 8 g total fat (1 g sat. fat), 33 g carb, 1 g fibre, 0 mg chol. % RDI: 4% calcium, 6% iron, 5% folate.

Variation

Chocolate Panforte: Omit citron. Increase mixed peel to 1 cup (250 mL). Add 2 oz (60 g) coarsely chopped bittersweet chocolate and 2 tbsp (25 mL) unsweetened cocoa powder to nut mixture.

Tips

Be sure to wrap the panforte in foil; wrapping it in plastic wrap will cause it to soften.

Using a candy thermometer is advisable when boiling the sugar and honey mixture. If you're using the manual test, be sure to keep a glass or bowl of well-chilled water right beside the pan in which to drop the cooked sugar.

Honey Cake

Honey cake is traditional at Rosh Hashanah, the Jewish New Year, which usually falls in the autumn. The main flavouring is honey, which symbolizes the hope for a sweet new year. Beating the oil into the eggs prevents it from sinking to the bottom of the batter and creating a dense bottom.

1⅓ cups	liquid honey	325 mL
1 cup	strong coffee	250 mL
1 tbsp	grated orange rind	15 mL
2¾ cups	all-purpose flour	675 mL
2 tsp	baking powder	10 mL
1 tsp	baking soda	5 mL
1 tsp	cinnamon	5 mL
½ tsp	nutmeg	2 mL
¼ tsp	each ground cloves and ginger	1 mL
Pinch	salt	Pinch
1 cup	chopped walnuts	250 mL
4	eggs	4
¼ cup	vegetable oil	50 mL
1 cup	granulated sugar	250 mL
	Icing sugar	

1 In small saucepan, bring honey just to boil; remove from heat. Stir in coffee and orange rind; let cool slightly.

2 Meanwhile, in bowl, stir together flour, baking powder, baking soda, cinnamon, nutmeg, cloves, ginger and salt. Remove 2 tbsp (25 mL) and toss with walnuts; set aside.

3 In large bowl and with electric beaters, beat eggs until lemon-colour; beat in oil. Gradually beat in sugar, beating until pale and thickened, about 3 minutes.

4 Using whisk, alternately fold dry mixture and honey mixture into eggs, making 3 additions of dry and 2 of liquid. Fold in walnuts.

5 Pour batter into greased nonstick 10-inch (3 L) Bundt pan. Bake in 325°F (160°C) oven for 60 to 65 minutes or until cake springs back when pressed and cake tester comes out clean.

6 Let cool in pan on rack for 30 minutes; invert onto rack and remove pan. Let cake cool completely. Sift icing sugar over top.

Makes 16 servings
Per serving: about 264 cal, 5 g pro, 10 g total fat (1 g sat. fat), 42 g carb, 1 g fibre, 54 mg chol. % RDI: 3% calcium, 10% iron, 3% vit A, 2% vit C, 15% folate.

Variations

Fruited Honey Cake: Substitute raisins or candied citron for the walnuts.

Spirited Honey Cake: Substitute 3 tbsp (50 mL) cognac for 3 tbsp (50 mL) of the coffee.

Dundee Cake

The Scottish city of Dundee is famous throughout the British Isles for this easy-to-make fruitcake. Unlike other dense, fruit-laden Christmas cakes, it has more cake and is notable for its decorative arrangement of blanched almonds on top. Be sure to plan ahead since this delectable cake needs to "age" for two weeks.

1 cup	butter, softened	250 mL
1⅓ cups	firmly packed brown sugar	325 mL
1 tbsp	each grated orange and lemon rind	15 mL
4	eggs	4
2 cups	all-purpose flour	500 mL
1 tsp	baking powder	5 mL
1 cup	sultana raisins	250 mL
1 cup	currants	250 mL
1 cup	chopped candied cherries or mixed fruit	250 mL
1 cup	whole blanched almonds	250 mL
2 tbsp	corn syrup	25 mL
½ cup	dark rum or brandy	125 mL

1 Cut circle of parchment paper or greased brown paper to fit bottom of 8-inch (2 L) springform pan or 8-inch (1.2 L) round cake pan. Cut strip to fit around edge.

2 In large bowl, beat together butter, sugar, and orange and lemon rinds until creamy. Beat in eggs, 1 at a time, beating well after each addition.

3 In separate bowl, stir flour with baking powder; stir in raisins, currants and cherries until separated and well coated. Gradually stir into butter mixture until well combined. Spoon into prepared pan, smoothing and levelling top.

4 Starting at edge, arrange almonds, rounded ends out and with sides touching, in tight concentric circles over batter. Gently press almonds into batter.

5 Place cake on centre rack in 300°F (150°C) oven; place shallow pan of very hot water at side. Bake for 2 to 2¼ hours or until deep golden and cake tester inserted in centre comes out clean. Let cool in pan on rack for 5 minutes. Remove from pan to rack; brush with corn syrup. Let cool completely.

6 Cut 24- x 15-inch (60 x 38 cm) piece of cheesecloth; soak in half of the rum. Lay cheesecloth flat on work surface; place cake in centre and fold up cheesecloth to enclose cake. Wrap in foil; refrigerate for 1 week. Brush with remaining rum; wrap and refrigerate for 1 week.

Makes 12 servings
Per serving: about 537 cal, 8 g pro, 24 g total fat (11 g sat. fat), 77 g carb, 3 g fibre, 113 mg chol. % RDI: 9% calcium, 21% iron, 18% vit A, 7% vit C, 16% folate.

Variations

Apricot Dundee: Substitute 1 cup (250 mL) chopped dried apricots for candied cherries.

Cranberry Dundee: Substitute 1 cup (250 mL) dried cranberries for candied cherries.

Tip

For longer storage, brush cheesecloth with 1/4 cup (50 mL) more rum after 2 weeks; overwrap in more foil and freeze for up to 6 months.

Almond Biscotti

Biscotti have taken the cookie world by storm. Originally from the small town of Prato in Tuscany, Italy, biscotti (which literally means "twice cooked") have been transformed into large and long cookies of every flavour – and we are all the luckier for this transformation. Ideal for dunking into coffee, tea or the more traditional *vin santo* (sweet wine), these nutty cookies contain little fat and few calories. Standing the cookies upright during their second baking ensures that they dry out evenly, giving them their characteristic crunchiness.

Ingredients

1¾ cups	all-purpose flour	425 mL
2 tsp	baking powder	10 mL
¾ cup	whole unblanched almonds	175 mL
2	eggs	2
¾ cup	granulated sugar	175 mL
⅓ cup	butter, melted	75 mL
2 tsp	vanilla	10 mL
½ tsp	almond extract	2 mL
1½ tsp	grated orange rind	7 mL
1	egg white, lightly beaten	1

Makes about 24 cookies

*Per cookie: about 115 cal, 3 g pro, 5 g total fat
(2 g sat. fat), 14 g carb, 1 g fibre, 25 mg chol.
% RDI: 2% calcium, 4% iron, 3% vit A, 6% folate.*

Variations

Chocolate Chip Biscotti: Add
½ cup (125 mL) chocolate chips to flour
mixture.

Double Chocolate Biscotti: Reduce
flour to 1½ cups (375 mL). Add ½ cup
(125 mL) sifted unsweetened cocoa
powder to flour. Omit almonds and
add ½ cup (125 mL) chocolate chips.
Dissolve 1 tbsp (15 mL) instant coffee
granules in vanilla. Omit almond extract
and orange rind.

Hazelnut Biscotti: Substitute ¾ cup
(175 mL) whole hazelnuts for the
almonds. Omit almond extract.

Tip

**To prevent crumbling when slicing
the partially cooked log of dough,
use a sharp chef's knife and cut with
firm, decisive strokes.**

1 To measure flour accurately, lightly
spoon flour into dry measure, without
tapping, until cup is heaping; level off with
blunt edge of knife. In large bowl, combine
flour, baking powder and almonds.

2 In separate bowl, whisk together eggs,
sugar, butter, vanilla, almond extract
and grated orange rind; stir into flour
mixture until soft sticky dough forms.
Transfer to lightly floured surface; form
into smooth ball.

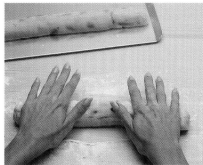

3 Divide dough in half; roll each into
12-inch (30 cm) long log. Transfer to
ungreased baking sheet.

4 Brush tops with egg white; bake in
350°F (180°C) oven for 20 minutes.

5 Remove from oven and let cool on pan
on rack for 5 minutes. Transfer each log
to cutting board; cut diagonally into ¾-inch
(2 cm) thick slices.

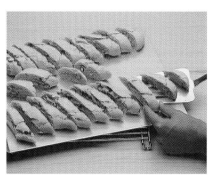

6 Stand cookies upright on baking sheet;
bake for 20 to 25 minutes longer or
until golden. Transfer to rack and let cool.
*(Biscotti can be stored in airtight container for
up to 2 weeks.)*

Candy Apples

Turn your kitchen into a fun, fantasy-filled carnival by delighting your youngsters (of all ages) with these crackling, crunchy, juicy candy apples. Working with sugar does require care, so keep pan handles turned away from prying hands. Use a thermometer to check for the appropriate stage and keep ice water nearby to stop the cooking as quickly as possible. Wearing rubber gloves can help remove any danger of burns while keeping all the fun in the project.

Ingredients

8	small red apples	8
2 cups	granulated sugar	500 mL
1 cup	water	250 mL
½ cup	corn syrup	125 mL
¼ tsp	red food colouring	1 mL

Makes 8 servings

Per serving: about 315 cal, 0 g pro, 0 g total fat
(0 g sat. fat), 81 g carb, 2 g fibre, 0 mg chol.
% RDI: 2% calcium, 8% iron, 1% vit A, 10% vit C,
1% folate.

Variation

Caramel Apples: Increase apples to 10. Substitute whipping cream for water and brown sugar for granulated sugar. Omit food colouring. Cook until hard-ball stage of 258°F (125°C) on candy thermometer, or until hard ball forms when dropped into cold water. When cooling pan in ice water, stir caramel with wooden spoon until smooth. Turn each apple in caramel 4 or 5 times or until well coated. Makes 10 servings.

Tip

Choose the reddest small apples available: McIntosh, Spartan and Cortland are all excellent choices.

1 Remove stem from each small apple; insert wooden stir stick for holding in centre of stem end. Set aside. Grease baking sheet; set aside.

2 In 12-cup (3 L) heavy-bottomed saucepan, combine sugar, water and corn syrup; cook over medium-low heat, stirring, for 8 minutes or until sugar is dissolved. Increase heat to medium-high and bring to boil, brushing down side of pan occasionally with brush dipped in hot water to prevent crystallization.

3 Boil, brushing down side occasionally but not stirring, for 15 to 25 minutes or until at soft-crack stage of 290°F (143°C) on candy thermometer, or until ½ tsp (2 mL) syrup dropped into cold water separates into hard but pliable threads.

4 Remove syrup from heat; very quickly stir in red food colouring. Immediately plunge bottom of pan into bowl of ice water and hold for about 15 seconds or until sizzling stops.

5 Holding each apple by wooden stick and tilting saucepan, swirl each apple in candy syrup until well coated all over.

6 Lift apple and quickly swirl over pan to allow excess to drip off. Place on prepared baking sheet; let stand at room temperature for at least 30 minutes or until hardened.

Classy Croquembouche

A croquembouche is one of the most impressive desserts that you can make. Its unparalleled elegance and stature are matched only by the sinfully exquisite pairing of creamy, slightly boozy custard with crispy, eggy pastry. Making a croquembouche takes time, commitment and a whole lot of love, and we have 11 steps here to prove it! But once you have finished the elaborate, towering masterpiece and spun its final jewel-like caramel thread, your sense of accomplishment will be such that you'll want to tackle just about anything!

Ingredients

Pastry Cream
(recipe, page 220)

Choux Pastry:

2 cups	water	500 mL
1 cup	butter, cubed	250 mL
¼ tsp	salt	1 mL
2½ cups	all-purpose flour	625 mL
8	eggs	8

Glaze:

1	egg	1

Caramel:

5 cups	granulated sugar	1.25 L
1 cup	water	250 mL

Makes about 28 servings

Per serving: about 371 cal, 5 g pro, 16 g total fat (9 g sat. fat), 53 g carb, 0 g fibre, 136 mg chol. % RDI: 5% calcium, 6% iron, 19% vit A, 0% vit C, 10% folate.

Tips

In Step 1, bring water just to boil but don't let any evaporate or you'll end up with a dry dough. Shape and bake as soon as the pastry is made for maximum expansion and lightness.

Unfilled puffs can be wrapped in plastic wrap and stored for up to 2 days or frozen in airtight containers for up to 2 weeks; thaw in refrigerator.

During assembly, if a puff won't stay perched, secure it from inside the cone with toothpick; remove toothpick before finishing top few layers.

If caramel begins to cool and thus thicken, place over low heat to keep warm and loose enough for dipping. If caramel begins to darken on heat, you can stir in 2 tbsp (25 mL) water and bring to boil; boil for 1 minute, stirring, before continuing.

Unhulled strawberries dipped in caramel or melted chocolate make lovely decorations for your "tree," and also disguise any gaps.

1 **Choux Pastry:** Line two 17- x 11-inch (45 x 29 cm) baking sheets with parchment paper, or grease and dust with flour. In heavy saucepan, bring half each of the water, butter and salt to boil over high heat; immediately remove from heat. Add half of the flour all at once; stir vigorously with wooden spoon until mixture comes away from side of pan in smooth ball.

Cook over medium heat, stirring constantly, for 4 minutes or until film forms on bottom of pan. Transfer to bowl; stir for 30 seconds to cool slightly. Make well in centre.

2 Using electric mixer, beat in 4 of the eggs, 1 at a time, beating well after each addition. Beat until shiny and pastry holds its shape when lifted.

Using pastry bag fitted with ¼-inch (5 mm) plain tip or with spoon, pipe pastry into 1¼-inch (3 cm) round by ¾-inch (2 cm) high mounds on pans.

Glaze: Beat egg with 1 tbsp (15 mL) water; brush half over pastry, flattening tips and making sure glaze doesn't drip onto pan.

3 Bake in 425°F (220°C) oven for 20 minutes; rotate trays. Reduce heat to 375°F (190°C); bake for 10 minutes or until golden. With knife, make small hole in bottom of each; bake for 5 minutes. Turn off oven; let stand in oven for 10 minutes to dry. Transfer to rack; let cool. With wooden spoon handle, enlarge hole in each puff. Repeat with remaining choux pastry ingredients and glaze to make 85 puffs in total.

4 Spoon Pastry Cream into pastry bag fitted with ¼-inch (5 mm) plain tip. Pipe into hole in each puff, squeezing bag gently until puff is filled with cream. Place on waxed paper–lined baking sheet. *(Puffs can be lightly covered with plastic wrap and refrigerated for up to 1 hour.)*

(continued on page 220)

5 **Caramel:** In deep heavy saucepan, stir sugar with water over medium heat until dissolved, brushing down side of pan with pastry brush dipped in cold water. Cover and bring to vigorous boil over medium-high heat. Uncover and cook, without stirring, for 17 minutes or until amber. Immediately remove from heat; place pan in bowl of ice water for 2 minutes to stop cooking. Remove from water.

7 Repeat with 12 more puffs, arranging with sides touching to form about 10-inch (25 cm) diameter ring. Continue to dip puffs, nestling each into space between puffs, angling inward and pressing lightly to adhere, to form second ring on top of first.

6 Let caramel stand until slightly thickened and not runny. Set pan on angle. Set serving plate on piece of paper. With tongs or hands, hold 1 puff at bottom with tip pointing out; working quickly, dip 3 sides of puff into caramel, leaving bottom and tip uncovered. Scraping off any excess caramel on side of pan, place puff, undipped side up and tip facing out, on plate.

8 Repeat with remaining puffs, making each ring slightly smaller than previous ring, to form croquembouche about 16 inches (40 cm) tall.

9 Let caramel stand until quite thick and does not run easily from spoon. Holding spoonful of 2 tbsp (25 mL) caramel over paper, tip spoon until large globule falls, trailing very thin unbroken strand of caramel. Working quickly, circle croquembouche with spoon, letting strand wind around croquembouche and cling to puffs. Repeat with remaining caramel. Store in cool, dry place for no more than 2 hours.

Pastry Cream

3 cups	milk	750 mL
3	eggs	3
¾ cup	granulated sugar	175 mL
¼ cup	all-purpose flour	50 mL
1 tbsp	cornstarch	15 mL
2 tbsp	butter	25 mL
1½ tsp	vanilla	7 mL
2 cups	whipping cream	500 mL

1 In heavy saucepan, heat milk until steaming. Meanwhile, in bowl, whisk together eggs, sugar, flour and cornstarch; gradually pour in milk in thin stream, whisking constantly. Return to clean pan. Cook over medium heat, whisking, for 5 minutes or just until boiling; cook, whisking, for 2 minutes longer or until thickened. Remove from heat; stir in butter and vanilla.

2 Pour into bowl; place waxed paper directly on surface to prevent skin from forming. Refrigerate until cool, at least 4 hours. Whip cream, gently fold into pastry cream with spatula just until combined. *(Pastry cream can be refrigerated for up to 3 days.)*

Acknowledgments

So many splendid, supportive and talented people were an integral part of this book that it's a shame all their names can't grace the front page.

I'd like to thank Elizabeth Baird, food director at *Canadian Living* magazine, for her unflagging support, energy, palate and boundless passion for all things culinary. It is because of her exceptional enthusiasm and commitment to the highest standards that the food pages in the magazine and the cooking lessons in this book are so beautiful and remarkably delicious. Her guidance over the past eight years has meant a great deal to me.

Senior editors Beverley Renahan and Julia Armstrong held my hand, with a sharp pencil in their other, throughout the process of compiling this book. They wove magic with my words and skilfully edited and proofread the manuscript until it was deemed worthy of their meticulous standards. They were a pleasure to work with and to learn from.

A pantryful of thanks is owed to the Test Kitchen personnel – associate food director Donna Bartolini, test kitchen manager Heather Howe and home economists Jennifer MacKenzie, Emily Richards and Susan Van Hezewijk – who spent their days developing and testing these recipes until they were perfect (and perfectly doable in your kitchen).

Thank you to Bonnie Baker Cowan, editorial director/vice-president, who believed in this book, was vital to its inception and stayed with its course over various incarnations. The invaluable leadership of *Canadian Living* publisher/vice-president Caren King is also greatly appreciated.

Much credit is due to the talented group of people who staff the *Canadian Living* art department, now under the able directorship of Michael Erb; their imprint enlivens so many of the cooking lesson photos.

Nutritional analysis for all of the recipes comes from the formidable team of Sharyn Joliat and Barbara Selley at Info Access (1988) Inc.

Collaborating with Denise Schon, Kirsten Hanson and Eva Quan of Denise Schon Books Inc. was a real treat. Their goal of making the book reader- and cook-friendly is evident on every page. Linda Gustafson, our gifted designer, worked tirelessly to achieve the same goal, bringing alive the learning process with her inspired selection and choreography of photographs, recipes and sidebars.

At Random House Canada, Sarah Davies, Anne Collins, Sheila Kay and Pat Cairns deserve a hefty dose of thanks and appreciation, as does Random House Canada president and publisher David Kent.

Finally, a personal and heartfelt embrace of gratitude goes to my husband, Skip Walters, for all his love, never-ending encouragement and willingness, at all hours of the day or night, to eat and listen. And to my mother, Zipporah Dunsky-Shnay, with whom my love of good food and of learning started.

Photo Credits

Fred Bird: pp. 12, 16, 17 (middle and right column), 22–27, 32–35, 38, 39, 42, 43, 48–51, 54, 68, 76, 77, 80, 81, 86, 87 (steps 1–4), 90, 91, 94, 96, 97, 99, 103, 106, 107–113, 118, 120–122, 124, 125, 131, 132, 134, 136, 137, 144, 145, 162–165, 168, 169, 180, 183, 186, 187, 195, 198, 199, 200, 201, 206, 214.

Doug Bradshaw: pp. 18, 19, 30, 62, 64, 130, 138, 142, 156, 192, 204.

Christopher Campbell: pp. 7, 11, 15, 17 (left column), 21, 29, 31, 37, 41, 55, 58, 59, 63, 65, 67, 69, 71, 75, 79, 83, 87 (steps 5–9), 89, 93, 101, 102 (middle and right column), 105, 115, 119, 123, 126 (steps 1, 5, 6), 133, 141, 147, 151, 153, 157, 161, 171, 173, 174, 175, 179, 181, 188 (steps 3, 5), 191, 193, 194, 197, 203, 205, 209, 211, 212 (steps 2, 5, 6), 213, 215, 219, 220.

Peter Chou: pp. 36, 100, 177, 202, 208.

Yvonne Duivenvoorden: p. 6.

Michael Kohn: p. 14.

Pat Lacroix: pp. 20, 72.

Michael Mahovlich: pp. 61, 92, 116, 117.

Vincent Noguchi: pp. 52, 53, 66, 88, 146, 158, 178, 182, 190.

Michael Visser: p. 28.

Michael Waring: pp. 44, 82, 172, 210, 212 (top left), 216, 217.

Robert Wigington: pp. 10, 40, 56, 60, 70, 74, 78, 98, 102 (left column), 104, 114, 126 (top left), 140, 148, 150, 152, 160, 167, 170, 188 (top left), 196, 207, 218.

A talented team of food and props stylists help make our cooking lessons a visual feast each issue, most notably Olga Truchan, Jennifer McLagan, Claire Stancer, Ruth Gangbar, Rosemarie Superville, Debbi Charendoff Moses, Julie Aldis, Christine Cushing, Kate Bush, Jill Snider; Miriam Gee, Maggi Jones, Shelly Tauber, Janet Walkinshaw, Bridget Sargeant, Susan Doherty-Hannaford, Debbie Boyden.

Index